The Toombs Oak,

The Tree That Owned Itself,

and Other Chapters of Georgia

The Toombs Oak,
The Tree That Owned Itself,
and Others Chapters of Georgia

By

E. MERTON COULTER

UNIVERSITY OF GEORGIA PRESS
ATHENS

Contents

v

Illustrations

Preface

THE nine chapters which comprise this book originally appeared in the *Georgia Historical Quarterly* and are here reprinted with a few slight changes and corrections. All relate to Georgia, and, therefore, have a unity in that respect. The first five chapters have a further unity in that they deal with Athens.

As for the other chapters, it seems to have escaped the knowledge of most Georgians, and others, too, that a sizable group of the Acadians who were expelled from Nova Scotia lived for a time in the Georgia colony, and even those who have written about John Howard Payne apparently did not know that the famous author of "Home, Sweet Home," had one of the great experiences of his life on a visit to Georgia. Probably the most horrible murder of the nineteenth century occurred in Georgia when almost the whole Woolfolk family was brutally slain. This crime occupied the attention of the whole nation, but by the middle of the twentieth century it had all but faded from the mind of man, except for a folklore song or two. Henry M. Turner, one of the outstanding Negroes of the last half of the nineteenth century and the early part of the twentieth, has been pronounced both a credit and a disgrace to his race. These foregoing four subjects complete this book of nine chapters of Georgia. Front matter, of course, and a bibliography and an index have been added.

E. M. C.

University of Georgia
Athens, Georgia

CHAPTER I

The Toombs Oak

TREES are one of the most majestic manifestations of the creative power of Nature. Under the spreading boughs of trees, God has been worshiped; religions, organized; sermons, preached; governments, set up; laws, passed; armies, commanded and encamped; philosophies, evolved; poets, inspired; iron, wrought; and orations, spoken.

Among the trees which have been singled out for immortality was the Toombs Oak, on the campus of the University of Georgia. It was in vigorous middle age when the University was founded in 1801 and three years later when the first commencement was held under the forest still covering most of the campus this tree was an on-looker, though all available evidence indicates that none of the exercises was held under its boughs.[1] At some time during its life it was honored with the name of Toombs—Robert Toombs, who was once (in fact twice) a student at the University, but destined never to be graduated there. Like the tree, Toombs was a Georgian, destined for great things before he and the tree should crumble in the dust—a Representative and Senator in the United States Congress, a secessionist in 1861 and a brigadier general in the Confederate army, "an unreconstructed rebel," a planter, a lawyer, and a great orator.

Toombs, full of life, mental vigor, and devilment, and with a high sense of honor, entered the University in 1824. The next year he was expelled for having disobeyed too many rules, but with his great diplomatic powers and argumentative skill, he got himself reinstated, but in 1828 he was finally expelled as the first act of the faculty in the new year.[2] He went to Union College, Schenectady, New York for his degree and thus made it possible for that institution to claim the honor of affording the Southern Confederacy its first Secretary of State in Toombs,

1

when at the same time another Union College alumnus, William H. Seward, was the Secretary of State for the United States.

But how did this great oak become associated with Robert Toombs? The story has often been told and in varying versions. Let a great American historian answer—Ulrich Bonnell Phillips, an alumnus of the University, graduating in 1897, and an author of a life of Robert Toombs. As the tradition goes, Toombs having been expelled a second and final time, turned up at the commencement exercises the following autumn, and "mounting an improvised rostrum under the tree at the hour when his fellows approved by the faculty had begun their programme of speeches in the chapel, young Toombs began an address in such vigorous tones, with such eloquent phrasing and such telling humor that the audience within began to quit their seats and drift out of the building to enjoy the novel occasion; and Toombs did not conclude his harangue until the speakers inside had been left with empty benches before them." And now this critical historian added, "Whether this tale be true in its details no man can say, but for many years before the disappearance of the old tree it was pointed out as the 'Toombs Oak,' the showpiece of the campus, and as such it was held in affectionate regard by the quickly succeeding generation of students. In the present writer's undergraduate days there in the middle eighteen-nineties its top had broken off and its middle was hollow with decay. As the seasons passed it then lost branch after branch until but a stump remained; and now one of the classes has placed a marble sun-dial to mark the spot where flourished the oak and the rebel Toombs."[3]

Another alumnus of the University, a journalist and a diplomat, and also an author of a biography of Robert Toombs, was Pleasant A. Stovall, who graduated in 1875. Writing in 1892 he said there was "still standing in the college campus in Athens a noble tree, with the crown of a century upon it." Using his imagination, he stated that the first college commencement had been held under its branches and that among the various other activities which had taken place there, the "student Toombs once stood and addressed his classmates," and that of all the happenings under the spreading boughs of "this monument of a forgotten forest," Toombs' name alone had come to be linked with it.[4] In this version there was no mention of Toombs' expulsion and of his tricky vengeance whereby he remained around for a half year and more for the commencement (or returned for the event) and delivered the speech which emptied the chapel.

There was still another alumnus of the University, Augustus L. Hull, historically minded but a banker and a treasurer of the University for many years, who wrote in his *Historical Sketch of the University of Georgia* in 1894 the old story of Toombs' expulsion and his commencement speech. He added one more touch to the old oak: "It has even been said that on the day of Mr. Toombs' death the old oak was struck by lightning and destroyed." Hull, who graduated in 1866, and should have remembered whether there had been a Toombs Oak tradition in his student days, did not indicate so, but passed this judgment as to its origin: "There is not the semblance of truth in the story. It was a fabrication of Henry W. Grady, who, in an admiring sketch of the great Georgian, wrote charmingly of his overwhelming eloquence and pointed it with a story drawn from his own vivid imagination."[5]

There is no doubt that Grady's eloquence caused him to stray from the actual facts now and then. As an example, in speaking of the Confederate monument in Athens, he said in his oration, "The New South," delivered before the New England Club, in New York, in 1886, "In my native town of Athens is a monument that crowns its central hill—a plain, white shaft."[6] In fact, this monument was neither plain nor one shaft. Its sides were carved with crossed rifles and a draped flag, and the shaft was made up of six marble segments resting on three blocks of granite superimposed on one another. So, Grady could easily have started the Toombs Oak story; but Hull seems to be in error in saying that it appeared in a sketch of Toombs which Grady wrote. Grady wrote two sketches of Toombs, which appeared in the *Philadelphia Times*, July 1, and November 20, 1879. In neither of these sketches is the Toombs Oak mentioned. It is not likely that Grady wrote

Toombs Oak. *Top.* In 1883. *Bottom.* About 1893.

other sketches of Toombs, but it is highly probable that he did originate the Toombs Oak story in some speech.[7]

Certainly the Toombs Oak had become a tradition on the University campus as early as 1886;[8] and when it is remembered that Toombs died in December, 1885 it must be assumed that Toombs had heard of the story. And how fervently one wishes that whatever comments Toombs might have made, had been preserved; but the record is as silent as the tomb of Toombs.

By the early eighteen-hundred-nineties, the tradition was flourishing with becoming dignity and sentiment, on the campus and throughout the state, wafted thence in song and story. At this time Toombs and the Oak had become inseparable personalities. Toombs had gone; the Oak was on its way to join him in memory. "Another limb of the famous Bob Toombs oak on the College Campus fell with a crash yesterday," observed the editor of the *Athens Banner*, in 1891, "and with each rain storm of spring and summer it seems that the stalwart oak is crumbling to decay." As if all did not know the story, still the oratorical editor reported it: "Who has not heard of the Bob Toombs oak and of its history? Who has not been told of the pleasing incident in the life of General Toombs when forbidden by expulsion to speak from the chapel stage with his fellow seniors, he cooly walked out of the hall and took his stand in the shadow of this great oak and charmed hundreds of Georgians with the magic of his eloquence, drawing them from the exercises from within?" Continuing he mused: "There is something touching in the parallel histories of the man and of the tree. Both were reared into prominence at the same moment; both have flourished among their kingdoms with lofty heads; both have fallen at almost simultaneous periods. Neither will soon be forgotten. Time will do its destroying work, will wrinkle fond faces and whiten golden locks, but in vain will it labor to dim the brilliancy of the name of Toombs or efface the memories that cluster around the venerable oak."[9]

It was difficult for Remsen Crawford, the editor of the *Athens Banner*, to keep from dreaming of Toombs and the oak in his newspaper writings, just as a student at the University a few years previously he had sat under the old tree and dreamed of Toombs: "Hear the handsome young Georgian standing there in the heat of passionate youth and wounded pride, driven from the college stage beneath the faculty's frown; hear him in magic eloquence delivered of a heart that was full by a tongue that was golden, pledge his life to the cause of his country, drawing crowds from out the chapel door to hear him plight his troth and mark its after keeping."[10]

"Gone—glimmering through the dream of things that were.

A school boy's tale—the wonder of an hour!"

It was still the year 1891 and the tree was going fast away. "What a history has that giant oak, and how it blends with the history of Georgia! I stood beside its mammoth body yesterday and thought about the past. I thought how pretty was the story— the tradition as it almost seems to me now—that tells how the old oak came into prominence. I fancied for a moment the picture: handsome Bob Toombs in the bloom of passionate youth standing there before the crowds that flocked about him to hear his memorable graduating speech. Cheer after cheer goes up testifying to the fire of patriotism and magic eloquence just kindled into a blaze." He then visioned Toombs dead: "The old tree seems to have been touched by the black robed messenger at the same time." And in his trance he concluded: "It is dead, too."[11]

But it is not quite so, for the era of the Toombs Oak poets now sets in as they beg of their muse yet a respite for this last noble monarch of the former campus forest: If it had a tongue,

"What secrets to the world thou wouldst impart!
Long mayst thou live, Oh proud and stately tree
And may the coming year prove kind to thee."[12]

The poet says that trees are immortal no less than people:

"O venerable tree, thy form dost yield
To the insatiable tooth of Time.
Full many a winter's wind thy bough
Has torn and bent thy giant trunk;
But like that grand old rebel who

Did give thee name, th' increasing storm
But firmer fixed thy roots. But still boast not
Thy strength; for though the tempest fierce
Thou hast withstood, thou, too, must fall
Before Time's sickle keen.
But lives not e'er to die
The atoms of thy grand old form
The substance of thy rustling leaves,
That like the noble thoughts, the lofty deeds,
Of thy name-giver await th' decree
Of their Creator, to be changed
Into a greater glory."[13]

And as death draws nigh in 1903 the poet sings:

"Now is the hour of thy last agony!
The sombre shades of death draw on apace
To fold thee in its darkness, and ruthless
Ruin strikes thee with shaft of dread decay."

He predicts that now for the last time the "Midas-touch of Autumn" has glorified the ancient tree "Ere the death-rattle of December winds" would scatter its glory.

"Full five decades have swept, with kingly tread,
Through the procession of the centuries,
Since Robert Toombs, fair Georgia's lordly son,
Strong as the fibre of thy sturdy heart,
And full of fire as thy green bark of sap
Stood at thy feet to blend his fame with thine."[14]

And finally the poet gives up as he sings the tree into immortality with its other self, the mighty Toombs, and points a moral:

"Like a relic from remote antiquity,
Shattered by age, with ivy overgrown,
Standing still, venerable and alone,
It yet possesses all its former dignity,
Devoid though of its pristine symmetry.
Its youth and friends of its youth are gone,
But it is not friendless and forlorn;
It still has its younger friends—this historic tree,

So let the future promise you, my friend,
An age free from remorse—a peaceful end
Of actual days. Let your life be
Unblemished like that of this old tree,
That when you're gone the friends you've never seen
May crown your life with memory's evergreen."[15]

And finally in July of the year 1908, despite the attempt of the clinging ivy to give it life, the high stump of the disappearing old tree, sans boughs sans life, collapsed. Relics were made of the sounder parts and handed down to alumni, to revere the memory of the Toombs Oak no less than of Robert Toombs himself.[16]

Chapter II

The Story of the Tree That Owned Itself

TREES no less than people have become famous in history and for as many reasons. A "Who's Who of Trees" would be equally as interesting as a "Who's Who of People," for in almost all cases, famous trees have become so by their association with people. One of the rare exceptions is the Big Trees of California, which attained their fame through their own efforts, unassisted by puny mankind.

Athens, Georgia, has been blessed with famous trees as well as with famous men and women; and among its famous trees one has long stood out as unique—"The Tree that Owned Itself." The story of this tree does not begin with the day it sprouted out of the ground from an acorn, though that day must have been at least a century before James Edward Oglethorpe planted his first English colonists on the banks of the Savannah River. It seems that sometime during the latter part of the nineteenth century the story of this tree took roots, first in Athens, then widespread over Georgia, and ultimately throughout the land.

As far as it has been possible to trace the story from historical records, it first appeared, unsigned, in the *Athens Weekly Banner* of August 12, 1890, occupying a prominent place with big headlines on the first page—a spot generally associated with exciting news:

"DEEDED TO ITSELF. A Tree in Athens which Owns Itself. Deeded to it Years ago—And the Deed May be Seen in the Records—It also owns Real Estate." [And then follows the story:]

"A tree a property holder. What do you think of that? Is it legal? If so, when the tree dies, to whom does the land belong? If not, whose is it now? It is certainly an exceptional case and nobody ever heard of such a thing before.

"There are only a few in the city who know it, as it was done so long ago as to pass out of the recollection of nearly all.

"However, it is true, as the record of deeds at the court house

9

THE TREE THAT OWNED ITSELF

From a photograph taken about 1900, now in Special Collections, University of Georgia Library.

contains the one giving the tree itself and all the land within eight feet of it.

"The tree in question is the magnificent oak in front of the residence of Major Stanley, and it seems to stand straighter and hold its head more highly and proudly as if [it] knew that it ranked above the common trees of the world which are the slaves of humans, and can be cut down and burned at the will of their owners.

"This majestic oak cannot be touched against it's [*sic*] will, but the trouble is to ascertain what it's will may be.

"And who is to be judge of whether it is willing to be cut down or not? It is a peculiar case. The facts as told us are these: Way back in the first part of this century the land containing the tree and that taking a good part of the vicinity was owned by Col. W. H. Jackson.

"Col. Jackson had watched the tree grow from his childhood, and grew to love it almost as he would a human.

"Its luxuriant foliage, and sturdy limbs had often protected him from the heavy rains, and out of its highest branches he had many a time gotten the eggs of the feathered songsters. He watched it's growth, and when on reaching a ripe old age he saw the tree standing in it's magnificent proportions, he was pained to think that after his death it would fall into the hands of those who might destroy it.

"Thinking thusly he came to the conclusion that the only way to be sure of its protection from the axe of the unsparing woodsman was to allow it to become its own master. And this he did. Going to the court house he had there recorded a deed, from which the following is an extract:

" 'I, W. H. Jackson, of the county of Clarke, of the one part, and the oak tree, (giving location) of the county of Clarke, of the other part: Witnesseth, That the said W. H. Jackson for and in consideration of the great affection which he bears said tree, and his great desire to see it protected has conveyed, and by these presents do convey unto the said oak tree entire possession of itself and of all land within eight feet of it on all sides.'

"This is certainly the most novel transaction yet brought to light, and the question now is, who owns the tree?

"Can an inanimate object be an owner? Of course you say no. Then who owns the large oak in front of Major Stanley's residence and the land within eight feet of it?

"The transaction certainly took place, for the deed recorded in the book of records speaks for itself.

"As it is now no one cares how the point would be decided if carried to law, as nobody would be benefitted.

"But it certainly is an interesting case, and there is no room for a great deal of speculation as to how such a point would be decided.

"It certainly is the most peculiar of all transactions, and we would like to know who owns that tree."

Among the questions which immediately arise is this one: Who was W. H. Jackson and how does he fit into the story? William H. Jackson was born in Savannah in 1786, the son of James Jackson, who was a great patriot of the American Revolution and afterwards governor of Georgia. William H. Jackson and his brother James were graduated in the first class of the University of Georgia in 1804. His brother James became a professor in the University for many years. William returned to Savannah, where he became a man of some importance. In 1813 he represented Chatham County, in which Savannah was located, in the lower house of the state legislature. It does not appear that he joined the legal profession, but that his interests were rather in the booming business of becoming a planter, with a lingering interest, though small, in politics. He soon moved up into middle Georgia and settled in Jefferson County, with Louisville as the county seat. He continued his services in the legislature, lower house, by his election in 1817 and 1818 to represent Jefferson County. And in 1821 and 1822 he was chosen to represent the county in the state senate.[1] In the latter year he became a member of the Board of Trustees of the University, and continued in that position for the next forty-two years.[2]

It is not known when he moved to Athens, but probably it was soon after his term of service in the legislature had expired. He had a special interest in this little educational center. In addition to having once been a resident of the town when he was a student in the University, he was now a trustee of the University and had a brother on its faculty, and he had married Mildred, a sister of a resident of the town, John Addison Cobb. Through this marriage he became the uncle of Cobb's two sons destined for great fame, Howell and Thomas R. R., both continuing to live in Athens. And even more, his son, also named James, within a short time would be ready for a college education, and there was no school of higher learning in the state except in Athens.

This James was graduated at the University in 1837 and was destined for some fame—a member of the lower house of the Georgia legislature, a judge of the Superior Court of the Western Circuit, a member of Congress, a judge advocate on the staff of General Stonewall Jackson in the Civil War, and an associate justice and later chief justice of the Supreme Court of Georgia.[3]

When William H. Jackson moved to Athens, with the aid of his brother-in-law John A. Cobb, he built a residence on a high tableland sloping off to a small branch beyond which to the east-ward lay the University campus. This land was owned by the University, though it must be assumed that he intended to buy it, and doubtless did enter into such an agreement, which, however, was never carried out, for in 1832 the University sold to Malthus A. Ward, a University professor, this tract of land, containing four acres, "being the same whereon Wm. H. Jackson now lives." Professor Ward had an additional expense, for before he could take possession, he was required to pay to Jackson, his wife Mildred, and his father-in-law John A. Cobb, $1,200 for improvements on the lot "at present the residence of William H. Jackson."[4] It was on this tract of land where the "Tree that Owned Itself" grew.

Jackson now moved out of the town of Athens, but not very far, for young James was growing up, and he must attend the University. He bought a plantation of 655 acres across the Oconee River, a few miles away, and moved there. In 1834 he charged the Georgia Railroad Company, now about to build its road from Augusta to Athens, the nominal sum of $5 for a right-of-way across his plantation.[5] It must be assumed that Jackson was not a very successful businessman, for ten years later (in January, 1844) the sheriff of Clarke County levied on Jackson's plantation to satisfy a mortgage on it held by the Bank of the State of Georgia, and sold it for $1,410.[6]

By this time his son James had been graduated at the University, had studied law, and had been admitted to the bar. He had begun the practice of law in Athens, but soon thereafter had moved to Monroe in the adjoining county of Walton. His father William, being sold out of house and home, doubtless moved to Walton County to live with his son. The important fact is that he did not continue to live in Athens or within the county of Clarke. Neither the United States Census, Population Schedule, for 1850 nor for 1860, lists William H. Jackson as a resident of Clarke County. So much for William H. Jackson.

Now, it is in order to return to the story which appeared in the *Athens Banner* of 1890, announcing the startling news that there was a tree in Athens that owned itself. A close reading of this story might well suggest that it was written as a hoax or a joke to set the lawyers a problem to wrestle with, or merely for the author to test out his faculties of imagination to while away some idle moments—and perhaps to help fill up that edition of the newspaper. The editor and the indefatigable newsgatherer of the *Banner* at this time was that inimitable T. Larry Gantt, whose journalistic tracks covered a considerable part of the states of Georgia and South Carolina during his long and unpredictable careers. As has appeared, William H. Jackson never owned the land on which the tree stood, and in fact never owned any land within the city limits of Athens. It was pure imagination which led the author of the story to say that Jackson "had watched the tree grow from his childhood," for Jackson was in his middle age before he ever came to Athens to live, and as a student he was there for only three years.[7] And if according to one account he did not come until 1829, and it is known that he moved out of Athens in 1832, he could not have noticed the tree over a longer period than three years. And likewise, it is certain that when "on reaching a ripe old age," he was not in Athens sitting under the shade of the old tree and concluding to deed the tree to itself. Furthermore he did not go to the Clarke County courthouse and have the deed recorded, for in addition to all other negative evidence, there is no such deed recorded in the deed books of Clarke County.[8]

But the story was a classic one, and why there were no re-verberations in the newspapers following the publication of this legal teaser, or denials of the story or commendations for the author in letters to the editor—all this silence is puzzling. And it is equally puzzling, if there had been some previous story about the tree, why it had never reached print before. Why had not Dr. Henry Hull, in his sketches of Athens, written for the Athens *Southern Watchman* during the year 1870, mentioned this beautiful story? If there had been a tree that owned itself it would have been a choice morsel for Dr. Hull.[9]

Five years later William H. Jackson at the age of 90 died at the home of his son James in Macon, Georgia. By this time he should have been as famous as the tree and for the same reason that the tree was famous; yet in the appreciative obituary in the Macon newspaper there was no mention of a tree.[10] And when his remains were brought to Athens to be interred in the Cobb lot in the Oconee Cemetery, the Athens papers were as silent as the tomb as far as the tree story was concerned.[11]

Athens had long been tree-conscious and had had for many years, trees to boast of. There was the weeping willow in the famous University Botanical Garden, presented as a cutting from the tomb of Napoleon on St. Helena, to William H. Crawford, who had given it to the University. There was also in the Garden an elm grown from a cutting brought by Malthus A. Ward from the famous Cambridge elm under which Washington had taken command of the Continental Army on July 3, 1775. And there was now in the Garden, a huge oak grown from an acorn from England brought to Athens by Ward, who, in addition to his other University duties, was the keeper of the Botanical Garden. The weeping willow had been blown down by a storm in 1882, but many cuttings had been plucked and set out by Athenians. Here were the famous Athens trees being written about in the 1880's, but there was no mention of a tree that owned itself. What a remarkable oversight, if there had been such a tree! And T. Larry Gantt was at this time editor of an Athens newspaper. Apparently he or whoever started the story in 1890 had not yet had the inspiration to write of a tree that owned itself.[12]

The story of the "Tree that Owned Itself," rather mysteriously continued to sleep for a decade, a fact little to the credit of Athenians either to their imagination or to their sense of the possibilities of promoting such a tree into national prominence. Albin Hajos, the town's artistic photographer, published in 1900 a beautiful booklet, entitled *Souvenir of Athens, Ga. Photo-Gravures*, in which he portrayed the attractions of Athens even down to such a prosaic thing as a rock crusher—yet he did not notice the "Tree that Owned Itself," though he did give a picture of another famous Athens tree, the Toombs Oak, on the University Campus.

Finally in 1901 in the Centennial Edition of the *Athens Banner* the Tree came to life in the same story which appeared ten years earlier, but not exactly in the same words. The story now was soon to begin to make headway. Back in 1884, Augustus L. Hull, a son of Dr. Henry Hull, had collected and published his father's sketches, in which there was no mention of the Tree, and in 1893 he himself had added some sketches, in which again there was no mention of the Tree, and then sometime before 1906 Hull added some more sketches and in that year he published all of the afore-mentioned sketches by both father and son, in a book called *Annals of Athens, Georgia, 1801-1901*. In this last work, according to the dates in the title, nothing happening after 1901 might be expected to be included, yet in fact events as late as 1906 were brought in—and now the Tree story sprouts out vigorously. Probably it was written around 1901, but it could have been as late as 1906. In the *Athens Banner* for December 21, 1906, the story re-appears. In all these stories the facts are the same but the language varies slightly as it does even in the quotation of the wording of the deed; but it is evident that all stories stem from the original account appearing in 1890. Hull introduces his story by saying "The following is taken from a paper now many years old,"[13] and the story that follows is quoted—though it is not the language of the 1890 story or of the 1901 account; but there is no reason to assume that it could have been a story published earlier than the 1890 one.

Henceforth, the tradition took on vigorous growth. Now enters into the story George Foster Peabody, a public-spirited citizen of New York but Georgia-born and a frequent visitor in Athens, where as a life Trustee of the University of Georgia he usually attended the commencement exercises of that institution. In 1906 he became so enamored of the beautiful sentiment of a tree owning itself that he provided the funds for erecting granite posts joined by chains to surround the tree, for depositing rich soil around its roots, and for the erection of a marble marker quoting part of the famous but fictitious deed.[14] Soon thereafter colored post cards were issued, in two series, one giving a picture of "The Only Tree in the World that Owns Itself, Athens, Ga." and the other, giving a composite picture of the tree and the marble marker.

The imagination of Athenians, which for a decade following the "discovery of the tree" in 1890 had seemed to be so stunted, now began to burst forth in the most unusual forms. In addition to the issuance of post cards, which was a natural development, the officials of one of the local banks, the Citizens Bank and Trust Company, artistically embedded in gentle tones in their blank checks "The Tree that Owns Itself."

As the fame of the Tree spread, the story took on a few variations from the original account. In 1922 a book published in New York, entitled *Historic American Trees*, stated that Jackson deeded the tree to itself "about a century ago," and that the deed was recorded in the town clerk's office. The author said further that the tree was about 350 years old, and in the following words she admitted the Tree to the fraternity of the great: "By virtue of being the first tree distinguished as a landowner it seems fully entitled to rank as historic."[15] And in 1935 the Forestry Service of the United States Department of Agriculture issued a bulletin entitled *Famous Trees*, in which appeared this repetition: "This deed, dated 1820, is recorded in the Town Clerk's Office."[16] This statement represents a time variation of at least fifty years in the date of the execution of the deed. The original stories represented Jackson as making the deed in his old age. Since he died in 1875, his old age came far beyond the year 1820, when he was in the prime of life. As a further comment, it should be noted that deeds were not recorded in the archives of town governments; and even if that were true for the town of Athens there would be no way now to verify the statement, for not since 1904 and probably for many years previously, have the town archives of Athens extended back of the year 1847.[17] Probably in making several changes in the location of the town hall, the early archives were lost or purposely discarded.

With the vigorous growth of the Tree tradition, there began to flourish likewise the legal teaser of the status of the supposed deed. One of the post cards in addition to giving the familiar story of the Tree being deeded to itself, adds: "This giant oak, possessor of itself, is now thought to be dying. If this fear proves true, the mooted question is, who will become the owner of the lot on which the tree stands and to which it holds a legal title. There are no little sprigs around the foot of the tree to grow into full-sized oaks, so it is certain that the heir cannot be a tree." One commentator, somewhat critical of the story, not knowing the life history of William H. Jackson, said: "It is believed that Judge Jackson [who was never a Judge] well knew that inanimate objects cannot hold legal title to themselves or to property, and that he merely made a poetic gesture in letting the newspapers publish the pretended deed."[18] There is no evidence that Jackson ever made a deed, to say nothing of "letting the newspapers publish" it. Undoubtedly the first publication of the deed was made fifteen years after the death of Jackson. And then there is this statement, made in 1906: "This deed was, of course, not admitted to record, and was invalid in law, but it was seen by a number of the older citizens of the city at that time."[19] This statement was designed to get around the fact that no such deed was ever recorded in the archives of Clarke County.

Law students became interested in this unusual legal tangle in which the Tree found itself. A student in the American University Law School in Los Angeles, California, contributed to a law magazine, published in Brooklyn, N. Y., an article entitled "A Legal Conundrum," in which she mistakenly calls William H. Jackson a former chief justice of the Supreme Court of Georgia, confusing him with his son James. She solved the conundrum by quoting from an opinion she received from an un-named associate justice of the Georgia Supreme Court, in which he gave the evident answer that an inanimate object had no standing as a person before the law, and, of course, could not be a party to a deed or other legal instrument, but he stated further that such a deed could be construed as divesting heirs of any property rights in the tree and the surrounding land and placing such rights ultimately in the public.[20]

All of the evidence seems to indicate that the Tree first came to be notable in 1890 and thereafter, and yet there is this puzzling fact: The Tree stood in the middle of Finley Street and was left standing when that street was opened up. There must have been something unusual about that particular tree to account for the sparing of the woodman's axe. But, of course, the date when Finley Street was opened up is of first importance. A map in the City Engineer's Office, made in 1852, shows Finley Street running slightly beyond the location of the tree, with no indication of a narrowing of the street or an unusual situation at that spot. But as this was a dead-end street, even on the map, it might well be assumed that the street was not actually opened until residences began to be constructed in that region. If this development did not take place until 1890, then it is perfectly evident why the tree was left—it was now being clothed with ownership in sentiment, as appeared in the *Athens Banner* story of that year. But if the development was earlier, then the puzzle is far from being solved, unless indeed, some imaginative writer concocted this story earlier than 1890 and published it in an Athens paper which the present writer has been unable to find. But if such a story about the tree had been published much before 1890, why was this Tree not included in the stories of the notable trees of Athens, being written in the early 1880's?[21]

As the twentieth century wore on, this Athens Tree was approaching, by estimation, its four hundredth birthday; and trees like people must finally come to the end of the road which time has marked out for them. The signs of decay which the Athens Tree showed greatly disturbed the Athenians, and they resorted to all known remedies, but as the Romans would have said, *Tempus edax rerum*. On the night of October 9, 1942, the "Tree that Owned Itself" of its own volition fell with a mighty crash onto the bosom of mother earth, awakening the slumbering populace in the neighborhood.

Athenians having known that this day must soon come, and having seized time by the forelock, had begun to care for the children of this great oak. Acorns which had been planted had sprouted and were growing into shapely saplings. Four years later, on October 9, 1946, the Athens Junior Ladies Garden Club in a formal municipal ceremony planted on the same spot which had been occupied by its parent, one of those saplings. The mayor presided, the sapling was christened, and it and the whole occasion were blessed in a prayer by the Presbyterian parson.[22]

The sapling took root easily and began to grow into stately beauty to emulate for the next four hundred years its parent, adding to its parent's fame of being the only tree that owned itself the further distinction of now being "The Only Tree in the World that Inherited the Land on Which it Grew."

"The Only Tree in the World that Owned Itself" had set a style before it passed on, a style which deprived it of the "Only" in its name, for trees in Georgia and in other states, even as far away as California were being deeded unto themselves.[23] And what difference should it make, whether William H. Jackson ever deeded to itself a tree which he never owned, whether he did so in 1820 or in 1870 or never did it at all! The sentiment is there, unique and beautiful. Athenians enjoy the honor of having nurtured this sentiment by clothing the tree with a personality and giving it greater protection than any formal legal document could ever have done.

CHAPTER III

The Birth of a University, a Town, and a County

THE twelve parishes into which most of Colonial Georgia had been divided were combined into seven counties in 1777, and the recently ceded lands north and west of the Ogeechee River were made into an eighth county, called Wilkes. These divisions were often referred to as the Constitutional Counties, for they had been created in the state's first formal constitution.

With the end of the Revolution and the increasing pressure of settlers against the Indian frontiers, in 1783, the very year of the Treaty of American Independence, Georgia was able to induce the Cherokees on May 31 and the Creeks on November 1, in identical treaties, to agree to a large cession of land lying to the northward and westward of the settled part of the state. Large delegations of "Head-men, Warriors and Chiefs" had come to Augusta to make these treaties. The description of the new boundary which was agreed upon to separate the Indians from the white settlers was repeated before the end of the century in a half dozen additional treaties, some made by Georgia and others by the United States: Galphinton, 1785; Hopewell, 1785; Shoulderbone, 1786; New York, 1790; Holston, 1791, and Colerain, 1796.[1]

1. Washington and Franklin Counties

Sooner than four months after the Cherokee-Creek cessions had been made in the Augusta treaties, the Georgia legislature proceeded to open these new lands to settlers in an act, beginning with an expression which was to become the usual form in legislation setting up counties: "Whereas it is necessary in order to strengthen this State, and for the convenience of the inhabitants, that new counties should be laid out and properly settled."[2] This act, passed on February 25, 1784, became memorable in the history

22

of the state, by starting the division of the state into additional counties which in numbers were eventually to reach the high water-mark of 161 before a slight recession began, and by providing for the establishment of a state-controlled university of higher learning. It divided this territory into two counties, named for George Washington and Benjamin Franklin, and set aside in each county 20,000 acres of land as an endowment for the university. The next year, on January 27, 1785, the legislature passed an act embodying a charter for a state university, the first of its kind in American history.[3]

The university was to wait sixteen years before it actually took root; but the settlers could not wait to enter onto these lands not even for one year or hardly a month. Land was on the mind of everyone, for it was the principal road to wealth or even to making a scanty living. Land laws had been passed from the days of the Colonial Trustees down through the period of the Royal governors and on into the Revolution, laws to make it easy for people to get land; for only land that was settled was valuable. The latest system under which people could secure land until Washington and Franklin counties were opened up was provided in an act of February 17, 1783. This law allowed every head of a family to receive 200 acres "without any other or further charges than the office and surveying fees." If he wanted more he could buy it in amounts and prices depending on how many members there were in his family, apportioning 50 acres for each member. The first 100 acres of this additional land would cost one shilling an acre; the second 100 acres would be one and a half shillings an acre; the third 100 acres, two shillings; and so on until the sum total might reach 1,000 acres. No one might receive more than this amount; but "soldiery and other troops" might have land according to whatever previous commitments had been made to them. Settlers might pay "audited certificates," and they must cultivate three acres for every 100 acres before they might receive the final grant.[4]

With the opening up to settlement of these good lands of Washington and Franklin counties, much of it lying along the

Oconee, Broad, and Savannah rivers and their tributaries, these prices were considered too liberal—and especially so in the light of the great pressure of people to enter upon these inviting scenes. Those who bought land in these new counties should now pay "in gold or silver . . . in Mexican or Spanish milled dollars" three shillings per acre (a dollar being rated at four shillings and eight pence). Half of the amount was due after two years and the other half at the end of a subsequent period of three years. No one should have more than 1,000 acres and he must settle upon his holdings within a year, and if anyone could prove that he had lived on the land for a year and had cultivated two acres for every 100 acres granted, he might be exempted from taxation on it for the next three years.

In addition to the commonality of Georgians, who might purchase land according to the announced rates and who must conform to the other stipulations as to cultivation and release from taxation, there were five specially favored classes who had gained their status by certain services during the war. (1) During the darkest days of the Revolution many people had fled the state, leaving behind the unterrified such as the legendary Aunt Nancy Hart. Those who remained to defend their liberties to the bitter end were given the reward of 250 acres of good land exempt from taxation for ten years, provided they were not guilty "of plundering or distressing the country." This class were allowed "Citizens Rights." (2) But any who "during their refugeeship, had served their country as good soldiers," were allowed an equal amount of land, and any who had been officers were allowed a greater amount according to rank. These rights were recognized by what were called "Refugee Certificates." (3) Those who had served in the Continental armies were given rights known as "Continental Certificates." (4) Any Georgians who had enrolled as minute men, but who were not in the regular service were allowed "Minute Men Certificates." (5) And the few who had served in the small naval forces were given "Marine Certificates."[5] All of these bounty land people were charged only the office fees "without any restrictions or delays whatsoever."[6]

A great triangle of land lying between the North Fork of the Oconee (or simply the Oconee, as it commonly came to be called) and the Apalachee (South Fork of the Oconee), which with the exception of the southern point lay in Franklin County, was reserved for a year "for the officers, seamen and soldiers" who were "entitled to land in this State by any resolve of congress or act or resolve of this State."[7] This land extended north and west all the way to the Indian frontier. It was later severed from Franklin County and erected into Jackson County, and the southern part of Jackson subsequently became Clarke County. In addition to this special consideration all soldiers and sailors, "officers of the medical department, refugees, and citizens," who were entitled to land "as bounties for their services" were given the right, wherever in the state they might settle, to elect to receive fifteen additional acres for each hundred in lieu of their special tax exemption.[8]

These Georgia lands were open not only to citizens of the state but also to citizens of any other state who should come "with an intent to settle and form an actual residence" and take an oath of allegiance to Georgia. They might have as much as 1,000 acres according to the general regulations and it would be held for not more than a year for them to enter upon it.[9] This provision was called forth not only for the reason that Georgia wanted to draw a large population from the other states to fill up eventually her vast domain extending all the way to the Mississippi River, but also to carry out a promise she had made to a group of Virginians who had been negotiating with the state before the end of the Revolution for a tract of land.

The principal leader of this group was the old Revolutionary veteran George Mathews, who had fought under Washington and had been wounded and taken prisoner at the Battle of Germantown. He had been exchanged in December, 1781 and had joined General Nathanael Greene's armies operating in Georgia. In February, 1783 Mathews and three other Virginians, George Rootes, John Lewis, and John Cobbs (or Cobb), petitioned the Georgia legislature for a "certain quantity" of land. A few days later the legislature promised that when it should "lay out one or more counties . . . a Square district or Tract of Land" of 200,000 acres would be reserved for fifteen months for these Virginians and the group they promised to bring to Georgia. Mathews had first in the preceding January petitioned for 1,000 acres of land for each of thirty or more families, agreeing that each 1,000 acres would be paid for at twenty-five pounds sterling.[10] But the legislature had seized the bull by the horns and had decided that if thirty Virginia families in that war-ravaged state were thinking of coming to Georgia, that probably 200 or more would be willing to come. So the 200,000 acre tract would accommodate 200 families taking the maximum amount of land allowed and if any should take smaller tracts, there would be room for more families in this special area set aside. Of course others might come and settle where they pleased; but it must be understood that the head right system applied to all. This movement should not be allowed to develop into a great land speculation or into a small principality within the state. But if the Virginians wanted to hold together as a group, they might do so in such a large area as 200,000 acres.

So in the act erecting Washington and Franklin counties the legislature kept its promise and agreed to set aside the 200,000-acre tract. These Virginians were given the right to "fix on the county and place wherein they would settle."[11] They were given fifteen months after the passing of this act to remove to Georgia and settle according to the terms of the act. When the Land Court opened in April, 1784 to issue warrants for land, Mathews, Cobbs, Thomas Napier, Francis Willis, and James Marks petitioned the Court to reserve their 200,000 acres, and it seems that they wanted the whole tract to be reserved in their names, apparently thinking that they would be allowed to administer the tract in their own way. The Court held that they must adhere to the head right rules. They asked to be allowed to appeal to Governor John Houstoun.[12] Their appeal was allowed, but, of course, the Governor could not go contrary to the law; so the Virginians forewent their rights to a special tract in Washington and Franklin counties, and proceeded to settle along the Broad River in Wilkes County, though a few procured land and settled in Washington and Franklin counties. In this Broad River country they became a remarkable element in the population of the state, for a generation. They provided three governors of the state and other outstanding leaders. With the advance of population around the Gulf and the rise of the states of Alabama, Mississippi, Louisiana, and Arkansas, many of these Virginians moved on into those states to assume important positions of leadership.[13]

The Virginians were not the only ones who were displeased with the Land Court which had been set up in Augusta in April. There was a great scramble for land warrants among a mob of people, who approached in numbers as many as 2,000, all hoping to hurry ahead to pick out the best lands. And although the Court was to sit for three months, people wanted their warrants immediately, and when there was some delay, a bully inflamed "by the juice of the cane," called in derision the Fat King (a name of a prominent Creek warrior), "kicked up a dust" and led a mob which broke into the small structure where the Court was sitting and scattered the warrants all over the floor and out into the streets.[14] When the excitement was over, the legislature provided that lands not taken up before February of the following year should be thrown open to settlers under the cheaper system set up in the act of February, 1783, whereby a head right of 200 acres was allowed free except for office and surveyor fees, as has previously been noted.[15]

Settlers now began to flock into this region, getting their lands surveyed, building their cabins, clearing their fields, and upsetting the Indians, who knew very little about boundary lines. Although this frontier line was being repeated in every treaty made with the Indians, it was never surveyed and marked out, and apart from the river boundaries on the east and the west and the settled area on the south, its exact location was about as vague to the whites as to the Indians. The only clear point on the northern boundary was Currahee Mountain, visible for many miles, across which the line went in a southwesterly direction to the head-waters of the Apalachee River (South Branch of the Oconee).

The Indians soon began making raids on these new settlements, scalping, burning, plundering, and carrying off horses and cattle, and now and then taking a few prisoners, especially children. The whites naturally began to retaliate, and frequently they were the aggressors to begin with. Raids against the Indians soon developed into full-scale war, carried on by the organized state militia. In 1787 Elijah Clarke and his son John in charge of a considerable force engaged an army of Indians on a creek flowing into the Apalachee from the west, then called Jack's Creek, but not for John Clark, and there inflicted a severe defeat on the Indians, killing at least twenty-five, but estimated by some participants to have been as many as fifty.[16] This defeat did not long stay the tomahawk of the Indians or mollify the temper of the settlers. The next year a party of Indians swooped down upon a cabin in the clearing on the Oconee and wounded two men, a woman, and a child, but they lost four or five of their number in this foray. And the spirit of an Aunt Nancy Hart, later to become a legend, must have been present, for "The woman who was wounded, it is said, did more execution than the two men—a proof she was not entirely unskilled in squirrel hunting."[17]

The Indians were especially active along the Oconee River, which in its upper stretches was far inside the ceded territory (the South Fork of the Oconee or Apalachee River, as it commonly came to be called, being the Indian frontier on the west). Soon after the Battle of Jack's Creek, they killed and scalped a lad of twelve, and killed a man in a small settlement called Greensborough and burned the buildings, a half dozen miles east of the river. On the Oconee near the Cedar Shoals, the site of the future town of Athens, the Indians stole a little girl about six years old, whose name was Tempest Ellice or Ellison. Years later James Seagrove, the Federal Indian agent, in dealing with the Creeks got her released in South Georgia, and according to his report, "This girl was taken from or near the Cedar Shoals on the Oconee, at the house of Mrs. Scarlet, about seven years past; she is 13 years of age, but does not remember anything of her family."[18] Down the river at Scull Shoals the Indians murdered six persons, a man, a woman, three children, and a Negro.[19] About the same time a war party appeared at another place on the Oconee and killed a man, his wife, their two children, and a Negro woman.[20] And such was the news along the Oconee. Farther northward and eastward in Franklin County the news was the same. Between the Tugaloo and Keowee rivers three Cherokees scalped a man, mortally wounded another, and carried off a string of horses.[21] About the same time another party of warriors killed two men and stole forty horses. A group of settlers hurriedly collected to go in pursuit but found that they could muster only "5 old muskets."[22] A Franklin County citizen reported that for protection "many of our fellow citizens" were fleeing into South Carolina.[23]

Governor Edward Telfair was not sitting idly by. He had been demanding from the Federal Government protection against the savages and was prepared to send an army of a thousand or more men into the Indian country, even though the Secretary of War was warning him that he had no right to start an Indian war. And yet Governor Telfair was conscious that not all the wrongs were being committed by the Indians. On March 9, 1793 he issued a proclamation admitting that the Indians had been guilty of much savagery, but he warned the settlers against invading the Indian country and committing violence against them "or from trespassing on the lands reserved to them for their hunting grounds, either by marking trees, grazing of flocks, hunting or following game within the before described territory. . . ."[24]

A certain D. M'Cluskey became a bit sarcastic over this proclamation. He said there was too much coddling of the Indians. The governor had now proclaimed that the white people must not cross into the Indian lands, and "he strongly charges and enjoins all persons whatsoever, not to suffer their stock (should they straggle across the line) to bite off any blades of Indian grass.— His next will probably prohibit our pigeons to cross the Appalachee River, lest, they, perchance, pick up a few acorns, and thereby prevent the Indian Bears and Deer from getting so fat as they otherwise do."[25]

About the same time, Judge William Stith in his charge to the Franklin County Grand Jury, using as much judicial temper as he could muster, referred to the savage situation which prevailed along the borders of the county and far into the interior. "We have experienced," he said, "a continued series of the most inhuman butcheries and robberies committed on our frontiers by those savage tribes, and as yet we have not been cheared [sic] with scarce a single ray of Federal Protection." If any of the citizens of Franklin County were to blame, the jury should find the facts and present them, for "offences against any Indian in amity with us is [sic] made a high crime by the laws of this state, as true and faithful representation (of facts) relative to the differences between the frontier inhabitants and the Indians being made, the world will determine on which side justice ought to preponderate. Therefore let the truth of facts be known, how much, and how long your citizens have suffered, and if they have been their avengers, whether they are justified therein by that great and first principle of nature, *self defence*."[26]

People were coming to Georgia in great numbers from as far north as Virginia and moving into Washington and Franklin counties and people already in Georgia were flocking in—all in spite of Indian dangers, which were as impotent against land-hungry settlers as was King Canute against the ocean tides. It took but two years to bring enough people into Washington County, which was the southern part of the ceded lands, to cause the northern part of it to be cut off and erected into Greene County (1786). Ten years later, the southern part of Franklin County was severed and set up as Jackson County.[27] Flood gates were open, and into Jackson County flowed a stream of settlers which, according to Judge George Walton, by 1801 had brought the population to "at least ten thousand, according to the census lately taken."[28]

2. Locating the University and Founding Athens

Forces were now converging on the southern part of Jackson County which would before the end of 1801 result in cutting off that part of the county and organizing it into Clarke County. The chief of these forces had its origin in the original law which authorized Washington and Franklin counties in 1784. It was none other than the setting apart of 40,000 acres of land in these two counties to be an endowment for the state university. Twenty thousand acres in 5,000-acre tracts had been surveyed in each county, and at least one of these tracts was in what was to be Clarke County. During the years preceding 1801 it had been as difficult to bring to a permanent location this university as it had ever been to bring to port the "Flying Dutchman." At first its location had been made at Louisville, in Jefferson County, but as the university was only a phantom it soon broke its moorings here and turned up next at Greensboro in that part of the original Washington County which had now become Greene County. Determined at last to bring substance to a phantasy, the sonorously-sounding Senatus Academicus, which was the governing body of this university-to-be, after vain efforts to get a quorum, finally met on June 17, 1800. It now decided that the university should be located somewhere in Jackson County and it appointed a committee of its own members consisting of five to visit the county and locate the hill from which the torch of learning should cast its beams both near and afar. On this committee were Abraham Baldwin, who had written the Charter of the University; Judge George Walton, who was one of those who had signed for Georgia the Declaration of Independence; John Milledge, soon to be governor of the state and subsequently a United States Senator; and Major-General John Twiggs and Hugh Lawson, men who had served their state well.

Losing little time, the committee soon organized itself for the journey from Louisville, then the capital of the state, northward to the very edge of the Indian frontier. Passing through Lexington, the straggling seat of justice of Oglethorpe County, probably the

second or third day out, they spent the night at a tavern just across
the line in Jackson County, and proceeded the next morning to
the Cedar Shoals on the Oconee River (the branch often called
the North Fork). They were looking not only for the hill of the
future classic shades, but also one in the midst of a flourishing
agricultural region where there would be plenty of wholesome
food for those one hundred scholars who were to occupy the
"wing of the university" for which they were instructed to let the
contract. And these were not all of their instructions, for they
were to pay particular attention to the healthfulness of the region—
there must be no miasmic vapors hovering over the region, like
prevailed in the sickly coastal region. And they were not to forget
to have a spring of cool sweet water bubbling out of the hillside.

For the next week and more the committee made trips to many
prospective sites in this lower end of Jackson County, and on the
Fourth of July, which had already come to be a day to be fittingly
celebrated, they happened up on a great group of settlers who had
congregated around a bold spring in the midst of one of the
5,000-acre tracts which had been set aside for the university endowment. These people were celebrating the day and in the midst
of the enjoyment of their independence they invited the Committee to participate. After providing "a suitable collation for the
entertainment of the Committee," they began the important business of drinking toasts. With the university in mind, they drank
to Josiah Meigs, who had recently been elected president, to the
state of Georgia—"May her literature keep pace with her agriculture and population"—and to Judge Walton, who was chairman
of this university committee; and as was the becoming thing to
do, Judge Walton retired to a distance beyond hearing the toast.[29]

By now the Committee had about made up its mind in the
selection of the spot where the university should be built; and
two days later the decision had been reached. It was to be on a
high hill on the western side of the Oconee River at the Cedar
Shoals, not very far away from that grove of trees and the spring
where the Fourth of July celebration had taken place. At this
place there seemed to be all the requirements necessary for the

growth of a thriving institution of higher learning. There was
the imposing hill sloping not too abruptly down to the river's
edge; there was the spring of water, in fact there were two or
three of them; there was plenty of wholesome country provisions
to be had in the neighborhood, with beef, pork, and mutton so
plentiful that it was supplying the Augusta market to a greater
extent than any other region. In fact on the very side of this hill
there were fields of flourishing corn, cotton, and potatoes, and
what was more (at least in the eyes of prospective students)
there were on this same hillside orchards of apples and peaches.
And even more than that—for combining sport with the procural
of food, there were besides, "the common lesser fish of fresh waters,
the shad, in their season," which were to be found in the river
"in great perfection; yielding a comfortable supply of this bounty
of nature, the delicious and healthful change in the food of man."[30]

And most of all, for one must live to enjoy the good things
of life, there were no low lands along the river from which
noxious vapors might arise, and those few which did come from
the water's edge were wafted eastward away from the university
hill. There was a pleasant breeze across the hill; the sky was clear
and at night the heavens were studded with twinkling stars. As
President Meigs said when he arrived to begin collecting and instructing his students, "If there is a healthy and beautiful spot in
Georgia this is one."[31]

The Committee was very effectively assisted in making their
choice by an old-time settler at the Cedar Shoals—old as settlers
went on this new raw frontier. He was Daniel William Easley,
a Virginian, who had at some unknown time settled in Franklin
County and had become sufficiently important to be named one
of the commissioners who were designated by the legislature in
1796 when it cut off Jackson County, to fix on the location
of the county seat; and he seems to have been the most important
one of these five commissioners, for until the site had been selected, "courts and elections" were to be held at his house.[32] Like
all ambitious men of his day he busied himself buying land and
developing likely spots, and it seems that he was so busied with

his land dealings and other activities that he and the other commissioners had no time to be selecting a site for the county courthouse—and it was probably convenient for him to have his home to serve as the spot where county government should be carried on. Two years later another set of commissioners were appointed, with Easley omitted; but these new commissioners were no more prone to act than Easley and his commissioners had been. So finally the legislature in 1801 appointed a third set of commissioners to choose the county site.[33]

It is not known how much land Easley owned in that part of Franklin County which was later to become Jackson, as the early Franklin County land records are fragmentary; but Jackson County records show that he was early in the market for land there. In 1797 he paid $500 for 237½ acres "on the North Fork of the Oconee River"; and on the 19th of March, 1800, for $897 he bought from William Few 693 acres "on the south west side of the North Fork of the Oconee River . . . it being a part of a tract of 1,120 acres granted to said Few" in October, 1785.[34] The land which Easley bought from Few lay in the vicinity of Cedar Shoals and was the site on which the University was to be founded and on which the town of Athens was to grow up, though it hardly seems probable that it included the Cedar Shoals, for by the summer of 1801, when the University Committee came that way, Easley had built a dam across the river to develop water power sufficient to run a flour mill, "a saw and common grist mill," and he expected to add soon to his growing industries a "cotton machine [gin]."[35] Also he had nearby two dwelling houses, one very new.

Easley was undoubtedly an easy talker and a real estate salesman par excellence (of the variety a hundred years later to win the sobriquent of "super"), for despite the 5,000-acre tract of University land, with that beautiful grove and bold spring, and despite the fact that the Trustees of the University had scarcely any money, Easley so captured the Committee and especially John Milledge, one of the Committeemen, that he sold them 633 acres— John Milledge himself paying $1,000 for it and donating it to the

University. But Easley was not so foolish as to sell all his land here, for of this land which he had bought from Few, he still had 60 acres of it left with whatever other holdings he had adjoining—all of this to hold for an increase in value when a town must inevitably grow up around this educational center. Immediately on buying this land, Milledge and the other Committeemen could think of no better name for their location than that of the great classical center in Greece—"and it was called Athens."[36]

Choosing the spot did not complete the work of the Committee. They had the further task of letting the contract for the first university building to house those hundred students who were expected to enroll within a short period of time. Thereupon they set aside 36½ acres for the University square or campus in the center of which enough land was cleared to begin the structure with Jett Thomas being awarded the contract for the wood work and David Gaddy for the stone and brick work.[37] Apparently the Committee had not been assigned the duty of planning a town, but, nonetheless, they took it upon themselves as a necessary part of their task in founding the University. So they laid off lots on the north and west sides of the University Square, and these with the additional lots which Easley and others sold were the foundations on which the town of Athens was built.[38] And so the University and the town of Athens grew up inseparable for a hundred years, but with the greater size of each thereafter the umbilical cord which had tied them together grew weaker, but, of course, was destined never to completely snap in two.

3. The Birth of Clarke County

But this exciting development of a university and the growth of a town in the southern part of Jackson County, causing a foregathering of more and more people with accompanying ambitions for greater things to come, led inevitably to the erection of a new county. So it was that on December 5 of this same year 1801, the legislature was prevailed upon to provide for erecting a new county to be called Clarke. As was the custom it appointed five commissioners and vested in them the authority to fix the site of the county seat in "the most convenient and central place." Until the commissioners should make their selection, courts and elections should be held at the house of Isaac Hill, who lived a few miles south of Athens.[39] Among these five was John Hart, son of the redoubtable Aunt Nancy who according to later traditions slew many Tories in the Revolution in the Broad River country, and who was soon to come and reside with her son before she moved on to Kentucky to join some of her Hart kindred.[40]

If it had not become the custom to appoint commissioners to select the county site when a new county was established, it seems that the legislature might well have designated the town of Athens with all its promise for future growth and influence. The only point of argument against it could have been the fact that it was slightly north of the center of the county. A year later the county business was still being transacted at Isaac Hill's house,[41] but it was not because a county site had not been chosen.

The commissioners, who in addition to John Hart were William Hopkins, William Strong, Daniel Bankston, and John Cobb, with commendable speed and energy (unusual with such commissioners), chose a site for the county courthouse and jail. On December 5, 1801 the county had been authorized; on the following New Year's Day they made their choice. It was only a stone's throw from Isaac Hill's house, on "a place belonging to John Cobb on the South Side of Coles [Calls] Creek above the said Cobb plantation." The Commissioners in making their report, said that the place was "known by the name of the big Spring and the Town we have named Watkinsville." Cobb generously "agreed to give up to the Commissioners above mentioned a certain portion of Land for a Town for the use of the public or County eight Lots, Six of which are to front the public square and two back lots and one Acre for building the Courthouse and Jail & five or Six Acres for a Common."[42]

More for its central location than for any importance it may have had as a settlement, the Commissioners chose this spot and let the contract for the courthouse and jail to the lowest bidder. Micajah Benge, a prominent landholder and speculator in land and a member of the first Inferior Court of Clarke County, was the lucky bidder. He contracted to build the courthouse for $589.99 and the jail for $570.79.[43] In March, 1803 the Commissioners examined the courthouse and finding it completed they accepted it and declared that it was now "open for the purpose of holding court."[44]

What Watkins was thus being honored in the name of this new town can never be known, for at this time Watkinses were probably the most numerous family in Georgia, and there seemed to be as many Robert Watkinses as there were later to be John Smiths. There was at this time a Robert Watkins who was a justice of the peace of Clarke County and there was a William Watkins who was buying and selling land in this vicinity when it was still Jackson County.[45] So this place most likely was named for the family rather than for any individual. Certainly after the name had come into use, the place was frequently for a few years referred to as "Clarke Court House."[46]

The courthouse which the commissioners had announced was "open" for court business, must also have been "open" in that it was without all of its walls, windows, and doors, for in the following September the Grand Jury gave as a presentment "that our public buildings are not finished," which very likely also had reference especially to the jail.[47] Whatever the status of the first courthouse may have been, it was found to be too unsuited for the purpose it was designed to serve, and it was soon sold to two men, who were so slow in paying for it, that suit had to be brought to force collection.[48] The Inferior Court at its January term in 1809 paid John Brown $8.00 "for the use of his house the present Term as a Temporary Courthouse."[49] By 1810 the new courthouse, which had been a-building for a time, was completed, and the Inferior Court ordered payments of a total of $900.00.[50] It made a final payment to John Smith of $13.50 for furnishings consisting of "five Windsor Chairs for the Court."[51]

But what of the jail—a building so necessary on the raw frontier? Benge seems to have been slow in constructing a jail. But something had to be done with prisoners, and as the Inferior Court in 1803 observed that there was no place near the court where "disorderly persons can be confined, either for contemptious behavior in court or for rioting in the court yard," it ordered the sheriff to "have a strong paire of Stocks large enough to contain at least three persons prepared near the Court house . . . on or before ten o'clock tomorrow morning."[52] The sheriff busied himself immediately, but whether or not he succeeded in having the stocks ready by the next morning, very shortly the Court ordered William Finley to be paid $4.00 "for building Stocks." These stocks seem to have been badly used by either those whose misfortune it was to be fastened in them or by obstreperous persons who feared their time might come; for the next year the Court ordered Jacob Williams to be paid $3.00 for repairing them—or as the official record had it, "for building over pair of stocks."[53]

Undoubtedly there was grave need for stocks, a jail, or even a whipping post as instruments in upholding the dignity of the court, for court days afforded an inviting opportunity for rambunctious frontiersmen and bullies to release their exuberance built up "by the juices of the cane or the corn," or to give vent to fancied wrongs long unpunished. In 1803 the Grand Jury presented Robert Fulwood for profane swearing and saying "if he had people to back him that he wd [would] be the first man to lay hold of the judge after court broke, & put him in the stocks." At the same time the jury also presented William Townsend "for profane swearing, and saying that he would let the Sheriffs Guts out, and saying that all the people in the Court yard could not take him."[54] In this same year of turbulence one Sanford Ramey created a scene at the courthouse by pulling "his butcher knife out of his shot bag belt and swore he would kill Nathanial and Burkett Deane." On his knife being taken away from him, he "said he would be damed if he would neither eat drink nor smoke until he had killed" them.[55] Two years later, to escape the stocks or a libel suit, one John Puryear swore that he never said that Thomas Greenwood "was a man of infamous character & and more especially I Solemnly deny that I ever Said Thomas Greenwood had stolen a Pair of Shoes in the state of Virginia or any other place and that he had been publicly whipped for the Same unless I was in a state of intoxication & knew not what I said." He further testified that it was his belief that Greenwood was a man of high character, honor, and integrity, in witness whereof he secured the signatures of Judge George Walton, one of the Signers of the Declaration of Independence, and William H. Crawford, destined for a brilliant career which led him to the very edge of the presidency of the United States.[56]

Stocks served the purpose of punishment for minor crimes and brief restraints against committing crimes, but for those guilty of more serious infractions of the peace and of the dignity of the court, a jail must be provided for their lodgment. In the course of a few years a jail was constructed, but as late as 1809 it was still in need of steps. It was in this year that jailer Joseph Brown was paid $11.00 for making steps for it.[57] Jails could also be used, and at this time were used, for people who by certain acts had committed no crimes as viewed by future generations—those people who unfortunately owed debts which they could not or would not pay. In 1809, two of those inmates of the Watkinsville jail for debts agreed to give up all their estate, real and personal, in return for their freedom. In a hearing set for one of them, he was freed after giving up every possession except his clothing, bedding for his family, the tools of his trade, and "the necessary Equipment of a Militia soldier."[58]

Probably the most celebrated of the petty crimes committed was one charged against a chief man in the early history of Clarke County. He was Micajah Benge, the contractor for the first courthouse and jail, who was a leader in the region while it was still Jackson County. In 1798 Benge and William Hopkins (later, as has appeared, one of the commissioners to locate the courthouse site of Clarke County), engaged in an important land transaction with Colonel John Cobb (or Cobbs), who was one of that group of Virginians who had asked for 200,000 acres of land. They bought from Cobb for $4,000.00 a tract of land a few miles south of the future site of Athens, containing 4,025 acres, and the next year they added to their holdings in that region.[59]

Benge alone bought various other tracts and in various dealings came into possession of large landholdings. He also sold land, selling in 1799 with the consent of his wife Sally, land that brought him $2,550.00.[60] Benge was important in other ways. A few months before Clarke County was set up, the Inferior Court of Jackson County appointed him as one of the commissioners charged with opening a road from High Shoals on the Apalachee River "to the Seat of the University of Georgia."[61] And when Clarke County came into being, as has been noted, Micajah Benge was made one of the original judges of the Inferior Court.

Probably Judge Micajah Benge let his importance get the best of him on one occasion, for all puffed up over the way in which law and justice were being administered, he "went on a binge." According to the language of the Grand Jury in September, 1802, he was presented "for profane swearing . . . also for profane Cursing the Juries . . . also for bidding his Maker dam the Legislature for passing a Law that the verdict of any damned fool jury of a Justices court Should be final & Decisive & also for wishing god to dam the World & also for abusing a professor of Religion."[62] Benge was finally brought to trial in the Clarke County Superior Court for this outrageous display of ill-temper, and was fined $5.00.[63] But Benge had not lost his standing as a principal citizen, for even before his trial he had been awarded one-sixth of the general tax "for the use of building the Court House & Jale."[64]

County government in these early days rested in the hands of the Inferior Court, the Superior Court of the Circuit in which the county lay, the justices of the peace, constables, the coroner, and the sheriff. The members of the Superior and Inferior courts were appointed by the Legislature and held court twice a year. The justices of the peace were nominated by the Inferior Court and commissioned by the governor. There were two constables for every captain's militia district, appointed by the Inferior Court. Exempt from being appointed to this position were "justices of the peace, clergymen, attornies, infants, lawyers, madmen, physicians, idiots, poor, old and sick persons." The people at large elected the coroner, who, in addition to the usual duties of that office, was directed to act for the sheriff whenever this official was an interested party in any litigation, and to arrest him if he committed a crime. The sheriff was elected by the people for a term of two years.[65]

The judge of the first Superior Court to meet in Clarke County (it being in the Western Circuit) was Thomas Peter Carnes. In a judge's address to the Grand Jury, which for many years was considered a document worthy of publication in the newspapers, he would most likely orate on the high principles of justice and liberty and give a lecture on the philosophies of government. In the first such address that Clarke County citizens heard, Judge Carnes considered it proper to pay tribute to Elijah Clarke, the Revolutionary hero, only recently dead, for whom the county was named. "The name given to this county," said he, "is a name of reverence veneration and respect. It perpetuates the virtues of a charactor [sic] making early exertions & those of the most indefatigable kind in the trying times of the revolution, when Virtue & Patriotism were the moving causes and the post of danger was that of Honour; this charactor allways [sic] shewed the most substantial and unequivocal attachment to the liberty of his country—never when called on either by the authority of the state, or pressed by the distress of his neighbors was he known to hesitate a moment. Philanthropy and good will to all who thought well of there [sic] Country's cause, were themes in which he delighted to dwell & no man would go further honestly to serve his country & fellow citizens than this character."

Nor could Judge Carnes forego referring to the place where he was standing and to the barbarous savagery which the Indians had inflicted on the early settlers in its vicinity. "It need not be told," said he, "that this spot where we now appear and in which the command of the Laws of our Country is the distribution of speedy & impartial Justice was a waste and howling wild where the Savages exulted in the war songs and tortures of some of our relations & friends and when the Tomahawk & scalping knives were lifted and directed with success against innocent captive women & children. I say that these things are unnecessary to be repeated, as every man who has had the experience of twelve or fourteen years on the frontiers will sufficiently bring to mind such dolefull scenes, and convince all such as have been conversant with them as well as those who observe the progress that a patriotic and virtuous exertion on there [sic] parts will in all events secure and promote their happiness and that the best conduct toward the attainment of those desirable situations is to keep the mind generally in the contemplation of the means by which they have been acquired."[66]

The authority which came nearest to looking after the varied needs of the people was the Inferior Court. Besides appointing the constables, this body also appointed tax collectors and receivers; it granted tavern licenses, as previously noted, and annually fixed the rates which might be charged the public; it directed the laying out of roads and building bridges; it had charge of the relief of the poor; and what came to be probably its most important function, it appointed guardians for orphans, bound out orphans and poor children, probated wills and settled estates.

As the incoming settlers sprinkled themselves over the landscape of Clarke County, the cry went up for roads; and as a result one of the most constant duties the Inferior Court had to perform was to have these roads laid out and bridges built across streams. There must be a road from Scull Shoals in the lower end of the county on the Oconee River across the county to High Shoals on the Apalachee River; the road from Cedar Shoals (Athens) to Cherokee Corner must be straightened out and improved; a road from Athens to the Jackson County courthouse should be built by the "nearest and best way"; there should be another road from Athens to the "flat shole" on the Apalachee River; a road must be opened up from Scull Shoals to "Clarkes Borough" in Jackson County—such were some of the roads which the Inferior Court was ordering during the first decade of the new county.[67] With the multiplicity of road laws and orders to build roads, the Grand Jury presented as a grievance that "the road laws have had so many amendments that the Citizens of this State cannot understand them," and it recommended that the legislature pass a new act.[68] As for the roads themselves they were scarcely more than clearings through the woods, with little or no grading.

In 1807 the Inferior Court gave leave to Peter Randolph and Thomas Hill to erect a bridge across the Middle Fork of the Oconee River, a few miles south of Athens on the road to Watkinsville, and it applied the tolls fixed by state law: foot passengers, 6¼ cents; a man or horse, 6¼ cents; a two-wheel carriage, 25 cents; a four-wheel carriage, 50 cents; a horse, 2 cents; a cow, a hog, or a sheep, 1 cent.[69] In ordering payments for services rendered, in 1802 the Court paid Bedford Brown $25.00 for surveying the boundary line between Clarke and Jackson counties—the chain bearers to receive $1.00 a day.[70]

Those persons receiving tavern licenses "must give security in fifty pounds for their keeping an orderly and decent house, with good accomodations for travellers, their horses and attendants."[71] A license running for a year cost $8.56¼, and the scale of prices fixed upon in 1804, which had to be "set up in the public entertaining room" follows:

"For a Well furnished Dinner with good Spirits $0.50
For a Well furnished Dinner without spirits 37½
For a Common Family Dinner 25
For a Breakfast with Coffee 25
For Supper with Tea 25
For Stabling a horse 24 hours 50
For Feeding a horse with grane and fodder 12½
For Lodging per night in good Bed 12½
For fourth proof Jamaica Spirits pr. H. [half] pt. 25
For West Indian Rum pr. Do [half pint] 18¾
For Northard [Northern?] Rum pr. Do. 12½
Cognac Brandy pr. Half pt. 25½
Peach Brandy Do 12½
Holland gin pr. Do 25½
Contenant [Continent?] gin [Do] 18¾
Whisky [Do] 12½
Cider pr. qt. 12½

Bear [Beer] 12½
Wine of good quality such as Sherry & Midara 25
Malag Tineruff & 18 1/3."[72]

And so, there was set going a new county, a new university, and a new town—and a county seat was located. Other towns grew up in Clarke, and one, Salem, later disappeared completely, with not even a ghost left. More than a half dozen other counties than Jackson and Clarke owed all or part of themselves to Old Franklin, and even Clarke County gave up its lower half to form Oconee County. It thereby became the smallest county in the state, but by this division Athens became a courthouse town. The "wing of the University," which was built on the Oconee River hill around which grew up the town of Athens, remained the whole University for more than fifty years and instead of accommodating "a hundred scholars," by the middle of the twentieth century it was striving to educate its thousands of students. And instead of being all of the University, it had become merely one of more than a dozen parts into which higher education had been grouped by the state and called the University System of Georgia.

4. Where the University Committee to Select a Site Met

A question of some interest being asked and agitated in 1959-1960 was: Where were the Committee staying when they made their selection of the site of the University? The answer to this question was of some importance, because there was standing at this time in the little town of Watkinsville an old dilapidated building, long known as the Eagle Tavern or Hotel and more recently referred to as Billups Tavern. The owner had presented it to the State of Georgia to be preserved as an historical monument, the common report being that the Committee had met there to make their final decision on the University location. Actuated largely by this supposition, Governor Marvin Griffin set aside $25,000 (later reduced to $19,000) to be used in repairing the structure and opening it to the public. Substance seemed to be lent to this supposition by a news item in the *Augusta Chronicle*, June 20, 1801 announcing that a committee had been appointed who were "to meet at Billup's tavern, the lower end of Jackson county, on the 29th instant, to select the site of the university; and immediately thereafter to contract for the building."[73]

Since it turned out that the Committee did not make its decision on the 29th, but a full week later, the news item is of little value as absolute evidence that the decision was made at a place known as Billups tavern; but it is proof that there was at some place in the lower end of Jackson County a tavern by that name. As county Inferior Courts licensed taverns, it seemed a simple thing to turn to the minutes of the Inferior Court of Jackson County to see if such a tavern had been licensed. It happens that only fragments of the early minutes have survived. This writer searched assiduously the loose pages that were left, but found no reference to Billups tavern. He did find that the Inferior Court had granted licenses to Cain Jentry, Rob. Fortinberry, Roderick Easley, and John Smith.[74] There was a John Smith who lived, in the early 1800's, apparently in Watkinsville or in its vicinity; and if Roderick Easley did not live there in the same period, at least he owned much of the land on or near which the town was to be built. Either one or, indeed, both of these men could have established their taverns in Watkinsville, before the place went under that name or afterwards, for it was customary for county Inferior Courts to grant licenses to almost any homeowner who applied. In 1960, there stood on the yard of the old tavern in Watkinsville a marker erected by the Daughters of the American Revolution in 1926 calling the old building Eagle Tavern and stating that it had been erected in 1789 as a blockhouse against the Indians. It is not known that the Daughters had any better proof for this statement than hearsay or their imagination.

There was a big spring in the vicinity and the place came to be called Big Spring. As settlers had keen eyes for springs of good water, this surely would have been a favored spot. Isaac Hill's house, designated as the first seat of justice in the law authorizing Clarke County, was not far away, but as for the development of a town here, there was none at this time. Not until January 1, 1802 was one planned, lots laid off, and the name Watkinsville adopted; and it appears that practically all of the land on which Watkinsville grew up was originally owned by John Cobb and Roderick Easley.[75] So there is no great likelihood that there was a tavern here in the summer of 1801 when the Committee was looking for a location on which to build the University. But if there was a tavern at that time, the Committee in ranging down in this end of Jackson County might well have stayed there a night or two. However, at any rate, there was no tavern at that time called Billups Tavern.

Whether or not there was a tavern at the site of Watkinsville in the summer of 1801, soon thereafter there must have been one or more, for with the seat of justice of the county being located here, a tavern became a necessity. In 1836 Richard Richardson came into possession of the lot on which the tavern in Watkinsville stood in 1960, it having previously belonged to Edward Lumpkin, who had bought it from George W. Moore.[76] Who built this tavern and when is not known, but it is on record that the tavern was called Eagle Hotel as early as 1843, for part of the Fourth of July celebration in Watkinsville that year centered at the Eagle Hotel—for according to a newspaper account the Watkinsville Independent Blues, after having listened to the reading of the Declaration of Independence and "a chaste and eloquent oration," at the church, "marched to the Eagle Hotel, and partook of an excellent dinner, prepared by the proprietor, Richard Richardson, Esq."[77]

On October 6, 1846, Martha C. Richardson, a daughter of Richard Richardson, was married to Edward S. Billups. Through this marriage the tavern later came into the possession of the Billups family and not until then would it have been called Billups Tavern, though the name Eagle Tavern (as indicated on the marker) persisted.[78]

But there must have been somewhere in the lower end of Jackson County in the summer of 1801 a Billups Tavern; and preferably as a place for the Committee to foregather, it ought to have been located somewhere on the road to Jackson County from Louisville, the capital of the state. The road which the Committeemen would travel led northward through Washington, Wilkes County and on through Lexington, in Oglethorpe, through Cherokee Corner on the county line into Jackson County, and across the Oconee River at the Cedar Shoals. And whether or not the Committeemen came as a group or singly, a tavern on this road would be the logical place for them first to meet.

Henry Hull, long a resident of Athens, soon after the Civil War, wrote historical sketches of the town, which were later published by his son Augustus Longstreet Hull as the first part of his book *Annals of Athens, Georgia, 1801-1901. With an Introductory Sketch by Dr. Henry Hull* (Athens, 1906). Henry Hull, who said that his memories of Athens went back to 1803, declared that the Committee had met at a " 'tavern' " which belonged to John Billups, "to locate the University."[79] He did not state where the tavern was located; but his son, who was equally historically minded and who graduated at the University in 1866, was more specific. In his *A Historical Sketch of the University of Georgia* (Atlanta, 1894) he stated that the Committee "met at Billup's Tavern on the Lexington road and thence made tours of inspection to various localities."[80] A. L. Hull learned of the location doubtlessly from his father, and inferred from common repute, that there was an old tavern just inside Clarke County (Jackson County in 1801) known as Billups Tavern; and that it was here that the Committee lodged and made its decision on the location of the University. For a century and more this tradition was handed down among people living in that region. The site of the tavern, which had burned many years previously, was being pointed out as late as 1925.[81]

As has been stated previously, no record has survived indicating that John Billups had been granted a license to run a tavern, though in the missing parts of the minutes of the Inferior Court of Jackson County there was no doubt such a notation of a license being granted to him. But the deed records of Jackson County, which are intact and complete, list a purchase of 200 acres in 1799 by John Billups in the vicinity of Cherokee Corner on Big Shoals Creek, which takes its rise north of the Lexington road.[82]

The same year he bought 700 acres lying farther to the north-eastward in Oglethorpe County, but at this time he lived in Jackson County and continued to live there (Clarke County after December 5, 1801) until some time between September, 1802 and January, 1803. At the latter date, he was listed in a deed record as being "of Oglethorpe County," where he spent the remainder of his life.[83]

In 1815, shortly after John Billups' death, there was advertised for rent, a house on "John Billup's Plantation," about ten miles from Lexington and six miles from Athens, on the main road between these two places. It was a two-story building, with four rooms on the first floor and two above "with a passage sixteen feet wide" and "a convenient dry Cellar." The overall measurements of the house were sixty feet by twenty-four. There was a storehouse on the place and a machine for cleaning cotton "which goes by water." The plantation contained about 300 acres of cleared land, and the house was "considered one of the best stands for a *Tavern* and *Store* in the upper part of Georgia."[84]

The evidence seems conclusive that the Billups Tavern referred to in the *Augusta Chronicle* was on the Lexington road between Lexington and Cedar Shoals, a short distance inside Jackson County at that time and was the building referred to in the advertisement. Undoubtedly the Committee lodged at this tavern on their way up from Louisville and it seems logical to assume that they made this tavern their headquarters, though not necessarily staying there every night while they were making excursions into various parts of Jackson County, selecting the site for the University, arranging to build a wing of the University there, and laying out lots for the town of Athens. If a tavern had been in the vicinity of where Watkinsville was later to grow up, the Committee might well have spent a night or two there while viewing that part of Jackson County, but it would be highly illogical to say that they went back eight miles out of their way to this tavern (if there was one there) either to make their final decision on the location of the university or to arrange for the first building and the town.

Undoubtedly the identity of the tavern where the Committe

made their decision could be established, if certain documents referred to in their report should ever be found. In the minutes of the Senatus Academicus session held in Louisville on November 12, 1801 appears the following entry: "Mr. Walton from the Committee appointed to fix upon the site of the University, and for other purposes, reported, and delivered in a journal of their proceedings with the several documents therein referred to, which were read and ordered to be filed. . . ."[85] What happened to this journal and other loose records of the Board of Trustees and of the Senatus Academicus is not known. Some clue is afforded by a notation pasted in the back inside cover of the Minutes of the Senatus Academicus: "Doct Church will herewith receive all the Records of the Board of Trustees and of the Senatus Academicus except the present vol of the Senatus, which is in the Executive office at Milledgeville. very Respectfully, Asbury Hull, June 13, 1857." Asbury Hull was secretary and treasurer of the Board of Trustees from 1819 to 1866, and Alonzo Church was President of the University from 1829 to 1859. If the Committee's journal was received by President Church, it was probably kept in the President's Office, which in 1903 was located in Science Hall. This building burned in the fall of 1903 with all the records then in the President's Office. If the journal had been received and had not been kept in that office, it might have been lost otherwise through carelessness. And it is possible that the journal was lost in the removal of the capital from Louisville to Milledgeville. And it is barely possible that the journal reached Milledgeville but was not included in the papers received by President Church, but was carried away when Sherman's troops plundered the capitol building and the state archives; or that it escaped Sherman and was lost in the transfer of the state archives to Atlanta when the capital was moved there or after reaching there was lost through carelessness.

Fortunately the date on which the Committee made its decision was recorded on the cornerstone of the first University building, in this inscription: "The Site of this Building was chosen on the VIth day of July, 1801, in the XXVI year of the Independence of the United States of America. George Walton, Abraham Baldwin, John Milledge, John Twiggs, and Hugh Lawson, a Committee of the Senatus Academicus of the University of Georgia, and for the benefit of the Institution the adjacent land was on that day given by John Milledge." This building was named Franklin College in honor of Benjamin Franklin, but it took on the name of Old College when other buildings were erected. Then the name Franklin College frequently came to be applied to the whole institution until after the Civil War, when the name University of Georgia became common again.

The original cornerstone, of marble somewhat eroded by time and the elements, is still to be seen, but not in its original position. In 1908 an outer wall was erected encasing the original building, and in the process of this work, the old cornerstone was placed on the level of the second story, and can today be read from the ground only by the aid of field glasses. The wording on this stone was recorded by Ulrich Bonnell Phillips, a tutor in the History Department and previously a student here, who wrote a sketch entitled "The Passing of a Crisis. A Study in the Early History of the University," which was published in the *Pandora. The University of Georgia, 1899.*[86]

It might be well to refer to some mistakes which have been printed about the founding of the University and to correct them. In the *Annual Catalogue and Information of the Martin Institute, for Males and Females. Thirty-Sixth Annual Session. 1896-97,*[87] the statement is made that Governor James Jackson was chairman of the committee to select the site of the University and that they first chose "Lookout Hill," later called "Mitchell Hill," in Jefferson (in Jackson County), where Martin Institute was later to stand. It is then stated further that John Clark was one of the Committee and that he insisted on changing the location to the Cedar Shoals site. As a matter of fact Jackson was not governor at this time and was not a member of the Committee; neither was John Clark. It is possible that the Committee ranged as far as the future site of Jefferson, eighteen miles west of Cedar

Shoals—and that supposition alone of all that appeared in the above statement, could be true.

In the *Atlanta Constitution*, October 19, 1958 appeared this sentence. "The school, first called Franklin College, was originally scheduled to be located at Watkinsville, 25 miles south, but the founders feared the effect of a tavern there upon the students so they moved the college to a rural section on the Oconee River."[88] Unfortunately there are four mistakes in this one short sentence. The University was not first called Franklin College; it was never located at Watkinsville; Watkinsville is not 25 miles south of Athens, it being only 8 miles; and there is no record that the founders feared the effects of the Watkinsville tavern life on the students, for there was at that time no town of Watkinsville and probably no tavern in the vicinity of what later became Watkinsville.

5. Some Reasons for the Sixteen Year Delay in Founding the University

Before closing this critique mention should be made of some reasons why the University, chartered in 1785, was not actually founded until 1801, sixteen years later. In the first place, during these years of dormancy, the control of the University was vested in a cumbersome and unwieldly body, which after a few years became more so on account of constitutional changes in the government of the state. The act of 1784 authorizing the counties of Washington and Franklin and setting aside 20,000 acres in each county as an endowment for "a college or seminary of learning," named the governor "for the time being" and seven self-perpetuating trustees to do all things "requisite and necessary to forward the establishment and progress of the same." The next year when the institution was given a charter, that document named six additional trustees, who should continue to exercise the right to fill all vacancies on their board, and also it added another group to be called the "Board of Visitors," which should be composed of the governor, the Executive Council, the speaker of the House of Assembly (there being only one house), and the chief justice.

At this time there were twelve on the Council, but as the population of the state should increase, more would be added. These two
bodies meeting together were to be called the Senatus Academicus,
and they were required to meet annually. The Trustees were to
meet separately as often as they deemed it necessary. The Board
of Visitors should exercise no functions and hold no meetings
except as part of the Senatus Academicus.

In 1789, four years after this mode of governing the University
had been set up in the charter, the state adopted a new constitution,
which omitted the Executive Council and added another house
(the Senate) to the General Assembly. With no executive council, there could be no Board of Visitors, and hence no Senatus
Academicus; and yet this situation was not remedied until 1800—
eleven years later.[89]

During all of this confusion, making it impossible after the first
four years to hold a legal meeting of the Senatus Academicus,
it is not to be much wondered at that the first meeting of this
august body did not take place until fourteen years (1799), after
it had been authorized—and then the meeting was not a legal one,
for it was not until the next year that the legislature in the Act
of 1800 made possible the formation of a Board of Visitors. For
the thirteen years following the granting of the Charter, the
Trustees met only twice, the first time in 1786 called forth by a
request of the legislature and the next in 1794, which was a wholly
illegal meeting, with only five persons present, although seven
were necessary for a quorum. Of these five, only two were bona
fide Trustees, the others being two judges and the speaker of the
house. This meeting was a laudable attempt to fill five vacancies
on the board with nominees who were to become valid if agreed
upon by absent members.[90]

The general policies affecting the University had to be agreed
upon by the Senatus Academicus, but there remained within the
power of the Trustees the transactions of much detailed business.
And it was in this connection that their first meeting was called
for by the legislature, in carrying out an act of February 3, 1786

which set up Greene County from a portion of Washington County.[91] One of the 5,000-acre tracts of University land lay in the central portion of this new county, and by virtue of that fact the legislature decided to locate the county seat on this tract and to authorize the Trustees to lay out a town, called Greensborough. After reserving land for the public buildings, they were required to sell lots and the adjacent lands, "that the money arising from the sale of the said lots and lands adjacent, shall be applied to the sole purpose of promoting learning and science. . . ."[92] Here was the beginning of the first monies which would make possible the actual establishing of the University; for at this time it seemed never to have been contemplated by the most public-spirited and educationally-minded citizens that there should be a direct appropriation for education.

The Trustees now became a sort of real estate board, busied with selling and renting out the lands with which the University had been endowed. They made the most of their first meeting, by setting up machinery for this purpose. The land was to be divided into equal lots of 100 acres each and rented to anyone for a period of seven years with rent free for the first four years if the occupant would agree to build a house on it not less than sixteen by twenty feet, plant sixty apple trees and sixty peach or pear trees, and clear ten acres. The rent for the last three years would be one-fourth of all he produced. He would have the preference of renting the land for the next period of seven years. The Trustees later increased the period to ten years and appointed an agent for each county in which the University owned land.[93]

Thus it is evident that the University was slow in getting started not only because the governing body was cumbersome and actually incapable of legally existing for a period of eleven years (1789-1800), but also because there was no money available. Therefore, there was good reason why there should be uncertainty as to the place where the University should be built. Yet in 1786, the year after the University had been authorized by its Charter, when preparations were being made to move the capital of the state from Augusta westward, the legislature designated a place to be called Louisville, and appointed a committee "for erecting of public buildings, and establishing the seat of government and the university."[94] At this time is seemed to be an assumption without argument from anyone that the University would be located where the capital city would be. But the lack of money and apparently the lack of enthusiasm on the part of Trustees, Board of Visitors, and consequently of Senatus Academicus, there was no action for the next four years while legal action could have been taken.

Finally on October 20, 1797 a resolution was circulated and signed by seven Trustees (evidentally without holding a meeting) filling six vacancies, and calling for a meeting to be held on July 1, 1798. On the second of July four Trustees appeared, but a quorum not being present, they adjourned to the next day, when seven members appeared. For the next two days the Trustees were in session. On the last day they reported that they had on hand $7,463.75, which they considered "sufficiently respectable to commence the building of the University." Taking on life at last, it seemed, they now called a meeting to be held at Louisville in early January following, "as a failure on their part will, in all probability be productive of consequences highly injurious to an Institution on the prosperity of which materially depend the liberty and happiness of the rising generation." And they pronounced the warning that anyone absent without a good excuse should be fined $20.[95]

On January 8, 1799, at the appointed time, only three Trustees appeared. No quorum being present the three met the next day re-enforced by one, but still there was no quorum. On the third day a quorum appeared and some valid excuses for absentees were presented and accepted. This was to be an active year. For the next three days they proceeded to business and tried unsuccessfully to bring about a combination which could be called the Senatus Academicus. Realizing that changes in the state constitution had made it impossible to carry out the Charter's method of forming the Senatus Academicus they suggested on January 12 that the governor, the judges of the superior courts, the president of the Senate, and the speaker of the house ought to constitute the Board of Visitors, and they resolved that the legislature be asked to pass "an explanatory act which will obviate all difficulties." A year later, on December 5, 1800, the legislature passed an act which amended the Charter, by the Trustees' recommendations and adding to the Board of Visitors all the senators except those from the counties which were otherwise represented in the Senatus Academicus. This act also named thirteen Trustees, all of whom were new except Abraham Baldwin, and deprived them of the old Charter provision of self-perpetuation. Also it withdrew the seat of the University from Louisville.[96]

In the meantime the Trustees had met again on July 2 and 3, 1799 and then adjourned to November 27. On this day they succeeded in holding a meeting of a body that called itself the Senatus Academicus, made up of eight Trustees and three state officials—the governor, the president of the Senate and the speaker of the house. The meetings continued through the 28th, 29th, 30th, and December 2. Apparently any meetings, though illegal or at least extra-legal, were considered better than no meetings at all.

On the last two days of this series of meetings (November 30 and December 2, 1799) the Senatus Academicus busied itself with trying to fix on a "temporary site of the University." It now assumed that one of the county academies might afford such a site. It voted on five academies, but none was acceptable to the majority. (They were Columbia, Hancock, Wilkes, Greene, and Jefferson).[97] The next day the vote was taken again, but with no choice. They now decided to postpone any further consideration until their next meeting the following year, and in the meantime to send out a letter to all the county academies in the state, asking for a statement of their funds and endowments.

The year 1800 was a busy time for the Trustees as they held their separate meetings and as part of the Senatus Academicus. When the Senatus Academicus convened in November it found reports from eight academies, and now it took up the matter of choosing a site for building a "wing of the University," indicating that it was to be a permanent location. In the meantime it seems to have been forgotten that Louisville had been designated in the Act of 1786 as the site of the University, or probably that law was considered obsolete, now that fourteen years had elapsed— the act of 1800 removing the site from Louisville had not yet been passed. Motions were successively made to locate the "wing" in Greene, Franklin, Hancock, and Jackson counties. Greene was agreed on and a committee was appointed to build a wing of the University there, to accommodate one hundred students.

Undoubtedly political considerations were running riot in the attempt to choose a site, and it was evident that the low country had no chance, for neither Liberty nor Chatham County, which had reported, was considered; and the legislature the next month in its Act of 1800, ignoring the fact that the Senatus Academicus had already chosen Greene, listed the counties in which the University might be located. All in the upcountry, they were Jackson, Franklin, Hancock, Greene, Oglethorpe, Wilkes, and Warren. On June 16, 1801, the Senatus Academicus met. It reconsidered the choice of Greene County, and decided that a majority vote (not a plurality) would be necessary for fixing "the permanent site of the University." The next day there was spirited voting, but only five of the seven counties listed by the legislature were put in nomination. The first vote was: Jackson, 7; Franklin, 3; Hancock, 7; Greene, 3; and Oglethorpe, 2. On the next vote Greene dropped out and did not re-enter. The contest soon narrowed down to Hancock and Jackson, with the latter finally winning 12 to 10, on the seventh ballot.

At this meeting there was announced the bad news that some thief had broken open a letter from the University treasurer to Abraham Baldwin in Washington, and had removed "a Post Note of the Bank of the United States for one thousand dollars." The Senatus Academicus offered a reward of $100 for the conviction of the guilty person. Also at this meeting the committee which had been previously appointed to erect the "wing" of the University in Greene County was now instructed to proceed to make a choice of the site in Jackson County where the University should be built and to contract for its construction. And so, as has been set forth already, the Committee began its search, with the results as detailed.

The delay of sixteen years between the authorization of the University and its founding had been caused by the governing bodies' lack of money, the difficulties and for a time the impossibility of their coming into being, and their lack of zeal for their task. And an over-all reason was the distempers of the times largely brought on by seven years of the devastating Revolution, a rapidly increasing population spreading out against the Indian frontiers with the resulting raiding parties back and forth, and widespread land speculations.

CHAPTER IV

William D. Wash, C. S. A., Bravest of the Brave

I N 1851 William D. Wash left his home in Newton County, Mississippi, to enter the Freshman Class of the University of Georgia, at Athens. It is not known why he by-passed his University of Mississippi, unless for the reason that it was just then getting started, or the University of Alabama, which had more of a reputation. Nor is it known why he did not keep going on to the University of Virginia, the best known of the Southern universities, or even why he did not stop short at South Carolina College (later the University of South Carolina) or at the University of North Carolina.

But his going to the University of Georgia should not be too much of a mystery, for that institution had graduated men who had attained national stature by this time; and he would be going to the first state university to be chartered (in 1785) and the second in point of actual beginning (in 1801)—the University of North Carolina had been chartered in 1793 and it had been able to open its doors in 1795.

The University of Georgia, like other universities of that time, had a curriculum heavily weighted with the classical languages and with considerable mathematics. The year was divided into three terms. The first term began in the first week of October and continued to the middle of December; with a month's vacation, the second term began in the middle of January and continued to the middle of April; and with no vacation the third term began immediately and continued to the first part of August. As a Freshman, Wash was required to take three courses during the first two terms and four during the third term. He had Latin and Greek every term. His Latin authors were Sallust, Ovid, and Horace; his Greek authors were Herodotus (no work specified), and Homer (*Iliad* and *Odyssey*). He took Algebra every term and

The University of Georgia as it appeared when Wash was there. From *Gleason's Pictorial* (Boston), May 13, 1854, page 297.

Geometry, the third term. His work during his Sophomore year increased to six courses every term, with Latin and Greek throughout, two Mathematics courses throughout, and to complete his schedule he took History, French, Reading and Oratory, Botany, and Evidences of Christianity. As a Junior, Wash had six courses the first term, four the second, and five the third. He had Greek the first term, and Latin the third. He had four courses in Mathematics scattered through the year, Natural Philosophy every term, and to make out the remaining courses he took Navigation, Logic, Rhetoric, Moral Philosophy, and Chemistry. A student having successfully progressed through the first three years, found his Senior year less crowded with courses—five courses the first term, six the second; and the third term was made up of "General Review." His Senior courses were Mineraology, Chemistry, Political Economy, Mental Philosophy, Astronomy, Geology, Civil Engineering, and Law of Nations; some of these courses were continued through the second term.[1]

It would appear that this curriculum should have kept any seriously-minded student busy through his waking hours; but there was much more to college than going to classes. There were two literary societies, which the students considered of vast importance in their education—in fact some felt that their literary society training was more valuable than their class work. There were early morning prayers that got students out before sun-up and one class to be attended before breakfast; and there was a whole booklet full of rules which must be obeyed every hour of the day and night. Disobeying these rules became a major activity of many of the students. But there seemed to be time for all these things, for the distractions of the twentieth century had never even been dreamed of.[2]

Like Tennyson's Ulysses, Wash became a part of all that he met—and he met everything which the University had to offer. He joined the Demosthenian Literary Society and progressed in its officialdom from doorkeeper to secretary, to president, in the meantime holding such committee assignments as: to repair the hall, on tribunal, to invite the "Athens Guards" to the Fourth of July celebration, on Fourth of July procession, committee to draw up resolutions on the death of a member, committee on appeals, on library, on alterations of the constitution, and on questions to be debated. Such activities suggest that he must have taken a prominent part in the debates, which sometimes lasted all night and into the next morning; but the librarians' records do not show that he read widely in the well-stocked society library, and no records of student reading in the University library remain, to indicate any activity there.[3]

Some of the students lived in the homes of faculty members and of townsmen, but most of them lived in the two dormitories, Old College and New College, which were under the supervision of unmarried members of the faculty, who resided there. Wash lived throughout his four years in Room 35, New College, which placed him in the very jaws of student brawls and temptations to join in the pastime of disobeying the many rules, either by design or forgetfulness. Students living off the campus had the protective screen of a home atmosphere. Wash was not of the reckless boisterous type, but he was not so meek as not to assert his manhood on occasion, and, was therefore, unlike Alexander H. Stephens, who twenty years previously as a student in the University seldom if ever got called before the faculty for infraction of some rule.

Wash was nineteen years old when he entered the University and was, therefore, of a maturity which he felt gave him the right to make most of his decisions himself. When a Junior he got into a dispute with Tom Daniel, a Senior, over some matter relative to the *Georgia University Magazine*, edited "Under the Patronage of the Senior Class." Daniel was one of the retiring editors and Wash had been elected as one of the editors for the coming year. As recorded in the faculty minutes, "The dispute gradually led to harsh words and finally to blows." This being a matter for the high court of the faculty to settle, it decided that both were equally "in the wrong," and fined each $5.00 and "put them on probation."[4]

The only other infraction of rules by Wash recorded in the

minutes of the faculty related to a trip he and six other students
made to Lexington, in the adjoining county of Oglethorpe—all
without first having got permission of the faculty to be absent
from their classes. Their purpose was to hear Alexander H. Stephens, now a member of the national House of Representatives and
of outstanding prominence in the nation. For this infraction of the
rules, Wash and his associates were asked to appear before the
faculty "and if they wished to do so to state to the Faculty what
excuse they had for violating a law of College by going to Lexington." As for himself, "Wash stated that he wished to hear Mr.
Stephens speak—that he considered him a great man and he would
probably never hear him again, that he *was of age* and had a right
to judge what was best for him, that he thought he received more
benefit by going than by staying, that if the same circumstances
should occur again he would do the same thing again." This was
forthright frankness which must have commended him and his
associates to the faculty, for the professors deferred action and
seem never to have revived the matter.[5] When Wash was graduated in 1855, the faculty selected him as one of the commencement
speakers.[6]

Wash distinguished himself in Mathematics and as remembered
by an acquaintance thirty-five years later "passed an exceptionally
good examination" for his degree of Bachelor of Arts.[7] Wash's
whole college career, including his manly answer on why he went
to Lexington, was a recommendation which led the Trustees to
appoint him in 1856 "Tutor of Mathematics," at a salary of
$1,000.[8] As an instructor in Mathematics, Wash gave ample
satisfaction to President Alonzo Church and his faculty and to
the University Trustees, but not always to some of his lazy
students. In 1858 he was made Recording Secretary of the
faculty and continued so throughout the remainder of his service
as a teacher. Also this same year, there appeared after his name
on the faculty list in addition to his A.B. the degree of A.M. At
this time this degree was not earned in American colleges, but
was honorary and could be easily got. The Trustees had this year
conferred the A.M. on a man of some distinction and noted in

their minutes that the "President is authorized to confer the same on all Alumni of this College, who may apply, and are known to be entitled thereto."[9] Although no record extant indicates that President Church conferred the degree on Wash, there seems to be no other explanation as to how he got it.

Wash seemed to have had few waking hours when he was not teaching or on some faculty duty otherwise, and it seems that he did not object to these burdens. As if teaching Mathematics to Freshmen, Sophomore, and Juniors were not enough classroom work for Wash, when there was need for assistance in teaching Natural Philosophy he was assigned to classes in this subject also. Such willing service could not escape the notice of the Trustees, who in 1860 resolved that he was "entitled to the expression of the Boards appreciation of the valuable services in instructing the Junior Class in Natural Philosophy and as a testimony of this appreciation," they paid him $300 extra salary, and resolved further "that he be made Adjunct Prof. of Maths & Nat Phil" at $1,300.[10]

Classroom work was only part of the duties a teacher assumed when he should join the University of Georgia faculty. In addition, if unmarried, he must reside in one of the dormitories to keep constant watch over the students living there, to visit their rooms unannounced at any time of the day or night, and to help put down fights and riots on the campus, and to enforce all the other rules that filled up the students' *vade mecum*. If a teacher were a man with a family he was expected to enforce any rules which he observed being violated, and since a majority of the professors lived in faculty houses on the campus, they found it difficult to escape these extra duties. In fact a teacher in the University was almost as much a policeman on the campus, as well as off, as he was an instructor in the classroom. An attempt to avoid these extra-classroom duties lay at the bottom of the celebrated disagreement between President Church and the LeConte brothers, John and Joseph, which resulted in John leaving the University in 1855 and Joseph the next year.[11]

Wash was duly respectful of authority and expected authority to be respected; and when he joined the University faculty and agreed to assume no less the duties of policing the students than instructing them, he expected to perform equally in both departments. No members of the faculty took more seriously his duty to police the students than did Wash, and he soon gained the reputation of being tireless at that work—a terror to the rule-breakers but in their more sedate and better natures, then and later, their ideal. Undoubtedly running down culprit students appealed to Wash's nature almost as much as it was an expression of loyalty to authority above him.

The agenda of cases before the high court of the faculty was mostly made up of Wash's prosecution of students for violating rules. This warfare which Wash and the students waged against each other subsided after four or five years, probably because Wash had gained the upper hand but more probably because there was being sniffed in the breeze the dangers of a shooting war in reality, as the secession of the Southern states began to loom up by 1860.

One of the first student outbreaks against Wash occurred within a few months after he had joined the faculty, but long enough for the students to have learned that they had a tough adversary in their new Mathematics tutor. A dozen assaluted his room in New College one night about one o'clock, first having tied his door shut with a rope. With a barrage of rocks and other missles they broke out his window panes, and the "damage upon the building was considerable." Wash soon managed to get his door open and then pursued the students to their rooms in Old College, and by observing the doors through which they scurried he learned their names. They were brought before the faculty, which expelled the ringleader and delayed action on the case of the others.[12] Seventy years later, a student not a member of the mob, remembered vividly this bit of the military history of his old alma mater.[13]

Another mob which Wash put down formed a few days after school opened in 1858. Soon after supper Wash heard "much boisterous noise" in and around Old College. He went out and dispersed the students and followed them into the building. He entered one of the rooms and was spoken to "disrespectfully and impudently." In one of the rooms he heard a student "propose to rock Bill Wash's room," but another student replied that "he would have nothing to do with it. Mr. Wash had always treated him as a gentleman." This gathering had been only preliminary to a bigger engagement in which Wash was soon to find himself. Later that evening a group of students gathered at an outhouse on the campus, "singing obscene songs and using profane language." As Wash approached he heard a student say "d--n him he better not come here." Undeterred by such empty bragadoccio, Wash flushed them and they ran. With his accustomed strategy he hurried to the dormitory and took note of the rooms; he found enough empty to implicate fifteen students. Only seven were found to be out of their rooms without permission, and of these seven, some were expelled and others fined $10.00 apiece.[14]

On visiting a student's room about eleven o'clock one night Wash found a group of students inside and on looking around he found a bottle of whiskey about three-fourths empty, which seemed to indicate to Wash that they had been drinking.[15] Wash's success in dispersing mobs made it easy for him to deal with single students. On one occasion, seeing a student out of his room when according to the rules he should have been inside, Wash found the student very obstreperous. The student refused to return to his room and insisted on sitting on the steps of Old College and he declared that he would not go inside "if you fine me $50." The faculty did not fine him at all, they expelled him.[16]

One night about 10:30 o'clock a student somewhat inebriated came into New College singing and pounding on the steps with a stick. When Wash came out to see about it, the student denied that he was noisy but admitted that he had been singing "but it was such a song as no one would object to." When hauled before the faculty he apologized to Wash and was let off.[17] Wash had a few encounters with student James M. Oliver, who was to become a captain in the Confederate army and to die in the service. First, Wash saw Oliver enter his room at night and reminded him that he was breaking a rule. Oliver replied that the rule was too rigid and that Wash was the only member of the faculty who enforced it. Oliver reported at the faculty trial that he meant no disrespect to Wash, and there the matter ended.[18] A week later Wash saw Oliver "entering a drinking saloon." The faculty admonished Oliver but did nothing further.[19]

Wash not only ranged over the campus, but cast an eye out into town. One day about 10:00 o'clock Wash saw some students sitting in a store; but they were excused by the faculty committee when they produced acceptable excuses.[20] Students knew better than to misbehave in Wash's classes; but a student on one occasion seemed to show considerable disrespect. He cleared himself by denying that he meant his actions as disrespectful.[21]

A recounting of Wash's police activities might seem to indicate that he was a strutting martinet; but the students more or less expected the treatment they got, for they knew the rules they were disobeying. And Wash's regard for the duties he had agreed to perform made it seem necessary that he perform these duties or otherwise resign. The full nature of the man, his sensitivity and his loyalty, as was to be later exemplified, should absolve him from charges of petty persecution of the students.

The election of Abraham Lincoln to the Presidency of the United States in November, 1860, created a profound effect throughout the South, and before the end of the year South Carolina seceded from the Union. The students at the University were upset and could muster up little enthusiasm for attending classes any more when the world they knew needed to be defended; and the professors were little less at ease. Before Lincoln was inaugurated, Wash resigned, but respecting the rule which required a six-months notice, he served on to the end of the calendar year, 1861. It was variously reported as to what object he had in mind, but whatever course his new activities might take, it was never doubted that he would direct them to the defense of the South; for he was a passionate believer in the rights of the states. The editor of the *Southern Banner*, one of the Athens newspapers, reported that Wash had resigned "for the purpose of practicing law,"[22] but in a reference by the faculty to his action it was stated that he had resigned "to enter into the military service of his country."[23]

The announcement of Wash's resignation softened any lingering harsh feelings the Junior Class might have remembered against him for his police actions on the campus. They held a meeting and expressed in a set of resolutions their high regard for him. They tendered their "heartfelt thanks for the kindness and courtesy which have ever characterized his deportment toward us"; they appreciated "highly his untiring efforts in endeavoring to advance the interest of the Class, both intellectually and morally"; and they resolved "with unfeigned regret that we dissolve our connection as Student and Professor, which has been of the most pleasant and profitable nature," and they hoped for him much success "in whatever field he may be called to labor," and further "may he meet with that success to which his talents so worthily entitle him."[24]

During the summer vacation, which began in the first part of August and continued to the first of October, Wash busied himself in politics. Heartily disagreeing with Governor Joseph E. Brown's obstructionist tactics toward President Jefferson Davis' Confederate policies, Wash became a delegate to the gubernatorial convention called to meet in Milledgeville in September (1861) to nominate an opponent to Brown. The convention nominated Eugenius A. Nisbet, who had introduced the secession ordinance which took Georgia out of the Union, and it selected electors for the November election of Davis for permanent president and Alexander H. Stephens for vice president.[25] The Davis-Stephens ticket had no opponents, but Brown won out over Nisbet.

In these exciting times when people on all sides were volunteering for war, Wash could not rest content to teach out his final term in the University without plans to enter the service. As was the custom, volunteers repaired to the standards of those leaders who were most appealing in their calls for troops; and there was keen competition in raising companies. Although still teaching, Wash was busily soliciting volunteers for a company he was attempting to raise. In early November the *Southern Watchman*, the other Athens newspaper, announced that Major Wash, "who has had a thorough military training, is anxious to lead a company into the service, either on the coast or elsewhere, for a term of six or twelve months, or during the war." He was well known in the community as a professor in the University and was "highly esteemed as a christian gentleman."[26] It is not known where he got his "thorough military training," or how he came to the title of "Major"; but most likely he got both as a member of the "Athens Guards," a local military unit for some years.

Wash was probably handicapped by his teaching duties in raising a company, for he did not succeed—doubtless he had entered the field too late. The "hot heads" had already volunteered and were on the firing line by this time. In his attempt to raise his company, Wash ran into trouble with Dr. James Camak, who also was trying to raise a company. Since Athens and Clarke County had been pretty thoroughly combed over, Camak "took to the wilds of Oglethorpe County" and got the promise of about thirty men for his company. When they came to Athens to be enrolled, Wash, not knowing that they had been recruited by Camak, tried to bring them into his company, and succeeded in enlisting a few. This activity led Wash and Camak into an argument in which slaps were exchanged, but friends prevented further hostilities. Years afterwards, Camak remembered Wash as "brave even to rashness, patriotic, self-sacrificing, and thoroughly imbued with the doctrines of State sovereignty."[27]

Undeterred by this failure, Wash, in December after his resignation had become effective, made another effort to raise a company. He announced that he was authorized by a colonel of a Georgia regiment (both unnamed) then in the field, to raise a company for three-years service. "Here is an opportunity," he stated, "for all who wish to serve their country in her present peril and take part in a revolution which is to fill an important page in history."[28] He failed again.

Wash now decided to return to his native state of Mississippi and join a company there. In June, 1862, these Mississippians were enlisted in John Morgan's famous cavalry. Wash now became one of Morgan's most dependable men, following him in his first Kentucky raid in July, fighting gallantly at Tompkinsville, Lebanon, and Cynthiana, and back in Tennessee at Gallatin; and in December with Morgan in his "Christmas Raid" into Kentucky.

General Braxton Bragg having made his ill-fated expedition into Kentucky in the late summer and being forced back, fought General W. S. Rosecrans' Federals at Stone's River the last day of 1862 and the first two of 1863. The Federals now back in central Tennessee made raids out of Nashville and Murfreesboro preparatory to their expedition against Chattanooga. On March 1, on one of their foraging raids they ran into a contingent of Morgan's men at Bradyville, about twenty miles southeast of Murfreesboro, and put them to flight, all except those whom they captured. Among the latter was Wash. He with the others were hurried off to prison at Camp Butler, near Springfield, Illinois. Although he had withstood the rigors of John Morgan's marches and fights, he was unable to withstand the rigors of this Yankee prison, and on March 27, within a few weeks of his confinement, in the words of one who knew him, he "succumbed to the horrors of a Northern prison."[29]

When Wash's former associates on the University faculty learned of his death, Chancellor Andrew A. Lipscomb called the faculty together in a special meeting on June 8 (1863) and read a letter from one of Wash's comrades. It was incorporated in the minutes as well as was the faculty tribute to Wash. Wash's comrade wrote that "he participated in all the trials, hardships and battles of the command." He continued, "I have often heard it remarked by his comrades that he knew no fear, nor have I any hesitation in saying that he was the bravest man I ever saw. He was as cool in battle as if he knew not what was going on. At Cynthiana, Ky., he was far ahead of his command, while showers of bullets came thickly around him, one of them taking effect in his cartridge box. At Gallatin, also, he distinguished himself for calmness and bravery." He added, "I have been intimately acquainted with him and take pleasure in bearing testimony for his Christian integrity, nobleness of purpose, and undaunted bravery. Many a time, I have heard his full, rich voice in camp, lifted to heaven in prayer. The high moral tone of his character won him the respect of all with whom he met."

The faculty then paid Wash this tribute: "To us, his former colleagues, these words read as the simple and truthful records of his daily life. We find here, the same forgetfulness of personal welfare—the same consideration to purposes dearer than self and holier than life—the same martyr-like loyalty, which have so often awakened our admiration. No man, whom we have known, had deeper springs of action; no one, a firmer trust in the self-sufficing-ness of principle to form a consistent and heroic character. But his crowning excellence was the simplicity, fulness, force, of his religious spirit, which, born of the spirit of God and fed in watchful nurture of all the offices of Christian duty, gave to his life that directness of purpose, that unity of thought, feeling and action, that subordination of self to the cross of Christ, which early matured it for the fellowship of a better world." In resigning to join in the defense of his country, "he exhibited the same high conviction of right, the same stern obedience of a magnanimous heart, which were profound elements of his nature no less than striking traits of his outward character."[30]

In addition to the tribute paid to Wash's memory by the comrade quoted by the faculty and the tribute by the faculty itself, Wash's comrades who were encamped on the "Banks of Cumberland, Russell co. Ky." on May 20th, passed a set of resolutions to be sent to the University of Georgia and to Wash's parents. They declared that in Wash's death "our country has lost one of her best and bravest sons, the cause of christianity one of its purest defenders, science and literature a shining light, while the old soldiers of Gen. John H. Morgan's command, who have followed their brave leader through many a trying field, will ever remember the name of Prof. William D. Wash as associated with all that is pure, manly, noble and brave."[31]

CHAPTER V

Slavery and Freedom in Athens, Georgia, 1860-1866

SLAVERY was a harsh-sounding word; but in Athens, Georgia, servitude was not as harsh as the word sounded, and, indeed, in Georgia as a whole, this lot of the colored man varied from hard labor to virtual freedom from it. Some of the laws relating to slavery were severe on their face; others guaranteed the slave protection against cruel punishment. In either case, the law might often, and did, operate as a dead letter, depending for enforcement on the attitude of the master or the sentiment in the community.

The slave, though a person, was still property, and being such, he could not own property. Anything the slave possessed belonged to his master; even a gift to a slave became the property of his master. A slave should not be taught to read or to write or to act as a clerk, whereby he might learn to do so. Nor could he work in a printing office in any capacity where reading and writing were necessary; but he might turn the crank on a printing press. It was against the law to sell to a slave writing paper or ink or any other writing materials for his own use. No white person might play cards or otherwise gamble with a slave. A slave might not work in a liquor shop where he would have access to strong drink; and no one might sell or give to a slave any spirituous liquors, except that a master might furnish his slave such beverages whenever he thought it would be to the benefit of the slave.[1]

Frequent references in the various laws relating to slavery (often referred to as the slave code) indicated how lightly slavery rested on some classes of Negroes, and in some cases, on all Negroes. There were such expressions as these: "each negro or person of color nominally a slave," "nominal slave," and "nominal slaves, or slaves who have purchased themselves."[2] Now and then a slave might hire himself out to a person not his master, until he was legally prohibited from doing so without a permit from his master. And in 1850 a law was passed prohibiting a master from allowing his slave to run around hunting someone to whom he might hire himself, unless he paid a fee of $100 for such a privilege.[8]

According to Georgia law the normal condition of a Negro was slavery, and, therefore, any Negro claiming to be a free person of color (often abbreviated fpc) must be able to prove himself to be so; and a Negro was defined as anyone with one-eighth Negro blood. This fact, of course, placed a severe handicap on such Negroes, and led unscrupulous white men to seize and sell such people as being slaves. A law passed in 1835 declared that since free persons of color were "liable to be taken and held fraudulently and illegally in a state of slavery, by wicked white men, and be secretly removed whenever an effort may be made to redress their grievances, so that due inquiry cannot be made into the circumstances of their detention and their right to freedom," it would now be the right and duty for the Justices of the Inferior Courts to take jurisdiction in such cases and make proper inquiry into the true facts.[4] And it became the duty of the Ordinary in every county to appoint guardians for all free persons of color who might reside in the county. As there was actually little distinction between a slave and a free person of color, except as to enforced labor, most laws relating to slaves applied also to the latter. Frequently the expression, "free persons of color" would appear in the slave laws, and where not, it was to be assumed that the application was there unless by the nature of the law it would not be logical.[5]

In 1860 there were in Clarke County (Athens being the principal town, though not the county seat) 11,218 inhabitants. Of these, 5,539 were white, 5,660 were slaves, and 19 were free persons of color. Of the last-named Negroes, thirteen were black and six were mulattoes. More than a third of the people in Clarke County lived in Athens, which had a total population of 3,848. Of these, 1,955 were white, 1,892 were slaves, and only one free person of color.[6] But these numbers were to be greatly changed during the war years, for there was a considerable increase of the slave population by planters allowing their servants to come to Athens, and very likely a majority of the free persons of color moved into Athens. Thus, it appears that in 1860, Clarke County as a whole had more slaves than white people, but that Athens had a slight majority of whites.

Before the Civil War broke out, Athens had developed the reputation of being a sort of "nigger heaven," for the slave seemed to have had little hindrance from running around over town as he pleased, and war conditions were to greatly intensify this situation. Sometimes Athens slaves were referred to as "Free Slaves," as was the heading to a protest written by "Justice" for the Athens *Southern Watchman* (one of the two town newspapers), and published two years before the war. Said "Justice" "there are more free negroes manufactured and made virtually free in the town of Athens in two months, than there are bona fide free negroes in Clarke and any ten of the surrounding counties." And all of this came about by the very best citizens of the town hiring to their slaves their time and letting them run loose seeking employment—all against the state law and the ordinances of the town. But the Negro thus set free "in nine cases out of ten, idles away half his time, or gambles away what he does make, and then relies upon his ingenuity in stealing to meet the demands pay day inevitably brings forth, and this is the way in which our towns are converted into dens of rogues and thieves." If the laws could not be enforced, then, this indignant correspondent advocated their repeal "and let every one who suffers from the depradations from these drones upon the honest portion of the community, be prepared at all times, to free himself from their encroachments by a judicious use of powder and lead."[7]

The election of Abraham Lincoln as President of the United States in November, 1860 threw a chill of fear into the hearts of Athenians and of Georgians throughout the state. Negroes knew something about the meaning of Lincoln's election, and white people now felt that their slave population was ripe for abolition emissaries to stir up a servile insurrection. A week after the election, a mass meeting was called in Athens, which resolved that an efficient police force be organized to patrol the town and that in addition there be organized volunteer policemen to patrol every ward in the town. It resolved also that the patrol system in the county, which had largely fallen into disuse, be brought to life and that its activities be stepped up beyond what had been the custom when the system first had been inaugurated throughout Georgia. The most practical work of this mass meeting, extra-legal to say the least, was to set up a detective force, called a vigilance committee "to examine into all alleged attempts at in-surrection among the slaves."[8]

As expressed by John H. Christy, the editor of the *Southern Watchman*, "Our object is not to spread needless alarm—far from it; but with the lights before us, we should be recreant to duty if we failed to warn the people everywhere to be on their guard."

"It is needless—indeed would be imprudent—to publish the facts on which we base our opinions; but they are of such a nature as to demand the exercise of prudent foresight in the prevention of any attempts at insubordination." Christy wanted it to be understood that the work of vigilance committees was not to terrorize the slave population, but on the contrary, "Humanity to the slaves, no less than the safety of the whites, demands the utmost vigilance."[9]

The constituted authorities were not asleep to the supposed dangers. The Grand Jury of Clarke County, in its presentments in 1861, recognized that there had been much "delinquency" in the patrols, and it warned them "to use great vigilance and care," to keep an eye on all strangers, and to watch over the movements of slaves.[10] The next year the Grand Jury observed that Justices of the Inferior Courts, Justices of the Peace, "and others charged with the duty of trying slaves for misdemeanors and crimes" had been too lax in the performance of their tasks, and it recommended the appointment of "Patrol Commissioners" in the several militia districts, apparently either to engage in patrolling or to direct the work of those who already had been appointed.[11]

Athens had been incorporated as a town in 1806 and it was to be governed by three Commissioners;[12] in 1815 the number was increased to five;[13] and seven years later two more were added.[14] In 1847 the government of the town was completely changed. Now an Intendant (mayor) and Wardens (councilmen) should rule over Athens. There were to be three divisions, called wards, with two Wardens elected from each, except for Ward Number One, which should elect three. The Intendant was elected by a city-wide vote.[15] The other town officials were a marshal, a deputy marshal, and a clerk for the City Council, which had the right to pass ordinances not in conflict with state laws and the constitution. On the touchy subject of slave control, the Commissioners back in 1831 had been given the right to pass all ordinances and rules "necessary for the government of slaves and free persons of color."[16] Under the rule of the Intendant and Council the Intendant was given the power to try all cases involving the city ordinances and the "good order and peace" of the city.[17]

As the town grew larger, more wards were added, and on special occasions additional marshals or policemen were provided. Starting out with modest boundaries, Athens in 1842 was extended two miles in every direction from Point Zero, which was the Chapel on the campus of the State University.[18] (The University had been founded in 1801 and the town had grown up around it.) The Town Hall was the seat of government. It was a two-story building, with the city market on the first floor, flanked by the calaboose, and on the second floor were the town hall and offices.[19]

The services provided by the city were elementary, but sufficient for that day and generation and the attitude of mind of its citizens, who believed that the Lord helped those who helped themselves. The streets were lighted by gas lamps; and to take care of them there was a lamplighter appointed by the Council, which generally awarded him a salary of $75 a year.[20] The streets were unpaved, of course, muddy in wet weather, and dusty in dry. To keep them in a passable condition, the city owned a mule, a cart, and a few necessary tools. To operate this establishment the Council hired annually a slave from some citizen slaveowner, at a cost of $130—more, nearer the end of the war, when Confederate money became less valuable. In 1862 the Council hired General Thomas R. R. Cobb's boy Joe "to work the streets, drive and take care of the town mule—he, the said Cobb, is to board and clothe said boy, and pay all physician's bills, if any."[21] Cobb was killed in December, 1862, at the Battle of Fredericksburg, but this boy Joe continued to work the streets in 1863, at least for a short time; but for most of this year a boy Lige was in charge of the mule and the streets. Boy Lige in January, 1865, was voted by the Council a reward of $50 "for his general faithfulness."[22] (It was customary to call any Negro, "boy," who was not old enough and respectable enough to be dubbed affectionately "uncle.") As the city did not own a stable, it rented one for the mule, generally paying $12 annually.[23]

To protect the city against fires, there was a voluntary fire department ("Hook and Ladder" company), to which the city made some small appropriations. There being no water works during the war years, the city depended on cisterns privately owned and several which apparently the city owned—one being under Broad Street opposite the University Campus. In those halcyon days of economy and simplicity, the total cost of the city government did not reach $5,000. The cost for the year 1863 was $4,200.[24]

Since there were few industries in Athens in which slaves might be employed, it was a problem for owners to find work for their slaves, and for the guardians of free persons of color to be responsible for their welfare. This was indeed, a problem, when it is remembered that there were almost 2,000 slaves in Athens in 1860. Of course, the great majority of them were used as household servants, yard boys, gardeners, carriage drivers, and in other capacities in keeping with city dwellers. For instance the Hull family, prominent in Athens from the beginning, subsisted four slave families on their lot. From these families the Hulls recruited a cook, a laundress, a nurse, a seamstress, a housemaid, a carriage driver, a gardener, and a few general utility hands. They had a plantation nearby, which could absorb some of their city slaves.[25]

To take care of some of the surplus Athens slaves, the City Council every year, in violation of their own ordinances and of state law according to the critics, allowed Athens slaveowners to pay a certain fee (generally referred to as a tax) and thereby let their slaves live away from the owners' lots. This dispensation also was allowed to the guardians of free persons of color. But any slave or free person of color who did not live on the lot of his owner or guardian and for whom the fee was not paid was required immediately to move beyond the city limits. It was the intention of the law that such persons must live on the lots of those who employed them, but evasions seem never to have been widely punished. Also it was possible for the employer to pay the fee instead of the owner or guardian. Naturally the guardian expected to be repaid, and so did the owner.

The fee varied with the individual slave or free person of color, depending on whether man or woman, on the ability of the person to perform labor (and hence on age), and with the progression of the war years. In 1861 Dr. Alonzo Church, former president of the University of Georgia, paid $10 each for his women slaves Caroline and Ann to live off his lot; and the Council (or Board as it generally denominated itself) tolled off at its February meeting in addition the following "free persons of color, and also . . . the slaves living separate and apart from their owner's, employer's or guardian's lot . . . Isaac Walker, free person of color, $25; Willis Parks, free person of color, $25; T M Daniel's girl, Caroline, $10; Billy Nance, free boy of color, $25; Milledge Nance, free boy of color, $20; T F Cooper's girl, Arra, $25; D H Alexander's girl Matilda, $25; Jonas Cochran, free boy of color, $25; Dr H C Billups' old woman, Dalla, $5; J I Carlton's man Caesar and wife, $10; R D B Taylor's old woman, Venis, $5; M E McWhorter's boy Jim and Wife, each, $15; M J Claney's girl, Julia, $10; J M Barnell's girl, Eve, $10; Athens Manufacturing Co.'s slaves, $50 [made cotton goods]; Wm M Morton's woman Dolla, $10; do do boy Jim, $20; George Morton, free boy of color, $25; L C Matthews' woman, $10."[26] Thus, it is seen that the fees ran from $5 to $25. During the year a few other slaves and free persons of color were allowed to live off the lots of their owners or guardians,[27] making about thirty or forty, all told.

The next year the fees per person were doubled;[28] for the year 1863 the fees for free persons of color amounted to $1,000;[29] in 1864 at least fifty-six slaves and free persons of color were allowed to live apart from owners and guardians, and the fees ran as high as $100 each.[30] During 1865 as long as the war lasted, the dispensation was still going on and the fees ranged as high as $500 per person.[31]

As this licensing system worked itself out, it set free to roam around over town with little hindrance from thirty to fifty or sixty slaves and free persons of color, looking for something to do for wages or to steal enough to pay their owners or guardians the license fees. Editor Christy made opposition to this system the recurring theme for editorials from the beginning of the war to its end. It was the cause of widespread thievery: "No man's property is secure so long as such numbers of lazy, rascally buck negroes are permitted to live off their master's premises.

"We venture the opinion that there is not another community of the same extent in the Confederacy where there is so much petty thieving as in Athens. No wonder a member of the Legislature from this place said a few years ago that this town had been converted by the negroes into a 'den of thieves.' "[32]

From every standpoint the system was bad. It was not only against the law, but also it had a bad effect on the other slave population which did not enjoy this liberty. "Everybody knows," he declared, "that negroes who are nominally slaves, but really free, will not work so long as they can find any thing to steal, and the dens established by the license system of the Council afford the best hiding places imaginable. The negroes are obliged to have something to eat—their inherent love of idleness prevents them from working, and stealing becomes a necessity." During the first half of the year 1864 Christy had lost through theft 100 pounds of bacon, beef worth $600, and two hogs worth $500 each—all because the City Council allowed "a lot of worthless negroes the glorious liberty of violating the laws." It was high time that a stop be put to granting these indulgences.[33]

Christy would grant this much: "We do not say that these pets do all the stealing—but we do say that the whole system tends to encourage theft, insubordination and other crimes among our negroes—and everybody knows this to be true."[34]

As the year 1865 came in, the Council again sold for a fee the right of Negroes to live off the lots of their owners, guardians, and employers; and Christy again attacked this group of law-makers for violating their own laws and the laws of the state. As a final resort he offered this advice: "Let us petition for a repeal of the Town charter—let Athens become simply '216th District G. M.'—let the patrol laws of the state be enforced, and then let us see if buck negroes cannot be whipped back to their owner's or their hirer's lots." The Council seemed to have been prevailed upon year after year in granting these indulgences, by Athens slaveowners who found some of their slaves a nuisance on their own lots and by slaveowners out in the county, who found that they could make more out of their slaves by sending them into Athens than they could by leaving them on their plantations. White men could not violate a law of Athens with impunity, said Christy, yet a "gentleman or lady of 'de African scent' can buy an indulgence to violate it openly three hundred and sixty five days in succession at from ten to fifty dollars hitherto." At this time Christy explained it cost a little more because of inflation.[35]

Besides stealing what other occupations were slaves and free persons of color engaging in? By now the "Four Horsemen of the Apocalypse" were appeaing over the horizon of Athens—certainly at least three of them, before the end of the first year of the war— the variety that was to be a plague for the next four years, Speculation, Inflation, Scarcity. And slaves and free persons of color were to have places in the picture. Before the end of 1861 Editor Christy raised the spectre: "It seems that the people have determined to destroy one another. Everybody is raising the price of everything, because salt, coffee, and a few other articles happen to be high! We fear the end of all this will be terrible! These exhorbitant prices are already doing greater damage to the country than old Abe's army can ever do. Our people are ruining the country. We have no fear of the Federalists. Their armies may be driven from the field; but the greedy, rapacious bloodsuckers in our midst, shielding themselves behind the letter of the laws which they daily violate in spirit, are determined to pursue a course which leads to inevitable ruin. Can nothing arrest them? Public opinion cannot, because the great mass of our people being guilty of some sort of extortion, are ready to tolerate it in others."[36]

These off-the-lot Negroes found ready employment in buying and selling foods and other products of farms and gardens. P. E. Moore, one of the Wardens in a Board meeting, raised the cry against this evil as well as others besetting the town: "The general demoralization of the town, from the unrestrained excesses of youth, and the night brawls of riotous adults, having increased to such a degree as to be a subject of general remark, and the stealing, trading and trafficking between negroes and trifling white people have become such an intolerable burthen upon the middle classes in town, and the surrounding farmers, that it is the emperative duty of this Council, to use every lawful means in their power to put a stop to it." He recommended that two policemen be employed to assist the marshal and his deputy in preserving order.[37]

In fact in November, 1861 the Council had sought to curb this trafficking by Negroes, declaring that no slave or free person of color might purchase or sell within the town or outside any flour, meal, corn, oats, butter, lard, chickens, turkeys, ducks "or any other fowls," eggs, apples (dried or green), sweet potatoes, or yams. Anyone found guilty after a trial before the Intendant should be fined $20 "or whipped or imprisoned." The fine should be paid by the owner or guardian, regardless of whether such person had given permission for such trafficking.[38] Later the Council amended this ordinance by adding "peas, beef, pork, bacon, cotton yarn, wool, jeans, cloth, or any other article or thing, except such articles as are usually made by slaves and vended for their own use only." The fine was now raised to as much as $100, and anyone informing on such trafficking should be allowed one half of the fine.[39]

Since much of the trafficking was being carried on at the instance of white traders and merchants, the Council about this time made it a fine of from $10 to $300 for any such person to send slaves or free persons of color out into the town to drum up any kind of country produce; and the marshal was directed to "whip all such slaves, or free persons of color, found drumming in violation of this Ordinance."[40] If a Negro might not drum for a merchant or other trader, then might he not set up a little business of his own? Apparently some were doing that, for near the end of 1863 the Council forbade any "slave, nominal slave or free person of color" to keep any store or grocery or to act as a clerk in any such establishment belonging to his master, his guardian or to anyone else. Any white person permitting this activity should be fined from $20 to $100; slaves should be whipped, and free persons of color and nominal slaves might be imprisoned for not more than one month.[41] Also the Council declared "that any white man engaged in buying or selling with a slave or free person of color, directly or indirectly, any beef, mutton, lamb, or any other article, at the market or in the town of Athens, be fined in a sum of not less than fifty dollars, to be collected as other fines."[42] This ordinance must not have been interpreted as forbidding free persons of color (at least) to buy from the keeper of the market or from merchants in the town; otherwise it is difficult to see how a free person of color could keep from starving to death, unless he lived by stealing.

Despite the very essence of the slave code that property could not own property, and, therefore, that a slave could not own anything, yet it seems that slaves acquired in some way vehicles and draught animals; and by so doing they came into competition with the white draymen of the town. At this time the Georgia Railroad (the only railroad reaching Athens) stopped on the east side of the Oconee River, not desiring to go to the expense of building a bridge and come closer to the heart of town. Therefore, quite a business grew up in hauling freight and passengers to and from the depot. To keep slaves and free persons of color from engaging in this activity, the Council enacted an ordinance stating that any such person operating for his own use or account a dray drawn by one and not more than two mules, horses "or other animals" should be fined $50 and given twenty lashes, unless permission had been granted by the Intendant. If the dray were drawn by three or more animals the fine should be $100 and thirty lashes.[43] This ordinance did not forbid Negroes from engaging in other transportation activities; but to discourage any hauling of freight or passengers in Athens, the Council in January, 1865, declared that any slave or free person of color "owning horses, mules, wagons, hacks, buggies or any other vehicles" should be taxed $100 each for every animal, $50 each for every two-horse wagon and buggy, and $100 each for hacks and carriages.[44]

The many rules and town ordinances would make it appear that the Negro population was well controlled, but seeping through all these regulations was the fact that the Negroes largely had their own way, for there were few policemen to enforce the rules. After nine o'clock at night no Negro was allowed on the streets unless he carried a pass; nevertheless, Negroes frequently might be found wandering around at almost any time of night. And, of course, Editor Christy, who carried the burden of complaining about conditions had something to say on this subject, using this headline, "Are the juvenile 'Buck Niggers' to govern Athens?" He answered in this wise: "As a voter and tax-payer, we want the question settled whether the respectable law-abiding tax-payers or the irresponsible juvenile negroes are to govern this town.

"These little miscreants gather in bands at the street corners and elsewhere on Sundays, and by their loud laughing, singing and boisterous talking, annoy quiet citizens. We have laid this matter before the proper authorities—an attempt has been made to abate this nuisance—but the police force is so small and the territory so large, that while these sable juvenile riots are being suppressed in one locality, they are in full blast in another! Nor do these imps of Satan confine themselves to noisy demonstrations in the street. They throw stones at hogs, cows and dogs, and even into the enclosures of quiet citizens, endangering the lives of their children.

"Now, this nuisance can be very readily abated, without the interference of the police, if the owners of these juvenile savages will see that they don't leave their lots on Sunday, except to attend church or Sunday-school. Will not our good citizens try the experiment?"[45]

Instead of complaining to the Council as Christy often did in his editorials, Athenians soon began to take their woes to Christy. When the war was far along and most of the eligible citizens were in the Confederate army, Christy noted: "A very respectable lady asked us the other day if the few white men left here had determined to permit the negroes to do as they pleased in the streets—remarking, that she had been frequently compelled to walk around crowds of these odorous gentry on the street corners, who showed no disposition to make way for her."[46]

Christmas times were especially vociferous occasions for the Negroes; a few extra policemen might be hired, and on other occasions as many as seven helped to patrol the town.[47] The Christmas of 1862 passed off quietly, but the " 'servile descendants of Ham' were, however, rather numerous for a day or two. It rained all day Saturday and this was a damper on the spirits of Sambo and Dinah."[48]

Negroes, like white boys, went swimming in the Oconee River; but neither blacks nor whites were allowed to swim in daytime in the river where it flowed through the main part of town (this being in the pre-bathing-suit era) nor in Trail Creek, a small water flowing into the Oconee in the middle of town. Violation of this ordinance carried a fine of $10 for whites and the penalty for Negroes was twenty lashes.[49]

Negroes on Sundays were not permitted to hire any horse, buggy, carriage, hack or other vehicle or to drive vehicles other than their owners' or guardians'; and any Negro so bold as to do otherwise would subject himself to thirty-nine lashes and imprisonment in the guard house until called for by his owner or guardian. Any white person hiring a horse or vehicle to "or driving any slave or free person of color" on Sunday should be fined not less than $50.[50]

But to make up for the prohibition against enjoying themselves riding around on Sundays, the Negroes seem to have taken advantage on weekdays of the opportunity of riding down to the depot to see the Georgia Railroad train come in and to ride back up the hill. Christy was indignant at this situation: "We are told that idle boys and buck negroes ride in vehicles from the depot, while wounded soldiers who have lost their limbs fighting for their country have to hobble over on crutches. We mention this thing thus plainly, not to offend any one, but simply to call attention to an evil which can be easily cured, and which, moreover, is a reproach to our town."[51]

Most of the Negroes in Athens were either Methodists or Baptists with some Episcopalians (and all worshiping in their special ways). They had their own churches, with the exception of the Episcopalians, who used the Town Hall on "Sunday evenings" (probably meaning afternoons), conducted by white members.[52] The meeting nights for the Negroes were originally on Wednesdays; but in 1863 the Council changed the time to Thursday nights.[53]

Negroes were allowed other forms of entertainment besides going to their funeral and burial exercises. In 1864 the Negro musician prodigy Blind Tom was brought by his master to Athens to give performances. After playing the piano to white audiences, in which, of course, no colored people were allowed, on his last appearance he performed "exclusively for servants"—no white people being allowed to attend.[54]

There were two serious disturbances in Athens in 1862 in which Negroes were the centers: one was a large gathering of them which might easily have led to a riot and the other was a lynching. In January a group, estimated at 50 to 100, gathered and showed their great joy at the defeat of one of the candidates for the marshalship "by throwing up their caps and hurrahing at the very top of their lungs." Even without this demonstration their assembling was against the town ordinances and was "outrageous; but we further give it as our opinion [said Christy], for negroes to be suffered to assemble by hundreds to make a public demonstration of their approval or disapproval of the election of an officer, is not only wrong in itself, conducive to insolence and insurrection, but that they should be permitted to do so in behalf of an officer elected especially to control them is insufferable." And added to all this criticism, he said, was the fact that "liquor was bought by white men, upon the occasion, and freely dispensed to the assembled negroes upon public streets."[55] It was strictly against town ordinances and state laws to allow Negroes to have liquors, and the Grand Jury of Clarke County had called attention to the fact that many persons had "been Trading & furnishing slaves with Spirituous Liquors and that too by a class of persons who exercise no salutary moral influence in the community, but on the contrary, corrupt and ruin our slave property and undermine the structure of all moral law."[56]

The Council ordered an investigation, but no report ever was submitted; or if it was it was not recorded in the minutes. Christy in his *Watchman*, however, called attention to the fact that about this time a group of slave musicians had given a concert in the town for the benefit of the Athens volunteers going to the Confederate army, and he could not refrain from throwing out the question, "What do the invaders of our soil think of this?"[57]

The lynching took place about a mile from town. A slave was brought into Athens from a nearby plantation to be tried for an assault on the wife of the overseer. Justice of the Peace Kirkpatrick held a preliminary hearing and announced the verdict sentencing him to jail to await trial in the Superior Court. An enraged mob immediately seized the Negro and placing a rope around his neck, led him down Broad Street and hanged him to a pine tree near the Georgia Railroad track. It was ascertained that the mob had feared that the owner of the slave might rescue him and sell him to someone where the crime was not known (the owner receiving no recompense for executed slave property) or that the court might delay the trial and make possible his escape. Christy, who had no prejudices favorable to Negroes, was prejudiced decidedly in favor of law and order, and admitting that "a negro guilty of the most revolting crime known to the law," as this one was, still should be tried and executed according to law. "There is no doubt about the justice of his punishment"; said Christy, "but we are utterly opposed to the *manner* of his execution. There can be no rational liberty which is not regulated by law. A deep and abiding respect for, and a rigid enforcement of the laws of the land, are, therefore, the greatest safeguard of freedom."[58]

Athens was not alone in Negroes seeming to take charge, for what happened in Athens was somewhat characteristic of many of the towns and cities of the Confederacy. Conditions in Richmond, the capital of the Confederacy, were worse than they were in Athens.

Negroes in Athens were not the only ones to create disturbances; white "Juvenile Depravity" burst forth now and then, as chronicled by Christy, the watchdog of Athens decorum: "One day last week, some half dozen small boys, from ten to fourteen years of age, were committed to the calaboose for petty thieving and perhaps other misdemeanors. We are not surprised at this. Our only surprise is, that the number did not reach fifty! So long as parents permit little boys to spend their time in idleness, and more especially in the streets—so long as they teach them that taking fruit, watermelons, &c., is not stealing—so long as they permit them to pelt hogs, dogs and cows with rocks—to throw rocks and bricks into other people's enclosures—to pull down young shade trees along the sidewalks—to tear down handbills and pull pailings off fences—and the thousand and one acts of villiany they are in the daily habit of perpetrating, it need not be wondered at that occasionally half-a-dozen of them are bagged for stealing! We can furnish a list of from fifty to a hundred boys in this place [who] will go to the penitentiary within the next twenty years unless they are hanged sooner, or (what is not likely) unless their parents cause them to amend their ways."[59]

The conscience of the City Council finally led to action. In July, 1863, it passed an ordinance declaring that any white boy throwing rocks or any other missiles "[through mischief or pastime] . . . at any other boy, negro or other thing" in the public streets should be fined from $1 to $10. And if the parent or guardian did not pay the fine the boy should be lodged in the calaboose. Any Negro boy guilty of this offense should be whipped by the marshal "without being tried . . . not exceeding twenty stripes."[60]

The peace of Athens was to continue undisturbed throughout the war except for its local disorders. No enemy troops ever came nearer than a half dozen miles, except as prisoners of war. In 1864 outriders of some of Sherman's cavalry brushed with Confederate troops in the vicinity and were badly crippled and some hundreds captured. They were brought through Athens on their way to the Andersonville prison and quartered on the University Campus, near Phi Kappa Hall, and guarded by the "Thunderbolts." The main group of prisoners numbered about 200, and for some days thereafter small groups of stragglers were brought through.[61]

Prisoners of war were not the only evidence that a war was going on, apart from high prices, scarcities, and local disorders. From the very beginning Athens had been a collecting point for volunteers throughout the surrounding country as well as providing all of her own able-bodied men. During the first two years of the war it was a familiar sight to see companies marching through the streets, off for the war. Later the casualty lists came in to be published in the local newspapers and many families were thrown into mourning. By 1864 one lady had lost her husband and three sons and a fourth was at home near death from the ravages of disease brought on by the vigors of army life.[62]

Refugees poured into Athens from invaded regions as far away as Mississippi, taking up all spare rooms in town and occupying the University dormitories, except for space allotted as a "Wayside Home," for soldiers passing through town. The University Chapel was used for hospital purposes.[63]

Even so, Athens after three years of war, had its dull spells, when no Negro boys were "whooping it up" on the streets and no white boys were throwing rocks at anything which moved, whether dog or hog or Negro boy. No one on horseback galloped headlong down any streets, for it had now been made illegal by the City Council for anyone to do so unless he were a physician or going for one. Violation by a white person led to a fine of $15 and if by a Negro a whipping was in store for him.[64]

Editor Christy in early 1864 found nothing to complain about, and in a woebegone spirit wrote: "Every thing has been so completely dried up by the war that we have not a syllable of local news—not a single incident worthy of a paragraph—this week. What is the matter? Will nothing happen to break the dull monotony? The boys have even abandoned their ancient amusement of running 'stray dogs' down Broadway with tin-kettles appended to their caudal extremities. 'Cat Alley' has dried up!— Cat Alley, which once could boast half-a-dozen *rows* per day. Even Cat Alley is quiet! Nothing disturbs the 'solemn stillness' except now and then a rickety ox-cart whose unlubricated axels make melancholy music! Our great thoroughfare which once was crowded with country wagons laden with the rich products of a generous soil, is now bare and desolate—its stores closed—the noise of trade hushed—nothing to break the stillness, save now and then the voice of some descendants of Abraham 'jewing' a countrywoman, whose butter and eggs he considers too high at $3 per pound and $1.25 per dozen!"[65]

The war was dragging out a slow course to its inevitable end— the destruction of the Confederacy. Ever since Gettysburg and Vicksburg, the two great tragedies for the Confederacy, both coming within the week of July 4, 1863, more and more people were realizing that the war was lost. But with some—and more than one might suspect—"the-hope-springs-eternal" attitude of mind still dominated to the very last. The South could not lose, for Robert E. Lee was at the head of the Confederate armies. Despite the fact that news hardly could have been worse for the past six months, when it reached Athens on April 26, 1865, that Lee had surrendered two weeks earlier (April 9th), it was considered incredible. But it was true, and Christy wrote, "Not a hero in that immortal band which composed the remnant of LEE'S forces will ever be ashamed to acknowledge that he belonged to the 'Army of Northern Virginia.'"[66] Even a week later Christy had not regained his composure: "The writer is free to confess, that after an experience of twenty-five years in the newspaper business, he has never before been so completely silenced—stunned—paralized—by rapidly-occuring events. He knows not *what* to say." But he could say this: "Rumors are as plentiful as blackberries in July. Our exchanges are filled with rumors. The passengers on the cars bring hundreds of rumors. It is rumor! rumor! everywhere!"[67]

Very soon there was something more than rumors; the people of Athens would be confronted with some hard facts, now that the war was over. Returning soldiers passing through and some equally needy whites and Negroes of the town, seized the small Confederate commissary here and ransacked it.[68] Why should they not do so, rather than wait for invading Yankees to do it? And the waiting would not have been long, for by May 4th Brevet Brigadier-General William J. Palmer swept down out of the mountains of East Tennessee and Western North Carolina, with the Fifteenth Pennsylvania Cavalry and other troops, trying to cut off and capture Jefferson Davis in his flight southward. He marched down Milledge Avenue and took possession of the town. While he was asking Brevet Major-General Emory Upton at Augusta what he should do with the Athens armory, with its 250 workmen "(mustered into the Confederate service and having their arms concealed)," and also what to do "with a large number of Confederate officers here, including several generals,"[69] his men were out over town pillaging homes and robbing the citizens. One soldier saw Patrick H. Mell, one of the University professors, sitting on his porch. Spying Mell's watch chain he asked him to come out, that he wanted to speak to him. When Mell appeared, the soldier pointing his gun at the Professor's breast, demanded his watch. Mell in a firm and quiet manner replied: "You may shoot me, sir, but you shall never have any of my property if I can help it. I am defenseless so far as weapons are concerned, but I will not yield one inch to you, even though you murder me." The soldier suddenly grabbed Mell's watch and made off with it. Mell was able to recover it before Palmer left, by going to him and protesting.[70] The General being more of a gentleman than his men, marched away a few days later, without destroying the armory or interfering with the workmen or with any officers he found in town.

Palmer and his men had come "in suddenly and unexpectedly as if they had dropped from the clouds," and they "passed away gradually until not one" remained. But even before Palmer had come and after he had left, there was excitement enough. Many paroled Confederate troops came through, including Basil Duke's Kentuckians and Tennesseans. "Fightin' Joe" Wheeler was not so fortunate; he came through as a prisoner. General William J. Hardee with his wagon train was in town for a day or two and Admiral Raphael Semmes was seen riding down the street on horseback—but probably not as good a horseman as a sea-fighter.[71]

Most Athenians did not know that an important part of the Confederate Archives had been kept in one of the classrooms of the University for a time, and that in the middle of June they were turned over to Brevet Major-General James H. Wilson, in command at Macon. These manuscripts were the journals and other records of the Provisional Congress of the Confederate States, which were in the keeping of Howell Cobb, who had been the Permanent President of that body. They were sent to Georgia where copies were being made (since they were not to be printed), and they were in Atlanta when Sherman was on his invasion of the state. To keep them from being captured they were sent to various places, including points in Alabama and South Carolina. They were finally brought to Athens, where they must have been stored previously, for Howell Cobb's home was in this town. Whether for the purpose of being used in the trial of Jefferson Davis, who was now in prison, or for their preservation as important historical records, Cobb wisely turned them over to General Wilson, who sent them with other Confederate archives.

which had been gathered up, to Washington in forty boxes.[72]

With deep regrets that the war had been lost and with the hard facts before them, there was nothing left for Athenians to do but submit with as much grace and sincerity as was possible. Christy in his *Watchman* advised all to become reconciled and to obey the laws, adding, "We are aware that it is very difficult for human nature to forgive and forget such wrongs as have been inflicted upon us during this cruel war—it requires time to forget such things."[73] And a little later there was a mass meeting of citizens of the town and of Clarke and the surrounding counties, which might be considered their formal surrender. They recognized that the war was over and they now submitted to the laws of the United States and its constitution "in good faith, as loyal and orderly citizens."[74]

Troops had been marching in and out of Athens since Lee's Surrender, but no permanent occupying garrison had come until May 29th when Captain Alfred B. Cree of the 22nd Iowa Volunteers set up a Provost Marshal government, making his headquarters in Phi Kappa Hall, on the University Campus, and instituting his "Watch on the Oconee."[75] Athens had been getting along governed by its Intendant and Council, with the last meeting of the Council on June 3rd until it met again on September 3rd.[76] There had been no term of the Superior Court from the upset days of August, 1864, until February, 1866.[77] Whatever little civil authority there was left did not clash with Cree's Provost Marshalship, for he was well received, since he had "urbane manners and polite and gentlemanly bearing."[78]

His duties were specifically to parole soldiers, to administer oaths of allegiance, to assist the civil government (but to be the final authority), to preserve order, and to set up whatever rules he deemed desirable. One of his first decrees was to order all paroled Confederate officers and soldiers not residents of the town to leave within twenty-four hours. Also anyone who was found wearing the Confederate uniform of an officer would be arrested and tried in the Provost Court; but anyone who could not procure civilian clothes might continue in his uniform if "all military buttons, trimmings or insignia of rank" were removed. Anyone having "fire-arms, powder and ammunition" was required to turn them over to the Provost Marshal.[79]

Captain Cree's urbanity caused him not to be looked upon with fear and trembling by the ordinary citizen or anyone else, and when he and his Iowans evacuated the town on June 19th, there were those who were loathe to see him go. He was succeeded by Major Euen and his command of the 156th New York Regiment.[80] By this time Athenians were becoming used to Yankee soldiers and seem not to have stood in awe of them or their officers. As a case in point, one day Major Euen drove up Broad Street in his buggy (which might seem unmilitary) and stopped for a moment to enter a store. Finding no hitching post, he remarked to a by-stander, "Watch my horse until I come out." A moment later a mischievous person clucked at the horse and started him off. When the Major came out and did not see his horse and buggy he chided the man for not "watching his horse," and he got this answer in a slow drawl: "I-did-watch-him-until-he-went-around the corner, and-I-couldn't-see-him-anymore-then."[81]

In October the guard again was changed in Athens. As Major Euen and his troops departed for the Georgia Railroad depot to entrain, they "presented a fine martial appearance marching down Broad Street, as they left."[82] Captain Beckwith with a part of the 13th Battalion of Connecticut Volunteers now took over the "Watch on the Oconee." Some of these troops endeared them-selves to the Athenians by assisting in saving the Town Hall from burning, and to show its appreciation the Council made a gift of $5 each to some of the soldiers and $2.50 to others.[83]

The military occupation of Athens, as such, came to an end before the year was out, when Lieutenant-Colonel H. B. Sprague of this Battalion on December 4th was appointed agent for the Freedmen's Bureau at this place.[84] Federal troops in Athens had not been considered a very great burden and there was little friction between them and the townsmen, though on one occasion there was some shooting but no one was killed.[85] Still, when the military authorities asked the Athenians to participate in the celebration of the "Glorious Fourth," it was decided that it would be "inexpedient, in view of our recent humiliation, our great losses of property, and more especially of men, to attempt a celebration this year."[86]

Yet Athenians were not sorry to see Yankee troops march away, and the University was more than glad to get rid of the burden it had had to bear, for the troops had been quartered in the buildings on the Campus, including the Chapel, which was used for various purposes and was left in shambles, with the seats removed, rubbish scattered everywhere, and the columns in front chipped by bayonet jabs and the bullets from rifle practice.[87] On account of this occupation and for other reasons, perhaps, the University did not re-open after the war until January 3, 1866.

How had the Negroes worked into this picture of the war's ending and the military occupation; how had the white population come to regard slavery; and, indeed, how had the Negro himself come to regard it? As the war approached its end it was pretty evident to all people who would stop to think, that slavery was on its way out—it was only a matter of how abruptly it would end. Some whistled in the dark like the man passing through the graveyard; others like the ostrich buried their heads in the sands.

Lincoln's Preliminary Emancipation Proclamation of September 22, 1862, and his final one of January 1, 1863, created a furor among high Confederate officials in Richmond, but the man on the streets paid little attention to it, and most slaves who heard about it did not get much excited. In Athens there was not a ripple. Yet some editors of Georgia newspapers by 1865 had begun to slant their thinking toward emancipation, which led unterrified Christy of the *Watchman* to say, "Five years ago the editor in Georgia who would have admitted into his columns an article squinting toward the abolition of slavery, however remotely, would have been hung with a grapevine, or at the least 'tarred and feathered.' "[88] And after Lee's Surrender he did not believe "that the Government or the people of the United States will attempt to reduce the 'rebellious states' to a colonial condition, or to force upon them the immediate emancipation of their slaves."[89] Disregarding entirely as of no effect Lincoln's Emancipation Proclamation, the City Council even after the war had ended continued to charge a fee to Athenians for allowing their slaves to live off their lots.[90] They would wait to see whether the amendment then before the country, which would free the slaves, would be ratified. But General Q. A. Gillmore, with headquarters at Hilton Head, South Carolina, whose Department embraced South Carolina, Georgia, and Florida, did not wait for the ratification of this amendment; for on May 15th he announced "that the people of the black race are free citizens of the United States."[91] This was the first attempt to give effect in Athens to Lincoln's Proclamation. In November (1865) Georgia wrote a new constitution for the state and in it she abolished slavery. The next month the amendment (the Thirteenth) was declared ratified and to be a part of the United States Constitution, which legally put an end to slavery throughout the country.

Freeing the slave did not automatically make him equal to the white man either in intelligence or in his ability to assume all the obligations of citizenship. Of this fact, Christy was very certain: "The different races of man, like different coins at a mint, were stamped at their true value by the Almighty in the beginning. No contact with each other—no amount of legislation or education—can convert the negro into a white man. Until that can be done—until you can take the kinks out of his wool and make his skull thinner—until all these things and abundantly more have been done, the negro cannot claim equality with the white race."[92] And if there was to be a meeting of the two races, it would have to be made in this fashion: "Although a negro cannot elevate himself to the white man's standards, a white man may very well lower himself to the negro level!"[93]

The slaves as they entered into their freedom were being given some good advice by all who wished to help them. General Gilmore in announcing that slaves were free throughout his Department advised them to go to work and avoid idleness, and he firmly declared that neither "idleness nor vagrancy will be tolerated, and the government will not extend pecuniary aid to any persons, whether white or black, who are unwilling to help themselves."[94] And Christy in his *Watchman* seconded this program: "Those who are able to work will now find it necessary to establish good characters for industry, sobriety, honesty and fidelity. When detected in his frequent delinquencies, Sambo will now have no 'maussa' to step in between him and danger. The time has arrived when he must 'tote his own skillet.' This will be rather hard upon him at first, but when he gets used to it the thing may work better than most persons suppose. . . . Under the new system the planter will hire only such as are willing and able to work—and when we say work, we mean work in earnest, and not the half play and half work to which many of the slaves have been accustomed. That has 'played out'—they will now have to work like white men."[95]

Many Athens freedmen found work with their former masters, but some despite all advice were determined to see if their freedom did not include freedom from work—and especially was this so for many who flocked into town from the surrounding country. When someone remarked to the cook in one of the Athens families, "Aunt Betty, don't you know you are free?" she quickly replied, "Mas' Henry ain't told me so yit." And Aunt Betty continued to cook for the family as long as she lived.[96]

Back in early May, when General Palmer had marched into Athens to stay for a few days, the country freedmen flocked into town in great numbers; but "as their reception was not altogether such as they had expected," they soon drifted back.[97] When a period of permanent occupation came with Captain Cree arriving with his troops, there was another hegira of freedmen from the country to town. The Captain took advantage of the situation to address the Negroes, in which he told them that loafing and idling around would do them no good, that they should go to work, and it would be best for them to work for their former masters, who knew best how to sympathize with them and their problems. If they did not work they should not draw rations from the government. According to the *Watchman*, "This address had a salutary effect. Country negroes have been very scarce here since its delivery. We understand they were very much disappointed, and think their freedom don't amount to much. The negro idea of freedom at present is, immunity from labor, plenty to eat and wear, and a good hot fire!"[98]

It was too much to expect all Athens Negroes to take the advice that was being so freely offered to them. Almost daily threats were "uttered by negroes who, as slaves, were vile, worthless and unruly, and now, as 'freedmen,' have added largely to their former stock of impudence." The better class of Negroes was receiving the respect and sympathy of Athenians.[99] The juveniles who had given so much trouble during slave times were no better now. These "juvenile 'American citizens of de African scent' frequently amuse themselves in our most public thoroughfares by an indulgence in the most abominable, loud mouthed profanity"; so it was reported.[100]

Thievery was now as rampant, if not more so, than during the war: "Every thing—fruits and vegetables, cereals and livestock, money and provisions, all kinds of property, everything of value— is stolen from day to day."[101] During one week in early June, from 50 to 100 Negro thieves had been reported to Captain Cree, and it was estimated that from 100 to 500 had not been reported. Cree's Provost Marshal government was doing all it could to stop thievery; and during one week 150 thieves were arrested for this crime.[102]

Captain Cree came and went, but thievery stayed for his successors to deal with. Various methods were used by the military authorities to contain it, but whipping as a remnant of slavery, was not allowed. Maybe Negro thieves could be shamed out of their crimes. At least it was tried. Two Negro thieves were drummed out of town "for some *slight irregularities* in their behavior—both of them having taken a fancy to other people's horses." They suffered one side of their head to be clean shaven, "the wool on the other side left intact." They were then encased in barrels, with sleeve holes cut out for their arms, with these placards attached, "I am a horse-thief." A drum and fife corps led them down the street, playing the "rogue's march," accompanied by a detachment of soldiers, and "a hundred or so juvenile freedmen following constituted the 'guard of honor.' "[103] Another Negro who was caught stealing was escorted out of town by a drum and bayonet corps, with both sides of his head shaved clean "so as to leave a ridge of wool about an inch in width, extending from the *os frontis* to the *os occipitus*, and presenting the most ludicrus aspect."[104]

On rare occasions Negroes engaged in threats which might have led to bloody encounters with the law. In the summer of 1865 the military authorities in Athens gave the county sheriff permission to raise a posse to prevent a gang of Negroes from proceeding across a bridge at Princeton with a large supply of meat which they had got from slaughtering stolen animals. A clash took place in which thirty of the gang were arrested and the meat seized, but the thieves assisted by other Negroes broke loose and re-seized the meat.[105] Around Christmas time there was a big demand among the Negroes for firearms, which led to this question: "What do they want with them?"[106] To foil any incipient uprising, the City Council authorized the employment of twenty extra policemen.[107]

Christmas time about the end of the year 1865 was an anxious time for white people, because of rumors that had been going the rounds that the Negroes were to divide up among themselves the property of their former masters about the end of the year. By mid-summer rumors were being spread among the Negroes in Athens and the surrounding country that there was to be a free barbecue in town, that a great speech was to be made to them telling them about things, that there was to be a free distribution of land and other property; and their minds were being abused with other fantastic tales. As a remedy, it was suggested that the "scamps who get up such 'cock and bull stories' ought to be tied up by their thumbs a few days."[108] So it was that now and then Athens overflowed with country Negroes, which led to this observation: "Can any body tell where so many idle negroes come from? Like the frogs of Egypt, they seem to be every where and in every body's way."[109]

For the very laudable purposes of taking care of the destitute, the United States had set up the Freedmen's Bureau following the war. Brigadier-General Davis Tilson, Assistant Commissioner, with headquarters at Augusta, in an order issued on October 3rd, warned Negroes that they must get jobs unless they were unable to do so or unable to work. He disabused their minds that there would be a distribution of land at Christmas or at any other time. Country Negroes flocking to towns would not be allowed to stay unless they could support themselves by work or other honorable means. The Bureau was acting as a labor agency, listing all jobs available and taking the names of Negroes looking for work. Contracts between employers and their Negro workmen would be in writing, and all were expected to obey the terms of employment. General Tillson declared in his order that all should remember "that it is the chief object of the Bureau to do simple justice to all persons, white or black—to aid to the utmost in securing to the employer permanent and reliable labor; and in restoring the state to its former condition of peace and prosperity."[110] Lieutenant-Colonel Sprague, having being appointed the local Bureau agent for Athens two months later, re-enforced General Tilson's order by announcing that all able-bodied freedmen "having no visible means of support" would not be allowed to go about in idleness, much less would they "be allowed to live by thieving." The Bureau always stood ready to find jobs for them.[111]

It took the Negroes a long time to learn what their freedom meant. Some of them never learned, but continued in a way of life that could have been in reality less satisfactory than the life they had led in servitude. True freedom was something which could not be given to them by law and decree! After all, it had to be earned. But for some generations thereafter, designing men for their own ends and idealists to bring pleasure to themselves in thinking that they were doing good, were by their actions and advice indicating that responsibility and respectability need not be earned.

CHAPTER VI

John Howard Payne's Visit to Georgia

JOHN Howard Payne was born in the City of New York on
June 9, 1791, but he spent much of his early youth in East
Hampton, Long Island. He was a precocious lad, especially interested in acting and stage productions. When thirteen years old
he surreptitiously edited a little publication, which he called the
Thespian Mirror. After a short residence in Boston and two years
at Union College, in Schenectady, he went on the stage and for
a time was almost a sensation. He acted in New York, Boston,
Philadelphia, and as far south as Richmond and Charleston. His
popularity having somewhat subsided, he set sail for Europe in
January, 1813, spending most of the following nineteen years in
London and Paris.

In England he continued his acting with great success at first,
but as he fell from favor he began writing stage productions and
for a short time he managed a theatre—so badly that he was
thrown into a debtors' prison, remaining there until he wrote a
successful play, which got him out of debt and, consequently, out
of prison. In England he became well acquainted with the elite
among actors and literary persons, the Kembles, Edmund Kean,
Samuel Taylor Coleridge, Sir Walter Scott, Thomas Campbell,
Robert Southey, Percy Bysshe Shelley and his wife Mary Wollstonecraft Shelley, and an expatriate American, Washington
Irving.

Payne became closely associated with Irving, and, in fact,
roomed with him for a spell in Paris. Always in debt, Payne was
helped out many times by his friend Irving. After Shelley's death
in 1822, both carried on a correspondence with his widow, and
Payne became so romantically inclined that he would have married her, had she considered their correspondence anything more
than a literary diversion.

Both in London and in Paris, Payne wrote plays and did considerable translating of French dramas and adapting them to the English stage. In 1823 he wrote a play, not his best one, which after a little rewriting he called *Clari, The Maid of Milan*. In this play, which Payne, on the instance of Sir Henry Rowley Bishop, the musical director of Covent Garden, converted into an opera, appeared this song, "Home, Sweet Home," first sung there by Ann Maria Tree. At first it was generally referred to simply as "Sweet Home." Payne sold this opera for 50 pounds, which, of course, included the song. It immediately became popular and in the course of time there was not a civilized country in all the world where it was not sung or hummed. The music, in which Sir Henry set Payne's lyric, seems to have been a tune which Payne had heard a peasant girl singing in Italy—and if that be true, Payne may be given credit not only for the lyric but to a great extent for the music itself. If Payne had in mind any particular place as the home, sweet home, it was undoubtedly his boyhood home in East Hampton, Long Island.[1]

The characteristics which were to distinguish Payne were well fixed early in life. He was sensitive and petulant with an instability of spirit, vacillating from achievement to failure. He was a romanticist through and through; his emotions were deep. He was an impractical dreamer of grandiloquent schemes and ideas, and utterly incapable of knowing how to manage money. He loved beauty and nature in its wildest forms. He loved his country and hated injustice wherever he saw it.

Having given to Europe all that he could and having absorbed all that Europe had for him, he returned to America in 1832, penniless. After a resounding welcome and a few benefit performances for him in New York, Boston, and Philadelphia, he was soon off on one of those projects "of a fertile rather than a practical brain."[2] He was now through forever with the stage and acting and play writing, but being literarily inclined he would continue to write poetry (romantic and lovelorn), but more particularly he would start the publication of a magazine. Since this venture gives the background of his visit to Georgia and the South, as well as, even more, an insight into his impractical dreaming and deep love of country, it is given here more than passing attention. He issued his prospectus, signing it August 26, 1833. It appeared both in pamphlet form and as an advertisement in newspapers. It filled almost two columns of a common-sized newspaper, in the smallest type used. In some places the language was a little involved, but plain enough generally.

Deeply touched by the welcome he had received when he landed at New York on his return from a residence of nineteen years abroad, he soon began to set that fertile but impractical brain to work, devising some way whereby he could be worthy of his country. As he expressed it: "By the double claim of natural affection and of gratitude, he has been impelled to examine, during the twelve-month of his recent residence at home, how he might best render himself worthy of his birthright as an American, and blend, with a provision to himself for the future, some advantage to his beloved country, of higher import than individual fortune or fame."[3]

The main purpose of his magazine was set forth in the following statement and question, first mentioning the vast amount of material American publications copied from European magazines: "Thus, the voice of Europe is heard incessantly in every corner of the North American Republic. In the meantime, who hears of our Republic in Europe?"[4] The magazine was to be literary and scientific—in fact to give a complete picture of American life excepting political and commercial. It was to have as contributors both Americans and Europeans, each group explaining themselves to the others. It was to be a sort of friendly competition which would give American writers, many of them only locally known, a European audience. Although Payne said that he would "endeavor briefly to explain" its purpose he lost some of his reasoning in its prolixity. He elaborated on ten ways by which his magazine would be servicable to the United States and four ways in which it would serve "the other side of the Atlantic."

Payne readily passed on from a love of his own country to the promotion of the brotherhood of man, "universal benevolence," as he put it. Continuing he said that "whatever tends to strengthen the brotherly feeling between nations, must hasten the great moment of general good will, to which the wonders which hourly meet our view are pointing. If the work now proposed can con-tribute in ever so insignificant a degree to aid the diffusion of sentiments so desirable, he who suggests it will feel that he has not lived for nothing."[5]

The magazine was to be edited in London, in a 32-page weekly edition, with the editor (of course, being Payne) making a trip back and forth across the Atlantic yearly. It was to cost sub-scribers $10 a year, and it would have the unusual title, which only the dreamer Payne could have thought up, *Jam Jehan Nima.* This was the name of a mythical Persian cup and its meaning was "The Goblet wherein you may behold the Universe." He hoped within three months to have secured enough subscriptions to enable him to set out on a journey to get more subscriptions, but primarily to gain a more thorough knowledge of his native land and, thereby, "to become her effective champion, as he has ever been her devoted and affectionate son."[6]

In late 1833 or the early part of 1834 Payne set out on his promised journey. He probably floated down the Ohio and Missis-sippi rivers, stopping and making inland trips as opportunities afforded. He visited Ohio, Kentucky, Indiana, Illinois, Missouri, Mississippi, Alabama, and Louisiana, before reaching Georgia. He arrived in New Orleans in late February, 1835, and was given a splendid reception.

Continuing his journey, he reached the Creek Indian village of Tuckabatchie in good time for the great display of the Green Corn Dance. He was much impressed by the festivities, and in a letter to his sister he described in great detail what went on. It seems that now, for the first time, Payne became interested in the American Indians. Displaying his romantic emotions, while watch-ing one part of the Green Corn Dance his eye caught a glimpse of the two daughters of the chief, "very elegant girls, but the eldest delighted me exceedingly." She was about seventeen or eighteen years old. He became personally acquainted with her and the chief. He called her Apotheola, though he called the chief the same name. During her dancing she kept her eyes on Payne, who said that someone "must have told her that I meant to run away with her," for he admitted that he had so said previously. Much to his regret he could not tarry longer to get better acquainted with her, for his guide through the forests and field into Georgia was leaving very soon, and so Payne had to "give up all hopes of ever seeing again my beautiful princess Apotheola." In describing the scenes and his experiences at Tuckabatchie, Payne could have been dealing in some light writing to his sister, but it is not assuming too much to believe that he was much attached to the Indian princess—and given a little time he might have been as willing to offer his heart to her as he had to Mary Wollstonecraft Shelley.[7]

1. Payne Enters Georgia

Payne reached Macon, Georgia, on August 9, 1835, and knowing no one in that town, he whiled away some hours by writing the long letter to his sister, describing the Green Corn Dance.[8] It is not certainly known where Payne's movements were for the next few weeks; but being now in a country fairly well settled, it is believed that he bought a horse and set out horseback for Augusta—heretofore he had undoubtedly been traveling by river boat and stagecoach as well as with parties on hired horses. In Augusta he probably saw Augustus Baldwin Longstreet, who edited there the *State Rights Sentinel*. It seems that Payne may have made an arrangement with Longstreet to write a few articles for the *Sentinel*, since *Jam Jehan Nima* was yet unborn.[9] But Payne had not yet given up hope that life might yet be given to his international weekly, for he had inserted on the front page of the *Georgia Journal* for September 22 his long prospectus of *Jam Jehan Nima*. This paper was published in Milledgeville, and undoubtedly Payne passed through this town, the state capital, on his way to Augusta.

Payne may have visited Savannah, though no evidence has been found to so indicate beyond the slim supposition that his next perfectly authenticated stop at Athens, had been suggested by someone in Savannah. The logic being that his host, Edward Harden, had been until recently a prominent resident of Savannah but had moved to Athens. A letter of introduction, which has persistently been stated he carried to Harden, most logically should have come from someone in Savannah.[10]

According to an Athens historian, writing sometime during the latter half of the nineteenth century, this personal note appeared in one of the city papers: "Our distinguished countryman John Howard Payne, Esq., the accomplished dramatist and poet arrived in this place a few days since from the South West."[11] Whether or not he had letters of introduction to Edward Harden, he soon made his acquaintance, and from all the evidence obtainable and from long-standing tradition, Harden invited Payne to be his house-guest. It is not known how long Payne remained in Athens, but certainly long enough to become a close friend of Harden's and even a closer friend of his eighteen-year old daughter Mary. Here were repeated the romantic stirrings in Payne's heart, which he had developed in an incipient stage for the Indian princess Apotheola, and earlier for Mary Wollstonecraft Shelley. This forty-four-year-old bachelor fell flatly in love with the eighteen-year-old Mary, and he may have proposed marriage to her at that time—if not, he was to do so later as will appear further on.

Sometime in September, Payne broke away from the hospitality of Edward Harden's home and his romantic attachment to Mary, and set out for the northern part of the state, whether more to see the wonderful mountain scenery which had been described to him or to study the civilization of the Cherokee Indians. At first he had planned to continue his journey northward through the Carolinas and Virginia, but, in his own account, "I was induced by the descriptions I had heard of the beauty of its

[Georgia's] mountain region, to turn somewhat aside from my road in order to seek the upper parts of the State: for I was anxious, in any thing I might write hereafter, to leave nothing which deserved admiration untouched."[12] He was thrilled by the majestic, roaring Tallulah Falls, the streaming bridalveil Toccoa Falls ("Tuckoah"), the high, leaping Amicolola Falls ("Amacooloola"), and the caves and mountains of the "Gold Region," including Currahee Mountain, which rose up out of the plains like a pyramid of Egypt. A person who had met Payne in Athens, writing almost a quarter century later, described how Payne had been carried away by the beauties of nature, which he saw on his trip.[13]

2. Payne Visits the Cherokees

According to Payne, "A mere accident led me among the Cherokees."[14] Somewhere in his rambles through Georgia he had met a "Dr. Tennille, of Sandersville," who got him interested in the Cherokees. "He suggested," wrote Payne, "that their history for the last 50 years, could it be obtained, would be one of extreme interest and curiosity, and especially appropriate to a work like mine."[15]

One account, undoubtedly imaginary, had Payne setting out from Athens in a two-horse carriage, with Governor Wilson Lumpkin, Edward Harden, and Samuel Rockwell.[16] These men accompanying Payne would seem highly improbable, because Lumpkin would soon go out of office (in early November) and would need to be on hand in Milledgeville to deliver his last message to the legislature; and there is no evidence that the other two might have been Payne's fellow-travelers. It is possible that Harden and Rockwell went part of the way (but not in a carriage) to put Payne on the road, but they would hardly have accompanied Payne on his mountain-scenery excursion. Furthermore, when Payne reached Cassville, in the Cherokee Nation, he received a letter of introduction to Principal Chief John Ross, from this same Rockwell, written on September 24th. By now

Payne had decided to visit Ross, and Rockwell in his letter said: "Mr. Payne's object in visiting you, is to obtain an insight into your national history & copies of such documents, as you may have in your possession concerning the traditions of . . . this oppressed People in order that if the race is to be extinguished, its history & that of the wrongs may be preserved."[17] Ross at this time was living in Tennessee, not far from the Georgia line, since he had been forced out of his home at Head of Coosa (Rome).

Payne's own account, however, if it is to be believed, would seem to put an end to all these suppositions and speculations as to how he entered the Cherokee Nation and as to his purpose in going: "In travelling through Georgia I, of course, heard frequent mention of the Cherokees; but I took little heed of what I heard. I considered the Cherokees, as they had been represented, as but the miserable remnant of a broken race, given up to all sorts of degradation; and I thought the sooner they could be transported beyond the bounds of civilization, the better for the world. Accident, however, brought me to some very different views of the question. I inquired more thoroughly. I determined to judge them with my own eyes. I purchased a horse, traversed the forsts alone, and went among them."[18]

Payne knew very little about the Indian problem, which was bothering the United States Government and especially Georgia. As he said later, "I knew next to nothing then of the Cherokees." He was no politician, though he considered himself a Whig, and he kept up little with public issues—his *Jam Jehan Nima* was to eschew all political and commercial news. Doubtless he did not know that the United States had promised Georgia in 1802 to remove the Indians from her borders as soon as it could be done on reasonable and peaceable terms—a phrase which Georgia considered a flat promise to get rid of them. Now in 1835, it had been a third of a century since that promise had been made and had not been kept. Georgia was restless and had been so for a long time. In piecemeal treaties the United States had got concessions from the

Indians at various times, but the Cherokees still occupied about ten million acres in Northwest Georgia, which they under the leadership of John Ross were determined not to give up.

Eternally prodded by Georgia, the United States had induced a faction led by Major and John Ridge and Elias Boudinot to sign a treaty on March 14, 1835, providing for all the Cherokees to leave Georgia for a new home in the Indian Territory (later to become the State of Oklahoma). John F. Schermerhorn, a clergyman, who had been a schoolmate of Payne's at Union College, had been the commissioner to make this treaty and he was now busying himself all the succeeding summer and fall in trying to induce Ross and the mass of Cherokees to accept it.[19] There had been much excitement throughout the Cherokee Nation, for Georgia had gone ahead and opened the Cherokee lands to settlers who had drawn lots under the Land Lottery System. In early summer a council attended mostly by the Ross faction was held at Red Bluff, where the treaty was rejected.[20] On the following July 20th and a few days thereafter, one of the greatest gatherings in Cherokee history took place at Running Water, a few miles north of Rome (originally called Head of Coosa), attended by about 2,200 Indians. The stated purpose of the meeting was to discuss the method of distributing the annuities due the Cherokees for this year; but Schermerhorn used every effort without avail to induce the Indians to accept the March 14th treaty.[21]

The next meeting of the council was called for the second week in October, to be held at Red Clay, just across the Georgia boundary, in Tennessee. The Cherokee capital was moved here from New Echota after Georgia had outlawed the Cherokee government. This was the situation when on September 28th, Payne rode into Tennessee and on to Ross's residence at Flint Springs, across the ridge, not far from Red Clay. On arriving there Payne had expected to spend only a day or two, copying records. Although his residence was a cabin of only one room, Ross invited Payne to be his guest if he "could put up with a rough fare." For the next two weeks Payne was engaged in copying Cherokee archives and succumbing to the convincing discussions Ross poured out detailing the wrongs the Cherokees were suffering. Although Payne said that Ross had not told him about the high-handed manner in which a Georgian had entered his house at Head of Coosa and seized it and his possessions and offered indignities to his family, yet Payne was duly impressed by the story and mellowed more and more toward the Cherokees and steeled himself against the governments of the United States and of Georgia. The climax of Payne's visit was to be attendance on the council meeting, which was to take place on October 12th.[22]

All of Payne's romantic nature and moral indignation was aroused as on October 11th he watched the Indians gathering on their way past Ross's cabin, going to the Red Clay conclave. "I cannot imagine a spectacle of more moral grandeur," Payne wrote, "than the assembly of such a people, under such circum- stances. This morning offered the first foretaste of what the next week is to present. The woods echoed with the trampling of many feet: a long and orderly procession emerges from among the trees, the gorgeous autumnal tints of whose departing foliage seemed in sad harmony with the noble spirit now beaming in this departing race. Most of the train was on foot. There were a few aged men, and some few women, on horseback."[23] It was esti- mated that between 1,500 and 2,000 Cherokees came together at Red Clay.[24]

Payne was properly conditioned to play an important under- cover part in the deliberations. To Schermerhorn and others, acting for the United States, and especially to the Georgia au- thorities Payne's activities appeared to be most gratuitous and outrageous meddling in a highly surcharged atmosphere. Payne was so emotionally stirred up over what he considered to be the wrongs heaped upon the Cherokees that he did not realize how he was pursuing a dangerous course. Right and justice must prevail, thought he, come what may. He and Ross had planned as their first attack on any attempt to have the March 14th treaty accepted, a challenge to Schermerhorn's authority to treat. They insisted that he had no right to negotiate, because first, he had no commission directly from President Jackson, but letters only from Secretary of War Lewis Cass. And secondly, because even if he did have the right to negotiate, he could not do so alone, because William Carroll, former governor of Tennessee, had been designated as the second commissioner and Carroll was not there—kept away by sickness.

Payne was ubiquitous, circulating everywhere among the crowd, singling out and buttonholing anyone who seemed to be concerned with the negotiations, telling them that there would be no treaty. That was definite; the Cherokees were not going to accept the March 14th treaty or negotiate any other one whose terms the United States Government would accept. Payne seemed to have enjoyed "having it out" with his old schoolmate Schermerhorn. He asked Schermerhorn for certain documents, and according to Payne, "He said he would gather them and send them to New York. I pressed him for them at once, — because I had already every thing from the other side and wished the entire evidence, for I mean to write a history of the Cherokees; and, added I, laughing, 'don't complain if I use you rather roughly.' I saw that he was chafed, although he forced a smile. 'No,'—replied he—'but if you do, don't complain if I return the compliment,' and he departed in apparent good humor, and I saw no more of the Reverend Commissioner."[25]

The Red Clay meeting was a complete defeat for the United States and Georgia. So complete was it that the Ridge treaty-making faction now joined the Ross faction and a united Indian nation definitely rejected the March 14th treaty and appointed delegates to go to Washington to carry on further negotiations. In characteristic Jacksonian firmness, "by the eternal," he would never again receive in Washington another Cherokee delegation. The Indians would have to make a treaty with Schermerhorn, accept the price offered for removal, and migrate beyond the

Mississippi. In late December, 1835 a council, attended almost entirely by the treaty-making Ridge faction, assembled at New Echota and made the Treaty of Removal; and during the next few years the Cherokees were being sent to their new home in the West.[26]

But in the meantime Payne was to reach the climax of his Georgia career. He had not completed copying the Cherokee archives at Ross's home, and at the Chief's insistence Payne returned to the Ross cabin after the Red Clay council broke up. Payne was especially desirous of seeing a complete file of the *Cherokee Phoenix*, an Indian newspaper, which had recently been suppressed by the Georgia authorities. On locating a file, Ross sent runners to fetch it, while Payne continued copying the Cherokee archives. On November 7th he was planning to make his departure two days later, expecting to return through Athens with the special purpose of seeing Stone Mountain, "a view of which had been one of the leading objects of my journey."[27]

The Georgia Guards were destined to interfere with this schedule which Payne had worked out. The discovery of gold in the Cherokee Nation in 1828 had led to an influx of people from the "ends of the earth," all expecting to become wealthy digging up the yellow metal wherever they could find it, without much regard as to whose land they were digging on. Great disorder was in the making, and to bring some control over the land, Georgia instituted a system of permits which made it necessary for anyone going into the Indian country to secure first a permit. But permits alone would not be sufficient; to preserve order a special force of soldiers must be set up. So it was that in 1830 Georgia authorized such a force and called it the Georgia Guard. They were to be organized as foot soldiers and mounted men "as the occasion may require," and to number not more than sixty. To properly lead and discipline them, the commander was allowed three sergeants and given permission to dismiss anyone at any time who was found guilty of "disorderly conduct." The Guards were given authority "to arrest any person legally charged with or detected in, a violation of the laws of this State, and to convey as soon as practicable, the person so arrested" to a justice of the peace or to a judge of the Inferior or Superior Court.[28] The well-known South Carolina novelist and man of letters William Gilmore Simms, visited the gold region of Georgia about this time looking for local color in writing his *Guy Rivers: A Tale of Georgia*. In bringing the Georgia Guards into his story he gave this description of them: "They were all fine-looking men; natives generally of a state, the great body of whose population are well-informed, and distinguished by features of clear, open intelligence. They were well-mounted, and each man carried a short rifle, a sword, and a pair of pistols."[29]

3. His Arrest and Release

These were the guards who hovered on the Tennessee border while a detail of United States troops preserved order at the Red Clay Council meeting, and these were the guards, numbering two dozen, who rushed into Ross's cabin about eleven o'clock on the night of November 7th and arrested Payne and Ross. According to Payne's account, he and Ross were spending the whole evening in writing and copying, with papers piled high upon a table, when suddenly "there was a loud barking of dogs; then the quick tramp of galloping horses, then the rush of many feet; and a hoarse voice just at my side shouted 'Ross! Ross!'" Soon the "room was filled with the Georgia Guard—their bayonets fixed, and some, if not all, with their pistols and dirks or dirk knives." Then an "exceedingly long, lank man, with a round-about jacket, planted himself by my side, his pistol resting against my breast." He was Sergeant Wilson Young, commander of the Guard. Then the Guard began gathering up Payne's papers and put Payne and Ross under arrest.[30]

Garbled half-truths and imaginary accounts, published at the time and later, characterized almost every aspect of Payne's Georgia experiences. According to an account published in 1882 Payne and Ross were seated before a fire in Ross's cabin, when in rushed six or eight Guards. Mrs. Ross, who was seated on a trunk filled with papers and some money, sprang up and began to scream wildly. Ross, conversing with her in the Cherokee language, quieted her and told her to sit down on the trunk, and so the papers were saved from the Guards. They now arrested Payne and Ross and took them to Milledgeville. As will soon appear, it was wholly erroneous to say that Payne and Ross were taken to Milledgeville and that the papers were saved from capture.[31]

Undoubtedly the most outrageously inaccurate account of the arrest was given by Williams Forrest, a novelist, in his book *Trail of Tears*. Although the book is labeled as a novel, Forrest says that for dramatic effect he has taken some liberties with chronology, "but this in no way violates the integrity of the text"—by which he must have meant that no liberties were taken with actual facts. This is his account of the arrest: The Guard rode up to Ross's house and killed two Negroes belonging to Ross and hanged two more for good measure. When Ross stepped out to save any others from harm, a Guard accosted him with this demand, "Now, squaw-man, I'm calling on you to bring out that Indian-lovin' songbird, that little ol' northern writin' man."[32]

The location of Payne's arrest was almost as varied as those who wrote about it. It was generally stated to be Ross's hut, but at least one contemporary account, had the arrest in the cabin of Sleeping Rabbit, a Ross henchman.[33] A later writer said that it was at Blue Spring.[34] It was evident to all who knew the facts, that a serious breach of state comity had been made by the Georgia Guard in going across the line into Tennessee to make the arrest. And yet Colonel William N. Bishop, commander of the Guard but not present when the arrest was made, took refuge in the long-disputed location of the Georgia-Tennessee boundary line, and stated that he had talked with a surveyor and that he was convinced that Payne and Ross "were found within the proper limits of Murray county, Georgia, where the arrest was made."[35] And a later writer declared that the boundary was so much under dispute that people were not sure whether Red Clay was in Georgia or in Tennessee.[36] And Benjamin F. Currey, who was "Special Agent for the Emigration of the Cherokees," and who was present at the Red Clay Council and knew thoroughly the political geography of the region, said that the arrest was so near the line as to make the question debatable, and, furthermore, that Tennessee had no organized government or control over the region. "Upon the whole," he said, "it is believed this arrest will supercede the necessity of arresting others."[37] A modern writer became so confused as to put the arrest of Payne at Head of Coosa (Rome), in Ross's old home, from which he had been driven, and stated that "Capt. A. B. Bishop," who "commanded the Georgia Guards," made the arrest; and this modern writer did not mention at all the arrest of Ross.[38] Sergeant Young, who actually made the arrest, lived long thereafter, to recount the details of this exploit, and to continue "a tall, gaunt, grizzled man."[39]

Having seized their prey the Guards were not long in making their departure, all on horseback. Payne and Ross rode together in the middle of the procession. When they set out, the night was "bright and beautiful," as Payne described their journey and also the period of his imprisonment, embellishing the account of his experiences far beyond what he could have remembered when he wrote his narrative. Soon a "wild storm arose" and the "rain poured in torrents," but the cavalcade sloshed onward, some of the Guards being "exceedingly capricious; — sometimes whooping and galloping and singing obscene songs; — and sometimes, for a season, walking, in sullen silence." When their boisterousness died down, Payne's thoughts began to turn back to an earlier and more propitious part of his life, and his "sweet home" song popped into his mind. And almost miraculously at that very moment Payne could "scarcely believe my senses" when he heard one of the Guards singing it. "What song was that I heard you humming?" Payne asked. "That?—" answered the Guard, " 'sweet home' they call it, I believe. Why do you ask?" Payne replied, "Merely because it is a song of my own writing, and the circumstances under which I now hear it, struck me as rather singular."

Payne then observed in his account, "My partner simply grumbled that he was not aware I had written the song." This episode and the time and circumstances of Payne's writing the song were to become the theme of an amazing variation of the facts, as will hereafter be recounted.

Later that night the group came to the home of Sergeant Young, which he ran as a tavern, and here they halted for refreshments and a little literary conversation between Payne and Young, who in his own way had done some unusual reading. The talk soon drifted to the writings of "*Marryboy*," which Payne soon devined was Young's way of pronouncing Mirabeau. Before their literary encounters were over, Young subscribed for *Jam Jehan Nima*. The procession was soon off again, and by the break of day they had reached their journey's end—twenty-four miles in about eight hours with a "coffee break" at Young's was making pretty good time. They had reached Spring Place, which Payne did not name, and he and Ross were imprisoned in a hut on the grounds of the Vann house, a pretentious residence, which had been built by James Vann, a Cherokee chief, but which Payne did not designate except to say that he and Ross were imprisoned in "a small log hut, with no window and one door." There were three bunks and a fireplace. Throughout the whole time of Payne's imprisonment, which extended over a period of thirteen days, guards were stationed around the building and door. There was a great deal of swaggering, horseplay, and rough frontier humor among the Guards—most of it directed toward Payne, so he recalled in great detail, giving many conversations which he remembered or improvised. He felt that the Guards were not bad men and might be made good citizens if given a chance; but he believed their leaders were beyond redemption.[40]

On the 15th of November, Colonel William N. Bishop, the commander of the Guard, who had been on a trip to Milledgeville, and of course, knew nothing about the arrests, returned and ordered Ross to be freed and allowed to take with him his papers; but he kept Payne in prison until the 20th, for he wanted to examine Payne's papers to see what he had been copying and writing in Ross's hut.[41]

When news of the arrests became known, the question immediately arose as to who had ordered them, and what the charges against the prisoners were, and why they were not taken to the civil authorities for a hearing as the law directed. Most fingers pointed to Currey as the person authorizing the arrests.[42] Payne asserted that Sergeant Young told him that Currey had ordered the arrests; but Currey vigorously denied the charge. He said that he was nowhere around at the time, "and if we had been, we had no control over the Georgia Guard."[43] A brother of John Ross, mixing up his facts, said that Currey had ordered Bishop to make the arrest and that Bishop had done so.[44] Whether or not Payne thought that Bishop had anything to do with the arrests, he knew that Bishop went through his papers when he had returned from Milledgeville and that he had not treated Payne civilly, and that when Payne asked him when he would be released, Bishop replied, "About Christmas." Payne in his best invective and sarcasm wrote what he thought of Bishop: "I have seen Napoleon Bonaparte—I have seen the Duke of Wellington—I have seen the Emperor Alexander—the Emperor Francis—the King of England—the King of Prussia—I have seen Ney—Rapp—Blucher—Swartzenburg—in short, I have seen most of the contemporary great men of Europe, as well as America; — but I have never yet seen quite a great a man as the Tavern Keeper, Clerk of the Court, Postmaster, County Treasurer, Captain, Colonel, W. N. Bishop."[45]

Payne and others attributed the arrests also to Schermerhorn, who repelled the charges as being "exceedingly unjust and incorrect." But Schermerhorn was not backward in saying that Payne "did interfere at Red Clay, in a very improper and unwarrantable manner, with the negotiations then pending between the Government and the Cherokee Indians, and I should have been perfectly justifiable to have had him arrested and removed from the treaty ground; and if I had known what he has since disclosed of the

part he acted there, I should have done it." He added that he was
at the time in Tuscaloosa, Alabama, and knew nothing about the
arrests until he read the news in the Georgia papers.[46]

A close analysis of all the known facts indicates that Currey
might have made some remark to Young that it would be well
if those plotters in Ross's hut were taken up; and with this hint,
Young proceeded.

Next, the question might well be asked, Why were they arrested? In an atmosphere surcharged as it was after the failure
of the Red Clay Council to accept the March 14th treaty and
in the light of what was already known about Payne's activities
at that Council, rumors flew thick and fast. Payne and Ross had
been "closeted, after the adjournment of the council, for at least
a week [in fact a great deal longer], just back of the Georgia
line within Tennessee,"[47] and there was a widespread feeling in the
surrounding region that they were concocting some conspiracy to
unite and incite the Indians and the Negroes to revolt against the
white people, and probably join with France in a war against
the United States, growing out of a bitter controversy over
American claims. Also, the Indians were being made to believe
that Payne "was a great man from England," and an emissary
from the English King, their traditional friend, "for the purpose
of enabling the Indians to resist the oppressions of the American
government."[48] The part which Payne played at the Red Clay
Council was well known and was enough to bring about his
arrest, and Currey said that no one could read Payne's own account
"without admitting that he had meddled in matters over which
he had no rightful control, and about which he was utterly unfit,
as a partisan and fanatic, to form correct opinions."[49] Payne had
been passing around charges that the United States Government
had been trying to bribe the Indians to sign the treaty and that
as much as $50,000 had been offered to Ross—proof of this charge
was confirmed in Payne's papers which had been seized.[50] And
Bishop declared that in these papers he had "found some very
improper and indiscreet statements in relation to the President,

our Government and State authorities and agents, the Georgia Guard; &c; and many bitter remarks concerning the Cherokee matter." All of this had been suspected, and now Payne himself had given the proof.[51]

One of the most dangerous charges that could be levelled against a person at this time was to label him an Abolitionist. One of the Georgia newspapers said that "rumor makes him an Abolitionist";[52] and Currey boldly asserted that Payne was an Abolitionist and that he had helped to distribute Abolition leaflets found in the Indian country.[53] This rumor, unfounded on fact, stuck; and years later an account of the arrest had it that Payne's shaving kit had been found wrapped up in a copy of the Abolitionist newspaper, the *Liberator*.[54] Payne denied that he was an Abolitionist or that he had ever seen an Abolitionist pamphlet, and now he saw how fortunate he was that he did not pick up one somewhere as a curiosity; for the possession of one at this juncture might "have cost me my life upon a scaffold."[55]

Also, undoubtedly the arrests were made to keep Ross and his delegation from going on to Washington in an attempt to induce President Jackson to allow a more favorable treaty, and they were made especially to satisfy curiosity as to what Payne and Ross had been writing and copying during all those weeks both before and after the Red Clay Council meeting.

Practically every charge against Payne which had been bandied around had either been made or accepted by Currey, who published them over his name in a letter written on December 1, 1835 to the editor of the Milledgeville *Federal Union*. He ended his letter with this sentence, "I hold myself answerable for its contents."[56] President Jackson was somewhat upset by Currey's public statement of these charges, and he called on Secretary of War Cass to ask Currey forthwith why he made the letter public and what his proofs of these charges were.[57] Using more than two months to assemble his proofs, Currey answered Cass through a long letter to Elbert Herring, Commissioner of Indian Affairs, dated April 16, 1836, accompanied by thirty statements, affidavits, and a copy of Payne's intemperate and incriminating letter of October 11, 1835, in which he berated President Jackson and Georgia, charged attempted bribery against the United States agents and bemoaned the barbaric injustices these governments were applying to the Cherokees.[58] Cleverly playing on the fact that Jackson was a Democrat, that the presidential campaign of 1836 was then warming up, and that Payne was a Whig and in touch with Hugh L. White's agents, who were passing the word around that if White were elected he would not remove the Indians—with these things in mind Currey wrote that Payne "was well understood to be an enemy of the Government, and to be busily employed in doing whatever he could to render unavailing the steps which had been taken to reconcile the Indians to the idea of removal."[59] He said further that no one could "doubt there was in the operations of Ross and Payne a settled design to connect the Cherokee question with the party discussions of the day."[60]

In the years before the telegraph, news traveled slowly—no faster than a horse could trot. Not until Payne and Ross had been released did it become generally known that they had been arrested, and then for a time the details were fragmentary and conflicting; but when the facts were learned there was a general outcry against the arrest of Payne. Ross's arrest was hardly noticed and few tears were shed for him, so low was the esteem in which the Georgians held him.

The Milledgeville *Southern Recorder* declared that it was "with feelings of the deepest pain and humiliation" that it learned of the arrest of Payne and that it was "outrageous."[61] It was informed that Payne had "suffered personal violence from the Guard, and was much injured by them."[62] The Milledgeville *Georgia Journal* was almost beside itself with anger. These "Vandals" had arrested "a gentleman of great celebrity, in the Literary World." It was a "gross enormity." Their reason seemed to have been "his copying certain documents relative to the manners and customs of the Indian Tribes, which their wiseacre of a leader, construed to be high treason against the State."[63] Because some of the papers were in French, "a language these armed kidnappers did not understand, their sapient leader concluded that they contained high treason to the State! Who could have believed that such Vandalism would disgrace the nineteenth century?"[64] After the news had been out for a few weeks this editor declared, "We hear but one sentiment from all quarters, of the State in regard to this wanton violation of personal rights, and bold disregard of the Constitution of the United States."[65] Beyond the limits of Georgia, the general opinion of Payne's arrest was typified in the Washington *National Intelligencer's* comment that "barbarous wrongs [had been] inflicted upon this respectable gentleman."[66]

The indignation of the press varied somewhat with how Whiggish the newspaper happened to be, for here propaganda could be made against the Democrats. Currey declared in early December that the "ephemeral excitement produced by the arrest of Payne and Ross" had passed off, "except with the disaffected politicians."[67] A person who had attended the Red Clay Council meeting and who was in Spring Place during the whole time of the imprisonment of Payne, declared that "he was kindly treated by the guard as well as the citizens."[68] The Democratic Athens *Southern Banner*, on first hearing of the arrest, felt that no doubt there was good reason for arresting Ross, but it was satisfied that Payne was not "creating a disturbance in the Cherokee country."[69] But on further reflection after receiving more details this editor concluded that the Guard was being unduly and unjustly condemned. The Guard had been a valuable force in preserving law and order in the Cherokee country for some years, and in the present instance its only fault was crossing into Tennessee in making the arrests. Payne should not have been surprised at getting arrested, and it was only the Ross supporters and Whig lovers who were raising so much dust over the affair. Payne "got himself into the difficulty under a full knowledge of all the circumstances with which he was surrounded—of the state of public feeling against Ross as the sworn enemy of Georgia—of the great anxiety of the people both of Georgia and of Tennessee for a treaty with the Indians, which he opposed, and of the strong prejudices existing among the people against strangers from the North."[70] Governor Wilson Lumpkin, whose term of office expired about the time of the arrests, as he looked back upon the times almost twenty years later, said: "The arrest was both premature and illegal, but the impertinent intermeddling of Payne was very unbecoming a stranger, a gentleman, or an author professedly collecting facts for history. He was the partisan, if not the agent, of Northern fanatics, whose avocation is to repent for the sins of everybody except themselves."[71]

When the news of the arrest of Payne and Ross reached Milledgeville, the legislature was in session, Lumpkin having recently been succeeded by William Schley as governor. Schley did not hear of the arrest until after the prisoners had been released; but he immediately sent a confidential agent to Spring Place to secure exact details. Bishop had reported to Schley that after examining Payne's papers he was convinced that there was insufficient evidence to hold Payne longer or to turn him over to the civil authorities.[72]

As soon as the legislature heard of the arrest it called on Governor Schley for any information he might have. He replied two days later, on November 30th, that he had no information except "the rumors of the day" and a letter that four Cherokees had written him.[73] The House appointed a committee to investigate the arrest of Payne—the Georgia government ignored Ross's arrest. The committee made a long report on December 18th, in which it gave a history of the Georgia Guard and condemned it for having violated some of the very definite instructions for its operation which Governor Lumpkin had given it when it was set up. It declared that the Guard had violated the Fourth Amendment of the Federal Constitution against search and seizure and it recommended the discontinuance of the Guard; and it severely criticized Bishop for not releasing Payne immediately: "Your committee would ask with feelings of mortification, why was he kept in custody ONE MINUTE beyond the time, when it was ascertained he had committed no offence?" It resolved that Georgia "highly disapprove" of Payne's arrest.[74] Payne was quite pleased with the report, writing, "The report I saw was creditable and in a much finer spirit than has been shown by some who ought to have known better in my own city—[New York]."[75]

Georgia had to apologize not only to Payne, but it was much more important to apologize to the State of Tennessee for having violated its territory. Payne had protested to Governor Newton Cannon, and Cannon reminded Schley of the seriousness of Georgia soldiers crossing into Tennessee, but he assured Schley that he believed the crossing had been done without Georgia's knowledge or direction. But he reminded Schley that he hoped it would not be necessary for Tennessee to station troops on the border. This was a mild letter, but the editor of the *Federal Union* thought that it was insulting and menacing and led people to "wonder, by what means" the Tennessee governor had reached "the high station which he occupies."[76] Schley's reply to Cannon was conciliatory and gave the assurance that those who crossed into Tennessee and made the arrest did so "without proper knowledge or reflection" and without the authority of Georgia.[77]

Payne was lucky that the contents of his letter or article dated "Cherokee Nation, Tennessee Border, Sunday, October 11, 1835" were not generally known when he was receiving the apologies and commiserations of the Georgia press and the legislature. This letter was written in Ross's cabin the day before the Red Clay Council meeting, and it seems that it was intended for publication. It was an intemperate and highly ill-advised attack on the United States and Georgia governments and a glowing defense of Ross and the Cherokees against their removal.[78] Payne was simple enough to think "It was such a paper as we see hourly upon our public affairs, only somewhat more gentle and conciliatory."[79] He declared that the United States had long been trying to bribe the Indians in their council meetings with many thousands of dollars, and as for Ross he had "resisted bribery in every instance, even in one amounting to fifty thousand dollars; rather than enrich himself by his country's ruin, he will remain poor, but honest. The agents insult him, still he goes on. The Georgia Guard watches for a pretext to make him prisoner, but the pretext is not to be found, and in some cases, where they would not be deterred by the fear of wrong, they are understood to have been held back through the fear of the people. It is rumored, however, that some attempt of the sort is, even at this moment, in contemplation."[80] The appearance of the Georgia Guard "reminds one of banditti more than of soldiers," he said in this letter,[81] but later after they had arrested him and he had got a closer acquaintance with them, he would like to apologize to banditti for having insulted them, by comparing them to the Georgia Guard.[82] As for the Cherokees and the progress they had made, "Georgia has hated them the more because of their civilization."[83] The governments of the United States and of Georgia threatened the Cherokees and they "now stand alone, moneyless, helpless, and almost hopeless; yet without a dream of yielding."[84] Payne had been hypnotized by Ross and his Cherokees.

Payne was deeply and emotionally upset by his arrest and imprisonment. When released he made his way on horseback, loaded down with all his equipment and papers (except this letter), going to Ross's cabin and on to Knoxville. When he reached Calhoun, on the north side of the Hiwassee River, he addressed a note to the newspapers, on November 23rd, calling on the people of Georgia to withhold their judgment until "a full and honest statement shall be submitted, the moment it can be prepared."[85] When not traveling on his more-than-one-hundred-mile journey to Knoxville, he was preparing his statement, at least in his mind, which was entitled "John Howard Payne to his Countrymen." He may have written it after he reached Knoxville. It was dated "Saturday, November 1835," which would make it the 28th, since the only Saturday in November, 1835 following the 23rd would be the 28th.

He had reached Knoxville probably sometime before the 28th. On December 1st he addressed a letter to Daniel Webster, now in the United States Senate, submitting to him "the statement of a gross violation of my rights as an American Citizen" (which presumably was his address "to his Countrymen") "in the hope that you will reflect whether there is not some way in which the outrage may obtain proper reproof from those high in the councils of my country."[86] The next day he wrote to S. L. Fairchild of Philadelphia, enclosing an account "of a great wrong I have suffered."[87] On the 5th he wrote to Edward Harden, who had entertained him when he was in Athens, saying that he had sent him a statement of the wrongs he had suffered, and added, "Have you ever known of a more impudent enormity?"[88] Payne's brother Thatcher, in New York, learned of the arrest, while John Howard was still in prison, and not knowing of his release, he wrote on November 27th to Secretary of War Cass to try to get him out. Thatcher noted that anyone knowing his brother's "pacific disposition and exclusively literary habits" would consider it "ludicrous" to attribute to him "any views politically dangerous, either in reference to Georgia or the United States in their respective relations to the Cherokees."[89]

Payne's address "to his Countrymen," which he considered his vindication but which many people used for his condemnation, was first published in the *Knoxville Register*, December 2, 1835, filling ten columns of the paper. Instead of making a short plain statement of fact, Payne soared away into a literary essay in which he used all the talents at his command, embellishing it with many conversations and minute details which he could not have recalled without notes—and there is no evidence that he took any notes while in prison. It was entirely too long and tedious to have served the purpose Payne intended, for a newspaper would not want to fill up most of an issue with Payne's statement, unless, indeed, it was a Whig paper and expected the address to be good propaganda against Jackson's Democrats. The editor of the *Richmond Enquirer* was moved sufficiently to read it and to become indignant over how the "suspicions of an ignorant and brutal guard were excited." The narrative, he said, was "amusing but too voluminous for re-publication."[90] The Macon *Georgia Telegraph* remarked that if "Mr. Payne succeeds in making his intended 'literary periodical' as uninteresting as he has this account of his capture, it will certainly be a remarkable work!"[91]

Payne ended his statement with an appeal to "People of Tennessee!"—"People of Georgia!"—"My poor fellow citizens throughout my native land!" "I will tell you and with my last breath, — if tamely you behold these things you are only slaves, — heartless, abject slaves, — and unworthy of the immortal ancestors who bravely fought and nobly died to make their country free."[92]

Attached to Payne's address "to his Countrymen" and published with it by the *Knoxville Register* was another address, "The Cherokee Nation to the People of the U. States." Payne had written this address at the request of Ross and the Cherokees after the Red Clay Council had adjourned. In it he attempted to use the imagery of Indian language, succeeding part of the time, but too often lapsing into long and involved sentences, which the Cherokees could not understand and whose meaning the ordinary American could not devine without, at least a second reading. It was to be sent out by runners for "the signature of every Cherokee within the country."[93] It was a plea for justice, for the right to remain on their 10,000,000 acres of land, but if they must go, then for a better price than Jackson was offering. Payne began it: "FRIENDS—Listen! The voice of thousands and of thousands, now speak to you in one voice. Listen! A nation asks it of you—Listen! We bring you no angry words. We would touch your hearts; for we think your hearts are good and, therefore, for your own sakes, as well as for ours, friends, we would have you listen!" And then, with the Indians being removed to the West, "Amid the universal hurricane, a small forest stood the desolation and yet remains. The wild tempest howls around it, yet it still stands. We are that little forest."[94] Those who went to the West were heartbroken and disappointed, and their "wail is on the night wind which pours its pestilential breath over the prairies of the far, far west."[95]

Few of the Georgia papers published Payne's address "to his Countrymen" and even fewer published this wail of the Cherokees. Payne not realizing that it was the length of his address which prevented it from being published widely, concluded that the United States Government was preventing its publication. Writing from New York in a letter to Edward Harden, March 22, 1836, Payne said: "The government agents seem to have been busy muzzling the press of our leading cities, in relation to my case, — but it is well enough known wherever it is necessary to be understood, and if occasion should arise, I am prepared to make it more so. — However, unless it can do service to the cause of the wronged or to the future honor of the country, it may as well be forgotten."[96]

Also Payne was complaining that nothing was being done to right the wrongs done him, either by the United States Government or by the Georgia authorities. True enough the legislature had soothed his feelings in its resolutions, but that was not enough. "Cannot Bishop—Young—& Currey be punished by a law suit? Is not Currey's letter actionable?" he wanted to know. "Surely it is a libel & a malicious one," he thought.[97]

On his way out of Georgia, when Payne had reached Knoxville he immediately found himself a hero. A committee informed him of their regrets that "your person and rights were violently outraged by a band of lawless soldiery." They invited him to "a public entertainment at the Tremont House." A public meeting was held at the courthouse, which passed a series of resolutions expressing their indignation at Payne's treatment and resolved to send them to the governors and legislatures of Georgia and Tennessee and to President Jackson. Payne thanked the citizens of Knoxville for their kindness and especially for their commiseration on this "wanton and arbitrary and lawless outrage, upon the sacred rights of an American citizen." He regretted that he would not be able to attend the public functions planned for him, as he found it "indispensible to pursue" his "journey without delay."[98]

Payne was now anxious to be on his way "homeward"—which

could have been no other place than his brother Thatcher's home in New York. Certainly he would not risk entering Georgia again after hearing the parting words he remembered Bishop having flung at him when he released Payne: "I order you to cut out of Georgia. If you ever dare again show your face within the limits of Georgia, I'll make you curse the moment with your last breath. . . . Sir, clear out of the State forever, and go to John Ross, G—d d—n you!"[99]

Payne was either frightened or made his friend Edward Harden, in Athens, think so, for he wrote him just before setting out that he would go mostly alone on horseback and he was not telling any-body the route he would take, but he would go to Charleston (and without him saying so, it is presumed that he would go on to New York by boat). As he had some baggage in Augusta, he would go to Hamburg (on the opposite side of the river) and "look in," but "Georgia I never enter again without a formal public invitation." This route, of course, would take him through eastern Tennessee, and western North Carolina and South Caro-lina. He was not too sure but what "these scoundrels" might try to stop him, adding the rather unnecessary heroic—"If the worst happens, I shall not be the first who has not lived out his time in a *free country*, and unless the nation awakens, I shall not be the last."[100]

4. *Payne Proposes Marriage to Mary Harden*

If Payne had not been arrested and imprisoned, it was his in-tention to take his road back through Athens by way of "the Stone Mountain of Georgia, a view of which had been one of the leading objects of my journey."[101] His direct route "homeward" would have been through eastern Tennessee and on into Virginia. Richmond was almost as near as Charleston, and from Richmond he would have had easy going on to Washington and New York. But, of course, as he said, he wanted to see Stone Mountain, and he had trunks to pick up in Augusta, and from Stone Mountain to Augusta the route would be through Athens—and in Athens his good friend Edward Harden would welcome him with the accustomed hospitality of the Harden home. And there can be no doubt that he was just as anxious if not more so to see Mary Harden. But this was not to be, for he never made the trip he had contemplated and he was never to enter the State of Georgia again.

But Payne and Edward Harden were to carry on a correspondence for sometime, Harden undoubtedly being a champion defender of Payne. On March 22, 1836, in answer to a letter Harden had written him in the previous December, Payne did not forget to express his friendship and continued interest in the Cherokees and his bitter enmity for Bishop, Young, and Currey. But his feelings were greatly tempered by "your daughter's flattering request about ['] Sweet Home.' " Mary had requested her father to ask for her a copy of this song, which, no doubt, she had played or sung for him when he was visiting in the Harden home. Payne replied in this letter: "I will write it out for her in my best schoolday hand whenever I find an opportunity in sending it post free. No one deserves a 'Sweet Home' better than she does—and no one would be surer to make any home, however sweet, still more so, by her goodness & her genius. But if I send a contribution for *her* Album she must make a sketch for mine." Then with a play on the traditional Yankee trading habits: "I belong to a section of the republic where we are not in the habit of doing things without large profits—in some places, to be sure, her request would be more than compensation—but in New York we look for per-centage by hundreds & thousands—I have caught the [infection?] & must treat with her in the spirit of New York speculation."[102]

This letter lays open a strong hint that Mary and John Howard had become romantically attached to each other, but there is no evidence that they corresponded with each other, beyond the fact that Payne did write out a copy of his "Home, Sweet Home," and did send it directly to her or to her father. It would be logical to think that he sent it to Mary and that Mary, being the most correct lady that she was, wrote to Payne, thanking him. But there is no evidence of any correspondence ever having developed between them, except a letter which Payne wrote to Mary, dated July 14, 1836. In that letter Payne poured out his romantic soul, but in the restrained etiquette of the times. After admitting that fortune had not smiled upon him, he wrote: "I am conscious of my own unworthiness of the boon I desire from you and cannot, dare not, ask you to give a decisive answer in my favor now, only permit me to hope that at some future time I may have the happiness of believing my affection returned, but at the same time I conjure you to remember in making up your decision that it is in your power to render me happy or miserable."

In an agitated state of mind, he left her, not having been bold enough while in her presence to ask her hand. Now he could not "contemplate the image of one too dear to me to resign for ever, without making an effort I was unequal to when in your presence." He had nothing to offer "but a devoted heart and hand," and whatever her answer might be, "fervent wishes for your happiness and welfare shall be the first of my heart—"

He closed with this plea: "I have felt it essential to my peace of mind that I should inform you of the state of my feelings satisfied that, that and your amiableness of heart will plead my cause— I intreat you to reply to this letter (if but one word) indeed I am sure if you knew how anxiously I shall await your answer, compassion alone would induce you to send me an early answer."[103]

Mary could not have been so heartless as not to have sent him an answer; and it must have been more than the one word "No." There were several reasons why the match would have been impractical. Mary was about eighteen and Payne was past forty five, yet this discrepancy in age need not have been fatal. But Payne's residence in Georgia would have been distasteful to him however much he might have tried to forget his bitter experiences in the state, and Mary's parents might well have looked with disfavor on Mary's life in poverty (even if in loving poverty) in the North; and logical tradition has it that Mary's parents objected to the match. An Athenian who knew Mary well throughout most of her life and was a pallbearer at her funeral said that "if Miss Mary's young heart was touched her father soon healed the sore."[104] And another Athenian, a spinister lady of great charm and culture, who also knew Mary, concluded that the "disparity of age was too great for any sentiment to be engendered on the part of the young girl for a lover so much older in years."[105]

Neither Mary Harden nor John Howard Payne ever married, and this fact has led to the most exaggerated exploitations and explosions in imaginary accounts of the Payne-Harden romance. Both have been made to spend the rest of their lives in pining away over a blasted romance. As for Mary her romance was never capitalized by feature writers in the newspapers and magazines until after her death, and her fellow-townsmen seem to have been oblivious of her romance. If Mary was much affected she kept it to herself. An Athenian who clearly remembered her during the time of the Civil War said that "when she appeared upon the streets she looked odd to say the least. . . . I knew her well and she honored me with her confidence. She was highly educated, extremely courteous and rather effusive in manner, honest, and sincere, independent and economical, *ex necessitate*."[106] That Mary Harden was more beautiful in personality than in looks, a glimpse at a fairly homely likeness of her would suggest.[107] It was a case of "Handsome is that handsome does."

Payne was by no means a Lothario, but to represent him as languishing away for Mary Harden the seventeen years of life left to him, is to ignore all the evidence. Payne could make love and almost as readily forget it, the record seems to show; but if he did hold in memory any one of his sweethearts it was neither Mary Harden, nor Mary Wollstonecraft Shelley, nor his Indian Princess Apotheola. If the statements of at least two close friends and biographers of Payne are to be believed, he did hold in fond memory to the very end a Boston lady to whom he was at one time engaged to be married. If either of these two biographers knew of the Mary Harden episode they were silent about it.

According to Charles H. Brainard, Payne told him "with deep feeling, the story of his attachment to a beautiful and accomplished lady of Boston, by whom his affection was reciprocated, and who would have become his wife but for parental objections."[108] And Gabriel Harrison, alluding to the same affair, said that it was "a romance of his early manhood" and that "Payne's over-sensitive nature never fully recovered from this blow, and to the last days of his life, he would speak of it in tones of sadness that excited the sympathy of the few friends whom he honored with his confidence."[109] In the light of these statements could it be that all of Payne's other love affairs were defense complexes against his deep love for the Boston lady whom he could not forget?

5. The Payne Legends

In Georgia without the song, "Home, Sweet Home" and Mary Harden, Payne's visit would be a forgotten episode of the Cherokee removal; without the song Payne would be unknown in America as well as throughout the world, where it is heard. Payne's love affair with Mary and the magical effects of his song have become folklore in Georgia, passing through many tellings and varying with the mood and the vividness of the imagination of the teller. Before Mary Harden's death the romance remained practically silent; the song, itself, held sway in the part it played in securing Payne's release. After her death the romance blossomed forth with the song as a necessary accompaniment.

The legends, always told as fact, began with Payne returning to Athens after his release from prison and sealing his love with Mary, presenting her instead of a diamond ring a pair of Indian moccasins and a walrus tooth. She said "Yes" instead of "No," but her parents said "No." Payne no longer a welcomed guest at the Harden home returns clandestinely and stays at the home of Madame Rosalie Renie Marie Claudine Josephine Yvron Vincent Dennis, de Kedron, de Trobriand, de la Perriere, Gouvain, a French lady living in Athens and a relative by marriage of the Hardens.

And Mary and John Howard carried on a correspondence for many years, with John Howard addressing his letters to Mary by way of Madame Gouvain. Their original courting days, before Payne became *persona non grata* with Mary's parents, were spent in idyllic bliss with music by Mary, with the colored servants singing "Home, Sweet Home," which suggests to Payne that when he found time he would write an opera with a Negro chorus in it.[110] As the same old Athenian who had known Mary Harden most of her life said, the love story "has been often told and oftner exaggerated."[111]

Just as exaggerated and incorrect were the reasons assigned for Payne's coming to Georgia, the time when he came, and the part played by Edward Harden in getting him out of trouble. It was frequently stated that Payne came to learn more about the Cherokees, when, in fact, as has already appeared, he was not interested in the Indians at all when he set out.[112] The time has been given as every year from and including 1832 through 1836—1835 being correct.[113]

Many of the romancers give Edward Harden credit for securing Payne's release, having him going to Milledgeville, where one writer has him seeing "Governor Troup" (William Schley, in fact, being the governor), and other writers sending him to Spring Place.[114] One writer deserves special mention for his having gone to the ultimate and correct source of proof—to the old family servant, Rob Roy, who at the advanced age of ninety, but with imagination undimmed, gave this version: When "ole Massa" heard of Payne's predicament, he saddled up three horses, one to be led, and he and Rob Roy set out, it being "unpossible to take a kerridge over dem mountain roads." When they arrived at Spring Place "Mister Payne looked mighty down in de mouf." They got him out, and while coming back he heard Payne "hummin dat 'Home, Sweet Home.'" "Miss Mary used ter sing it an' I almos' cry ebery time I hear her." In about a year Payne comes back again and when he "lef' de last time he was here he jest cried like er chile."[115] That Edward Harden aided Payne, another writer cites as proof an entry in Harden's diary which he made relating to a case he argued in Carnesville (far from Spring Place or Milledgeville) in 1834 (the year before Payne came to Georgia)—"Carnesville, April 14, 1834. Plead the case of Payne for Terrell."[116]

Imagination ran riot even to a greater extent and became embedded in the folklore of the region, in relation to "Home, Sweet Home"—when it was written and the part it played in bringing about Payne's release. Some of the confusion about the time when he wrote the song came from the fact that he did write a copy of it for Mary Harden; and the fact that he did not copy it into Mary's elegant Album but sent it to her at her request after he had left, indicates that Payne's romantic encounter with Mary in her home had not been too serious.[117] It was easy for the unthinking ones to assume that Payne had given Mary the original manuscript (written in Paris thirteen years earlier) instead of making a copy for her; and the less unthinking ones began retailing the story that Payne had originally composed the song in the Harden home. It is probably true that Payne interlined a love letter in the copy he made for Mary, but she never showed it to anyone in her lifetime and after her death it disappeared and led to the unanswered question for years thereafter: "What has become of the original copy of 'Home, Sweet Home,' given by the author to his Southern sweet-heart?"[118] It was often stated that it was buried with her at her request, and it has been as often denied.[119] It is true that "Home, Sweet Home" was sung at the graveside after Mary Harden had died in 1887 and was buried in the Oconee Cemetery in Athens.[120] The Athens *Weekly Banner-Watchman* in recording her death paid tribute to the little lady, who never married, and noted: "Probably not a half dozen persons outside of Athens knew that the quiet little house on Hancock avenue held this remarkable lady, and many a resident of Athens even had lost sight of this aged and unobtrusive person."[121]

Although some writers have asserted that the only copy of "Home, Sweet Home" in Payne's handwriting was the one he gave Mary Harden, it seems that Payne wrote about as many copies as Lincoln did of his "Gettysburg Adress." There is a copy in the Schaffer Library at Union College (believed by some people to be the original, but not so accepted by authorities) and the lyric is cast in bronze on the inside of the Payne Gateway to the College Grounds.[122]

In addition to the myth of the Harden home being the place where Payne composed the song, it has been asserted by the ignorant that on entering the prison cabin he threw up his hands and in anguish sarcastically shouted, "Home, Sweet Home," and then while in prison composed the song. The most bizarre account has it this way: Payne was visiting in Spring Place and "got on a drunken spree and was arrested." While in prison awaiting trial he composed the song, and on his way to the trial he sang the song so pathetically that he was realeased without being tried. And according to this same account Payne later said that while he lay in jail the song kept going through his mind and that he "got up and asked for a candle and wrote it off on paper borrowed from the jailer."[123]

The first suggestion of the magical effects of "Home, Sweet Home" was made by a newspaper editor while Payne was still in prison and before any of the many accounts came out, including even Payne's own version. The *Cassville Pioneer* on November 20, 1835 said, "We guess it will be a fortunate escape of Mr. Payne if he is dismissed without a passport from Judge Lynch. Nothing but his being the author of 'Sweet Home' will shield him from the just indignation of the Guard."[124]

A resident of Athens who met Payne when he visited there, in his reminiscences, written forty years later, remembered Sergeant Young having told this story (which he or Sergeant Young had badly mangled): A detail of about a dozen of the Georgia Guards was scouring the hills in 1832 or 1833 looking for lawbreakers when they ran across a pensive man, "idling along through the woods" admiring the scenery. They asked him his name and demanded his permit. He did not seem to know what was meant by a permit. They arrested him and continued on to the headquarters of Colonel Sanford (!!), the commander of the Guard, but being overtaken by night they pitched camp, and around the camp fire, engaging in a little horseplay they began to tease Payne by saying that he would certainly be hanged the next day but that they believed they would be rid of him by hanging him immediately. Becoming mellowed by whiskey, they began to sing "Home, Sweet Home." Payne remarked, "Gentlemen, I composed that song." The next day when they reached Colonel Sanford's headquarters, after a few minutes conversation, Sanford freed him.[125]

A humorous version, told by Payne himself according to the narrator, had Payne in prison. The sentry in his rounds began to hum "Home, Sweet Home," whereupon Payne asks:

" 'My friend, do you admire that song?'

'Don't I, stranger,' was the reply. 'Next to Old Hundred and Hail Columbia, its the prettiest song that ever was writ.'

'Well do you think the man who wrote that song could be a spy and a traitor?'

'Dern'd if I do; I'd lief believe that Gen. Washington didn't write the Declaration of Independence.'

'Well, I wrote it.'

'You did? What yer name?'

'John Howard Payne.'

'Jerusalem!' said the soldier, 'that's the very name! It's printed on the song! Hello, Captain, come here; you've made a cussed mistake. This feller ain't a clock pedlar nor a missionary. Its the man as writ "Home, Sweet Home." I say, let's ask him to licker and then let him out. I'll stand security he'll not run away.'

'And, indeed,' " continued the narrator, " 'they did let me out, gave me the best of treatment, and I saw enough of the real character of the right people, and heard enough of the true state of the affairs to prevent my regretting my capture and imprisonment by the Georgia Guard.' "[126]

These Payne stories were being manufactured in the North as well as in Georgia. According to an account in the New York *Home Journal,* Payne came to Georgia to see the Cherokee Green Corn Dance in Allatoona, and while on his way there he was arrested by the Georgia Guard. At the camp fire that night the sentinel "to keep himself from falling asleep, would alternate between cursing, drinking, chewing, and singing." When he struck up "Home, Sweet Home" Payne said, "Friend, I am the author of that song!" The sentinel, quite surprised but believing him, said "Well, by—, if you are the author of that song you have no business to be kept here. Do you see that horse? Just you mount that beast and make yourself scarce."[127]

A version coming neared the facts than most accounts, represented Payne with arms pinioned being marched along between two soldiers with cocked pistols. As they proceeded, one of them began to sing "Home, Sweet Home" and on finishing, remarked that he would give $1,000 to see the author of it. Payne said that he was the man. Thereupon they unpinioned him and allowed him to travel in comfort.[128]

Another account rather badly mixed up, but carrying out the motif of the song's miraculous power, had Payne and Ross under arrest (Ross was generally unnoticed in these stories), on their way to Milledgeville. As they set out it began raining and they spent the whole night getting there—[rather fast traveling if the arrest had been made near Red Clay, 200 miles away.] About midnight one of the soldiers began humming "Home, Sweet Home." Payne remarked, "Little did I expect to hear that song under such circumstances and at such a time. Do you know the author?" "No," said the soldier, "do you?" "Yes," answered Payne, "I composed it." "The devil you did! You can tell that to some fellows, but not to me. Look here, you made that song, you say; if you did—and I know you didn't—you can say it all without stopping. It has something in it about pleasure and palaces. Now pitch in and reel it off; and if you can't, I'll bounce you from your horse and lead you instead of it." Payne not only repeated the whole song, but also sang it "making the old woods ring with the tender melody and pathos of the words." The soldier was not only convinced, but also captivated. He remarked that the composer of such a song would never go to prison if he could help it. When they reached Milledgeville, and a hearing was held, Payne and Ross were released. Payne said that they had been turned loose because of Ross's captivating conversation on their way there, but Ross insisted that they had been saved by the magical power of "Home, Sweet Home."[129]

Payne continued his interest in the Cherokee Indians for some years after his Georgia adventure and after they had been removed to the Indian Territory, west of Arkansas. In 1840 he visited them and wrote an account of a court trial, which was published in the *New York Journal of Commerce*.[130]

Never able to keep ahead of his creditors, Payne in his poverty was able in 1842 to secure an appointment as consul to Tunis, when the Whigs were in power. After the Whigs had been thrown out by the Democrats in the election of 1844, President Polk recalled him in November, 1845. Payne now encamped in Washington, trying to get a reappointment. At one of Jenny Lind's concerts in Washington in December, 1850, attended by President Fillmore, Daniel Webster and other members of the cabinet, as well as by many other celebrated guests, she spied John Howard Payne in the audience. Turning to him she sang "Home, Sweet Home" with such electrical effect on the audience that Webster was seen to weep. If Payne's Whiggishness had not been sufficient, Jenny's singing "Home, Sweet Home" got Webster to support a reappointment of Payne as consul to Tunis. His reappointment came in March, 1851—on April 9, 1852 John Howard Payne died in Tunis and was buried there.[131]

William W. Corcoran, who had long known Payne, could not rest easy as long as Payne slept in a strange, foreign land. He provided the means for bringing Payne's remains back to his native country. The ship reached New York on March 22, 1883, and the coffin was taken to City Hall, where it lay in state for a day. There were "upwards of twelve thousand people" who passed by. Gabriel Harrison, who had written a biography of Payne in 1875, and had known Payne intimately for many years, "laid a wreath of immortelles on the coffin. A lady who noticed this expression of affectionate remembrance took a red rose from a bunch of flowers at her throat and dropped it within the wreath."[132] Payne's remains were taken on to Washington and interred in Oak Hill Cemetery.

The myth-makers were to get in one more round. Taking advantage of the lady laying the red rose on Payne's coffin in New York, a writer in 1958 identified the lady as Mary Harden, "who'd left Athens heavily veiled, slipped in among the crowd paying homage to the man she had all but worshipped and laid 'a red rose for love' on his casket. Then she vanished quickly."[133] The fact was that in the very week the red rose was being laid on the coffin, Mary Harden was spending a day with her cousin Evie Jackson, in Athens, Georgia, almost too feeble to leave her house, to say nothing of traveling to New York.[134]

No one should blame much a newspaper editor who in 1871, after calling attention to the many conflicting stories about John Howard Payne's song and his romantic affair with Mary Harden, for coming to this conclusion: "History, we are convinced, is not worth much. We have witnessed such gross perversions of the history that has been made during our own time, that we are convinced that that coming down from remote antiquity should be received with many grains of allowance."[135] The only criticism that can be attached to the editor is that he was not discriminating in judging the reliability of the sources of his information. He was probably thinking of his own profession in recording information, where every man (and woman, too) became a historian, by merely choosing to be so.

CHAPTER VII

Henry M. Turner: Georgia Negro Preacher-Politician During the Reconstruction Era

I N Henry McNeal Turner the elements were so mixed and the contradictions in what he said and did were so many that by selection and repression he has been made to fit the picture of either a great leader or a consummate scoundrel. One writer has declared that Turner was "the greatest Negro who ever lived," and another has said that he was an "intellectual genius, . . . [a] fiery orator, . . . daring and unique."[1] A more factual description characterized him as being of "a coarse nature, his manners and movements . . . crude," and held that "he cared nothing about his dress or personal appearance." Further, he was eloquent, though with a gutteral voice, and he was given "to angry tirades and bitter sarcasm against both Negroes and whites."[2] Indeed, he was emotional, extravagant and unrestrained, and had a prodigious memory; it was said that he was able to memorize "a dozen chapters of the Bible in one evening."[3] These were estimates after his death.

While living he was referred to as "a very smart speaker," "a very strong partisan,"[4] and an "incendiary Negro preacher."[5] In a hearing in 1871, Senator Thomas F. Bayard, Sr. of Delaware asked a witness whether Turner was "entitled to belief in his statements on a subject in regard to which he has any feeling or prejudice?" He received the reply: "I should hardly think he was."[6] A fellow-Republican of Turner's was more explicit in his assessment: "We knew him to lie; we knew him to drink whisky; we knew him to be profane; we knew him to be immoral; we knew him to be sacrilegious."[7] And he added, "We have seldom known a man who gloried so much as Turner at seeing 'his name in the papers.'"[8]

1. Early Years

Turner was born on May 1, 1834, near Newberry Courthouse, South Carolina. His mother was said to have been the daughter of an "African king" or probably just an "African prince," who was sold into slavery in Colonial times, but who was freed by the British, as they did not believe in enslaving royalty. Somewhere along the line of Turner's ancestry a strain of the white man's blood entered, for Henry was a mulatto—a yellow Negro, never referred to as black. When he was quite young, his father died and the youth now went to the cotton fields to work, though he was not a slave. Soon his mother moved to Abbeville, and there Henry worked as a servant in a lawyer's office and was taught to read and write.

Turner had a talent for making speeches and in a slave society the only road open for his oratory was in the ministry. He joined the Methodist Church in 1848 and in 1853 he was licensed to preach. He was soon on the road, preaching in the South wherever permitted and was often heard by white people. About four years later he turned up in St. Louis and decided the next year to join a Negro church organization, the African Methodist Episcopal Church. Continuing as an itinerant preacher, he was soon sent by his bishop to Baltimore, where he decided to add to his education by studying in a school there, English grammar and the three foreign languages of Latin, Greek, and Hebrew.

His steady progress in the ministry led to his appointment in 1862 to be pastor of the Israel Bethel Church in Washington. Here his fluent, fervid, and sometimes flamboyant oratory gained him considerable notoriety and led some of the Washington politicians, including Congressmen, to visit his church. With the Civil War now in full blast, Turner saw a wider field for his activities and for Negroes in general. He advocated the enlistment of Negro soldiers and set out to raise a Negro regiment. On September 10, 1863, President Lincoln commissioned Turner chaplain of this regiment, "the first man of color ever commissioned a chaplain in the United States service," according to a New York journal, which stated further that "he fears no man and nothing,"

REV. H. M. TURNER, CHAPLAIN FIRST UNITED STATES COLORED REGIMENT

and described him as having "yellow complexion and very sharp features."[9]

2. *Preacher and Politician in Georgia*

With the close of the war, Turner's active military service came to an end, when his unit, the First United States Regiment of Colored Troops, was mustered out. President Andrew Johnson now appointed him chaplain in the regular army and assigned him to the Freedmen's Bureau in Georgia. Just what his duties were and how long he remained with the Bureau he left vague in recounting this period of his life, merely saying that he was with it "for some time, and not receiving the respect . . . [he] thought was due" him, he resigned.[10] It is not difficult to imagine that his difficulties with the Bureau officials arose out of his desire to spend all of his time in organizing the Negro churches in Georgia and promoting the Negroes' position in the Republican Party, which was now in the process of being organized in the South.

At one time or another Turner was minister of a Negro congregation in Macon, where he made his home, but he traveled widely over the state in assembling and welding together his church and party, for many of his meetings were as much political as religious. In his organizational work he boasted that he had traveled 15,000 miles through Georgia and had spoken 500 times, and had done more work in the political vineyard than any five men, with the exception of John E. Bryant, the Radical leader, of Augusta. His activities consisted of establishing Loyal Leagues and other political clubs, making speeches and writing campaign documents, and promoting conventions. In an absurd boast, he said of one of these documents, "it took four million copies to satisfy the public."[11] Testifying before a Congressional committee in 1868 he said that he knew conditions in Georgia as well or better than anyone else and that he had traveled and lectured "as much and probably more than any other man in Georgia."[12]

In the religious field, Turner said that he was a "missionary agent and presiding elder of the district," but could not keep from adding that he had "taken a leading part in republican politics."[13] Under his jurisdiction were twenty-seven preachers, and he himself held every year from eight to ten camp meetings, "where from two to three thousand people gather. There is not a week," he added, "but what I am from forty to fifty, and a hundred to two hundred miles from my home."[14]

One of the troublesome problems that came up in Turner's district was the dispute over the ownership of a church building in Macon, which in ante-bellum times the white Methodists had built for their Negro members. When the war ended the Northern Methodists sought to get control of the building and when the case was finally settled in favor of those who had built the church, someone burned it. A Negro servant of a white family living within a few hundred yards of the building, said that he saw a Negro running from the building and that it was Turner; but when an indictment was sought, the Negro denied that he had made the statement.[15]

Carleton B. Cole, a native of Massachusetts and Superior Court Judge of the Macon Circuit, testified in 1871 that Turner's leadership during the past year had been "more political than religious,"[16] and that the Negro preachers had almost entire control of their congregations in political affairs. "I think they control them," he said, "and that their preaching is often political in character." He believed that Turner was their chief leader and that he had more control over them than any other Negro.[17]

When the war ended and a great mass of former slaves were now free to go and come as they pleased, Southerners hoped that they might be able to direct these freedmen into the paths of responsible citizenship and not hold out false promises of the millennium to come overnight. In early 1866 a meeting of the Equal Rights Association of Georgia was held in Augusta, composed of Negroes and whites, which worked out a conservative program, and asked its delegates to advocate among their people back home. It recommended that only educated Negroes should have the right to vote and called on the delegates "to inculcate the principles of honesty, industry and sobriety; to persuade their brethren to entertain kind feelings to their former masters . . . and to disabuse the minds of the masses that they are to be allowed to vote, or were to gain possession of lands without paying for them what the owners may ask."[18] It is not known whether or not Turner was one of these delegates, but at this time it probably represented his point of view.

But as Turner's point of view was subject to change and he had no qualms of conscience in contradicting himself, it was not long before he was in the camps of the Radicals, who were determined to gain power in the former Confederate states and bring about a social and economic revolution. And as the Radicals began organizing the Republican Party in Georgia and taking control from any conservative Republicans, they saw that the Negroes would have to be their main reliance and that, therefore, all Negroes should vote, for few could qualify as educated. Turner was soon on all important committees and his oratorical powers suggested him as the perfect messenger to the black masses to instruct them on their rights and duties under the Reconstruction Acts which were passed in 1867.[19]

But Turner still prized the good will of white Southerners, and for that reason he sometimes laid himself open to deceit, hypocrisy, and double-dealings. About this time he announced that he would make a speech at Indian Springs and he invited all the Negroes in the surrounding country to come. In his audience was Judge Cole, who reported that Turner "made as conservative and satisfactory a speech as any man of his education and intelligence could have done. It was advice and counsel to the black people to be quiet and orderly, to work, telling them that they were now dependent upon their own exertions, and they must take care of themselves. It was such a speech as met with my entire approbation."

But that was not the whole story. Turner passed around the word secretly among the Negroes that he would make another speech that night and only Negroes were to be present. Judge Cole managed to hear part of it, and "it was entirely a political speech for the purpose of organizing a political party and cautioning the Negroes against being influenced in any manner, shape, or form by white people, and to band themselves together for their own protection." Then it was, said Judge Cole, that he lost faith in Turner.[20]

Turner was wise enough to know that whoever controlled the Negroes controlled the Republican Party in Georgia, for the vast majority of Republicans would have to be Negroes, since most white people belonged to the Conservative or Democratic Party (Conservative often being used instead of Democratic). In 1860 there had been about six hundred thousand (591,550) white people in Georgia, three thousand five hundred free Negroes, and more than four hundred and fifty thousand (462,198) slaves. The proportion of Negroes to white people was probably not much different when the war ended. After the Reconstruction Acts of 1867 had been passed, disfranchising many whites, a majority of the potential voters in Georgia was Negroes.

The natural tendency of some Negroes to vote the Democratic ticket out of respect for their former masters and regard for their advice, was sternly combatted by the Negro leaders. Bodily violence was less often offered against Negroes attempting to vote Democratic than were ridicule, threats, and social and religious ostracism. This news item appearing in a Republican newspaper (Republican and Radical being synonymous at this time) was indicative of the ridicule: "Gabe Daniel, the nigger Conservative candidate for the Convention, has retired from the political arena until the next election. Meanwhile he will be engaged in cobbling up old shoes, and destroying rot gut whiskey. A first class one horse dray will always be called into service to convey him to his residence after each day's devotion to the 'stomach inflamation producer.' "[21]

As a majority of Republicans was Negroes, they expected the party to slant all programs in their direction. Their constant efforts to capitalize on their Republicanism were to nauseate white Republicans, to bring about a rift in the party, and ultimately to lead to its destruction. By 1871 a white Republican had come to this conclusion: "So far, since the freedom of the slave, the Negro has had but one object—self. He accepts the labor of his white friends as a matter of course, and he works for nobody but himself. He cries out for equality before the law—equal rights and privileges—yet, he is the last to grant the same thing he asks for."[22]

Even in the light of some of his double-dealings, Turner was for the first two or three years much more conservative in his political philosophy and programs and in his desire to be on good terms with the white people than were such other Georgia Negro leaders to Aaron Alpeoria Bradley, Southern born, formerly in the penitentiary in New York, and Tunis G. Campbell, Sr., who had had grandiloquent ideas about setting up a Negro kingdom on the coast of Georgia. As late as 1868 Turner could call Alexander H. Stephens "one of the greatest men, if not the *greatest*, man in the South, today, and one for whom I have the utmost respect";[23] and he favored having Jefferson Davis pardoned.[24]

When the two parties were about to hold their conventions to nominate candidates for the presidency, Turner suggested that if the Democrats offered a better plank for the Negroes than the Republicans did, then he would wait and see what to do. This attitude led a Republican to say that "we see, plainly enough that it is his intention to try to betray the colored people of Georgia, into the toils of the Democracy."[25] As a member of the Constitutional Convention of 1867-1868 Turner voted for a poll tax of one dollar to be levied for "educational purposes" and he advocated that after a common school system was in operation the right to vote should be based on certain educational requirements.[26] Also he favored the removal of all voting disabilities which Congressional Radical legislation had imposed on white Southerners.[27]

Turner was smart in more ways than one. He saw the danger to Negroes and to the Republican Party in having ignorant and illiterate Negroes run for office; for it was part of the clever maneuverings of the Democrats to have such Negroes elected to office and thus discredit Negroes in general and their party. In certain instances, he tried to get white Republicans to run for office in preference to Negroes; and he himself refused to be mentioned for Congress in 1868, saying that it was not yet time for Negroes to seek election to that body. But the Democrats, tossing out the apple of discord, replied that the white Radicals wanted all the offices, and that Turner had better run, for "*Now* is your time, my colored friend, or *never.*"[28] Of an important Negro who was aspiring to Congress, Turner said, "I have seen this ignoble piece of humanity, and tried to converse with him, but I found him to be so exceedingly low in the scale of intelligence that no one but a maniac could have been entertained by his wild farrago."[29]

Turner liked to announce publicly that he got along well with the white people. "As an individual," he bragged, "I must say that the whites have listened to me very attentively, and none of my meetings have even been disturbed."[30] And as a general summing up of his relations with the whites, he said in September, 1868: "So far as I am personally concerned, no man in Georgia has been more conservative than I. 'Anything to please the white folks' has been my motto, and so closely have I adhered to that course, that many among my own party have classed me as a Democrat. One of the leaders of the Republican party in Georgia has not been at all favorable to me for some time back, because he believed that I was too 'conservative' for a Republican."[31] He liked to praise Macon and its citizens in these earlier years of the Reconstruction period. In December, 1868, he declared that the mayor, though a Democrat, was "an honest, upright gentleman; and our municipal officers generally are dignified, intelligent and faithful officers"; and he supposed that "the best moral sentiment prevails among all the citizens, [as] anywhere in Georgia."[32]

In 1868 Turner attended the Washington Conference of the African Methodist Episcopal Church, a meeting of national importance. Before going, he approached the editor of the *Macon Telegraph* and asked him whether he would publish in his paper accounts of the proceedings of the conference, explaining that many of his congregation in Macon read the *Telegraph* and would be interested in news of the conference, which he would be glad to send.[33] The editor agreed, and Turner sent several dispatches.

Realizing the amenities in the situation Turner was very careful not to wound the sensibilities of the white people who would read his accounts, and he was a little patronizing toward them as he described some of the events. In the first place, he said the conference was getting more publicity than the impeachment trial of Andrew Johnson, which was then in progress. As for the conference, "Such an array of corpulent Negro preachers and black Bishops were never seen in this place before." Several new bishops were to be elected, and Turner modestly noted that his name was among those who were being mentioned for this honor, but as for him, he "would look as comely in a Bishop's paraphernalia as a mule under the diadem of Pope Pius IX."[34] He later noted that three bishops had been elected and that he had been urged to accept one of the positions, "but I stated, in plain words, that I was not fit for the exalted position, nor would I submit to ordination if elected. Whatever made them think I were fit or worthy to be a Bishop, I cannot tell, yet nothing but a peremptorial refusal prevented it."[35]

He reported that the conference was trying to raise the standards of the colored ministry and "to break down the idea that formerly prevailed among our people, *that ignorance was a pulpit prerequisite.*"[36] Here in Washington in the midst of the politically-charged atmosphere, Turner wrote that someone was passing the word around that he was "a rebel, and is not, therefore, entitled to the confidence of the Republican party." Turner answered, "But if the poor cowardly dog, be he white or black, knew how little I cared for his smartness, he would drop his tail, like another hound, and stop yelping about me."[37] This rumor was not sufficiently regarded by the conference to prevent Turner from being appointed on a delegation to wait on Thaddeus Stevens, the extreme Radical now on his deathbed, and to pay their respects to him. Knowing the odor in which Thad was held by the white Southerners, Turner diplomatically cut short his account of the visit, saying merely that Thad was "weak, fragile, and statuary in appearance" and "How he does [manage] to live is to me a wonder." Turner had been selected to make the concluding address to Thad, but he made no mention of what he said in his dispatch to the *Telegraph*.[38]

Turner concluded his letters to the *Telegraph* by stating that

J. M. Brown had been elected bishop for the South, and in an ingratiating spirit he said that he was glad Brown had been elected, for the new bishop was a Southerner and understood Southern customs. Turner hoped that the bishop would settle in Macon, for "our white citizens would respect his position as much as in any other part of the country—especially so since he is no politician."[39]

3. In Political Office and Out

On one occasion when asked what his occupation was, Turner answered, "I am a minister of the gospel and a kind of politician."[40] He was to play hard in both fields. In the first he was to go far; in the latter, after a good beginning, he was to be expelled. With the disappearance of the Republican Party in Georgia after 1871, there was no place for Turner or any other Negro in Georgia politics.

At the end of the Civil War, the reconstruction of the former Confederate states, under President Andrew Johnson's moderate policy, led to a Radical repressive program, devised largely by Thaddeus Stevens and Charles Sumner, and carried out under the Reconstruction Acts of 1867. The Johnson plan had not required Negro suffrage, and the new Georgia government had not volunteered it. The Radicals now under their new plan were determined to get political control of the South, and to succeed in doing so they saw that they must give the Negroes the right to vote and deny it to as many white Southerners as possible. To carry out these "reforms" the Radical Congress set aside the state governments in the South and called for constitutional conventions to devise new documents to usher in the new day.

The election in Georgia was held over a period of five days from October 29 to November 2, 1867, and resulted in the choice of 169 delegates, among whom were 37 Negroes. Turner was one of them. The convention met in Atlanta on December 9th and continued until the following March 11th. The document that was turned out was much better than most white Georgians expected or would admit, and was made so largely by the fact that moderate white Georgians in the convention held a restraining hand. So obstreperous did the New York ex-convict, Aaron Alpeoria Bradley, a Negro delegate from Savannah, become that the convention finally expelled him. Tunis G. Campbell, Sr., another Negro delegate, was less offensive and served out the time of his election. Turner was even more restrained and played little part in the debates, but he was a conservative influence and stood for such sound principles as an educated electorate.[41] Probably the most garralous delegate and almost constantly on the floor was George W. Ashburn, a white delegate from Columbus. The other Negro delegates were automatons, never speaking and always voting as they were told.

Soon after the convention adjourned, Ashburn rushed back to Columbus, bent on organizing a campaign for his election to the United States Senate by the legislature which would soon be chosen under the new constitution. Turner was out for election to the legislature from Bibb County; but in late March he was on a visit to Columbus, the county seat of Muscogee County, to help Ashburn, when on the last day of the month Ashburn was murdered about a half-hour after leaving the stage on which Turner had made the principal speech. The Ku Klux Klan was accused, though never proved, of committing the murder. It became a celebrated case in Radical Georgia politics. Turner charged that he himself would have been murdered if the assassins could have found him. He reported that bitter feeling had been aroused among the Negroes and that if the leading men "among us" had not quieted them down, "I believe they would have perpetrated violence on the whites, and perhaps set fire to the city."[42]

Ashburn was dead, but Turner still lived, and he with other former delegates to the Constitutional Convention were in the race now to profit from their handiwork, by securing election to the legislature. When the votes were counted it was found that the Negro office-seekers had done very well. Three had been elected to the Senate and twenty-nine to the House of Representatives. Turner was among the latter.

The legislature met on July 4th, and it was not long before there were rumblings in both House and Senate over the presence of Negro members, for the understanding had been general that the right of a Negro to vote did not give him the right to hold office. But before this issue arose in the Senate, the notorious Aaron Alpeoria Bradley, a member, was expelled on the grounds that he had served a term in the New York penitentiary on conviction of a felony. Later the other two Negro Senators were expelled as being ineligible on account of their color.

The Negro members of the House had been expelled even before the Senators but not before Turner was able to take some little part in the legislative proceedings. Characteristic of his service in the Constitutional Convention, he was in the House not garralous and disruptive. He introduced two bills of a progressive nature, neither of which was passed. The one called for an eight-hour day for laborers and the other was designed to prevent common carriers "from distinguishing between white and colored persons in the quality of accommodations furnished."[43]

On August 26th a resolution was introduced in the House declaring ineligible for membership the twenty-nine Negroes. The only two Negro members who had been active in the legislative deliberations were Turner and James M. Sims from Chatham County. The other Negro members had not opened their mouths except to vote "yes" or "no" as directed, and they were now in this crisis to remain silent and let Turner and Sims do the speaking. These two took up practically the whole time of the House during the last two days before the vote on the resolution, which was held on the afternoon of September 3rd, and resulted in its passage by 83 ayes to 23 nays. They had spoken "much to the edification and delight of their black brethren and sisters, large numbers of whom have crowded the lobbies and galleries on the two days they have been speaking."[44]

Turner closed the argument for the Negroes, which a reporter considered "perhaps the best speech that had been made on his side."[45] First he was allowed two hours and then his time was extended to the adjournment of the morning session. He knew when he began that it was a foregone conclusion that he and his fellow Negro members would be expelled, and this thought seared deeply his very soul and helped to change his outlook on life for the rest of his days. He felt angry and hurt that the regard he had had for white people had got him so little. He argued that the action of the House would be illegal, citing documents, from the Declaration of Independence on down. He did not see why the color of a man's skin should have anything to do with the question. Take the skin off a white man and a Negro, and a person could not tell them apart. "The Anglo-Saxon race, sir," he said, "is a most surprising one. No man has ever been more deceived in that race than I have been for the last three weeks. I was not aware that there was in the character of that race so much cowardice, or so much pusillanimity." He warned that this event would "be remembered by posterity for ages yet to come, and while the sun shall continue to climb the hills of heaven." And he announced that he would not defend a country which did not defend his manhood: "I will not raise a musket to defend" it. "You will make us your foes;" he continued, "you will make our constituency your foes. I'll do all I can to poison my race against Democracy. . . . This thing means revolution."[46]

Turner and his associates composed a protest and asked that it be entered on the journal, but the House refused to receive it "until said protest is corrected,"[47] which probably meant that the House considered it intemperate and filled with misstatements. The Negro members, headed by Turner, now walked out in a body, and the New York *Nation*, undoubtedly referring to Turner, said, "One of the colored delegates, in retiring, warned the 'carpet-baggers' of their approaching doom, and shook the dust off his clothes in a figurative and contemptuous manner."[48] Before leaving, Turner said that he hoped he would receive his salary up to that time and that he expected ultimately to get it for the whole session.[49]

Turner always prided himself on his education and especially on the fact that he had studied Latin, Greek, and Hebrew; and now for a person of his intellectual stature to be expelled from such an ordinary body as the Georgia House, rankled deeply. In fact, in his speech before the expulsion vote was taken, he bragged that he could read the Bible in as many languages as could one of his opponents to whom he was referring; and it became almost a custom of his to use this device in trying to belittle an opponent. This fact led a fellow Republican to observe that Turner had "bluffed large assemblies on various occasions, by offering to 'read the Bible in as many languages as any one present.' "[50]

Burning with indignation, Turner now decided to enter politics with a vengeance and carry the fight to the enemy, referring to the legislature as a "lawless conclave."[51] He formed the expelled members into a group termed the "Civil and Political Rights Association," and called for a convention of Negroes to meet in Atlanta to consider ways and means to save their rights. The convention met actually in Macon on October 6th and continued for three days. Turner was elected president. Thereupon he delivered a long address castigating the legislature for expelling its Negro members and declaring that it had "made Georgia, the Empire State of the South, a hiss and a bye-word among her sister States, and a disgrace to the Union." He called on Negroes to organize Civil and Political Rights Associations throughout the state.[52] The meeting before adjourning passed a series of resolutions and a memorial to Congress, which Turner was glad to take to Washington.[53]

The expulsion of the Negro members from the legislature had created a furor among the Radical Congressmen in Washington. Their excitement was aided by the presence of Turner and of Rufus Bullock, who had been elected governor under the new constitution in 1868. Adding to the worries of the Radicals over what was happening in Georgia was the fact that the state had voted for the Democratic candidate for president in the November election. The powerful Committee on Reconstruction decided to hold a hearing on the "Condition of Affairs in Georgia," which began in December, 1868. Among those testifying were Turner, James M. Sims, and Amos T. Akerman. All agreed that "a reign of terror" was going on in Georgia and that it needed the attention of the Federal Government. Finally a year later (December 22, 1869) the state was remanded to the mercies of the military authorities and General Alfred H. Terry was put in charge of the state—if it might be so termed. Bullock now called for a reconvening of the legislature, the one from which the Negroes had been removed, and Terry took charge of it. He threw out the white members who had replaced the Negroes, adding a few expulsions for good measure, and reseated the Negro members.

Turner was now glad to be back in his old seat, feeling the satisfaction that he who laughs last laughs best. He seemed to have lost some of the resentment he had against the "Anglo-Saxons," which he expressed on his expulsion, for he introduced a resolution, which was passed, offering sympathy for the sufferers from the recent fire in Richmond, Virginia.[54] Also, he introduced a bill, unsuccessfully, calling for an amendment to the Georgia constitution to allow women to vote.[55] But Turner was not now in good standing with a faction of his party, for his appointment on the Penitentiary Committee led to this caustic comment by one of his Republican enemies: "This is giving a rogue a great advantage. He is paid nine dollars a day, and given authority to examine the institution, outside and in, and is thus enabled, at the expense of the State, to mature plans to escape should Justice ever overtake him."[56]

4. Trials and Tribulations

If, as it was said, Turner could memorize a dozen chapters of the Bible in one evening, he was woefully negligent in not paying more attention to the sixth chapter of *First Timothy*, in the tenth verse of which appeared these words, "For the love of money is the root of all evil." Undoubtedly one of the weakest spots in Turner's character was the part he let money play in his life. It was charged that when in the legislature he supported someone for an appointment, "he was sure to want to *borrow* some money of him."[57] He was constantly trying to borrow money from his friends but he could never be induced to return it. A Federal Commissioner, and, of course, a Republican, testified that he had loaned money to Turner "a great many times," and that Turner always promised to return it, but he "never done what he agreed to do." "That," said the Commissioner, "satisfied me that he was not a truthful man."[58]

J. Clarke Swayze, a Macon newspaper editor and a Federal Commissioner, and a Republican, became one of Turner's most bitter enemies and pursued him relentlessly. He compiled a devastating bill of particulars against Turner and published them in his newspaper, the *American Union*. He charged Turner with being a forger; "a patron of frail women, according to evidence in Court"; a thief, "having stolen $30 from a letter addressed to another person"; and a swindler, having collected money for subscriptions to the *American Union* and never turning it in, and also having collected money to rebuild a church which he said the rebels had burned and never accounting for the money, and additionally having collected $70.00 for a church bell "and that money nor the bell has ever been heard of since." He was "a common blackguard . . . [and] a sponge upon the charity of an ignorant and credulous people, whom he keeps blinded with his pompous assumptions." Swayze issued this challenge to Turner: "The foregoing charges are true, and to prove them to be so, we have only to say that we challenge Turner to contradict them. If they are not truths, they are libels and lay us liable to him before the law, or personally; and we dare him to make the issue."[59]

Swayze said that Turner was "one of the smartest negroes we know of anywhere."[60] In this respect, he said that Turner was frequently calling conventions of Negroes so that he could take up collections from them to be used in publishing the proceedings, but they were never published.[61] "A few sharks like Bryant and Turner," said Swayze, "get the poor ignorant country negroes wrought up to such a phrenzy with ideas of their greatness and importance and then tell them to meet together and elect delegates to a convention, to take some grand movement into consideration, and one of the inseparable conditions is that the delegates go to the convention with plenty of money."[62] Turner called a labor convention of Negroes to meet in Macon in October, 1869, in which he took a prominent part. Swayze was led to comment: "Within the recollection of the 'oldest inhabitant,' he is not been known to have done an hour's labor. He is simply a vagrant, and sponges and begs his living from the laboring people."[63] For a short time in 1868 Turner was cashier of the Macon branch of the National Freedman's Saving and Trust Company.[64]

Trying his hand at a little burlesque, Swayze published now and then a "Sermon by Rev. Tarheel Kinky Head," in one of which appeared this sentence: "In de meantime Brudder Zip Coon go round wid de hat an take up a kollection for de benefit ob our decomposed Brudder Turner, who am busted an muss hab money fur to bi beere wid."[65]

Turner never answered these charges nor sued anyone for libel; but many years later he said that he had "been arrested and tried on some of the wildest charges and most groundless accusations ever distilled from the laboratory of hell," and that witnesses had been paid $4,000 to try to swear him into the penitentiary.[66]

Turner was undoubtedly smart, but not smart enough to keep the ragged side of his character in check. The venom which Swayze poured forth against him seems to have had its beginning in the appointment of a postmaster for Macon. Ulysses S. Grant, who became president on March 4, 1869, had fallen into the hands of the Radicals, and in promoting the Radical Party in the South he began filling the post offices with Negroes and Radical whites. Swayze had groomed himself for the Macon position and in his campaign he had secured a list of names signed to a petition asking for his appointment and had had Turner carry it to Washington. Turner now proved how smart he was by substituting his name for Swayze's—and he received the appointment. When Swayze was told that Turner had been appointed, he "reckoned not," but later when he found out that it was true, he was said to have exclaimed, "Turner has taken advantage of me, d--m him."[67] Turner might well have succeeded without this dishonorable trick, for Charles Sumner was said to have been strongly behind Turner.[68]

There was bitter opposition in Macon to the appointment of Turner. It was reported that with "the exception of but one white man in this community, and a few negroes, our citizens have felt greatly wronged and unjustly injured by the appointment of the negro H. M. Turner to the postmastership of Macon."[69] An Athens editor wondered whether Grant "or any other sane man" supposed "that the interests of peace" could be "promoted by sending an incendiary negro as an office-holder among a peaceable law-abiding people?"[70] And a Columbus editor was led to comment that "since the appointment of Turner the niggers of the country have developed quite a fondness for the postal service, one for which they are less qualified than any other."[71]

An Augusta editor in his comments alluded to the fact that Turner was at this time deeply in trouble: "It would certainly be a bitter mortification to President Grant if this negro Turner, whom he appointed to office in the face of such strong opposition for no other cause than that he *was* a negro, and a desire to humiliate the people of Georgia, should be convicted of a felony so soon after his installation in office."[72] This trouble related to money, the love of which was one of the principal failings of Turner. If he knew his Shakespeare as well as he liked to boast of knowing his Bible, he probably remembered what Iago said in *Othello*, "Put Money in thy purse: . . . fill thy purse with Money," and was heeding that advice with all his powers. And he seemed to have had few scruples whether it was good or "bad money."

Turner's first dealings with money, at least suspicious if not "bad" or counterfeit, was in connection with his managing the money affairs of a Negro widow in Macon. It seems that she had been hoarding a $100 bill for some time, and then one day she asked Turner to take it to the bank either to deposit it or get it changed. The banker told Turner that it was counterfeit and handed it back to him. Turner then took it to several other banks, which refused to accept it.[73] There were suspicions that

Turner had other interests in the bill apart from looking after the widow's affairs, for there was a rash of counterfeit money spreading widely over the country after the war.

This was merely a surface indication of Turner's involvement in the money business, and got him into no trouble. His difficulty grew out of his entanglements in a theft of $12,000 from the office of the Comptroller of the Treasury in Washington. A Negro messenger in that office, by the name of James H. A. Schurman about two years previously had stolen this money, which consisted of unsigned National Bank Notes, eighty $100 bills and eighty $50.00 bills. They were on the First National Bank of Jersey City, and were awaiting the signature of the proper officials of that institution. Schurman and Turner were old friends, and it was charged that Turner and others had signed the names of the bank officials.[74]

Turner had been living an immoral life, and one of his concubines was an illiterate Negro woman, who by her own testimony was "a lewd abandoned character," Marian Harris from Hancock County. She got around considerably and appeared in Philadelphia in the summer of 1869, and ran into her friend Turner, who was there attending a meeting of Negro preachers. She was also friendly with Schurman and admitted that she had entertained both of them in "a bad house" there. She now became mixed up in the money business of these two principals, who were desirous of passing into circulation these Jersey City bank notes, which were counterfeit only in the sense that the signatures were spurious.

She soon came into possession of an amount which she at various times stated was $1,800, $1,500, and $1,300; and she was as devious in telling how she got the money as the amount of it. She first said that Turner had given it to her in Philadelphia with the understanding that she should return to him $60.00 in "good money" for every $100 she had received; then she said that Turner had given it to her in Washington to carry it back to Georgia for him; again she said that she had found it on the seat of the railway car on her way back to Georgia. She then changed her story to say that Schurman had given her the money, that he had put it under her pillow at "Turner's house in Philadelphia," that Turner had not been at the "bad house" with her but it was a "blackman"—that is, Schurman. She varied her story further by saying that she had found the money in the street and that she had spent some of it in Philadelphia, that she had "put it off on a Dutchman."

When Marian Harris reached Augusta on her return to Georgia she decided to spend some more of that "bad money," and thereby she ran into the toils of the law when Lieut. J. B. Purcell of the police force arrested her and turned her over to the Federal authorities in Atlanta. In the hearing there, in addition to the varying stories she had told Purcell and in her testimony at the hearing, there were found in her baggage an incriminating letter from Turner and some of the "bad money."[75]

A summons immediately went out for Turner to appear in Atlanta for a hearing. Now, in great perturbation and consternation he went to Swayze's office (Turner and Swayze up to this time being on close and intimate terms as members of the Republican Party) and said, "I am ruined, . . . ruined politically, religiously and every other way." He confessed to Swayze that he had given the Harris woman the $1,800 to keep for him (that he had laid it down on the seat of the car which they had taken from Washington back to Georgia). He had given it to her to carry for him, fearing that if he should be killed and this money found on him, his memory would be ruined. Now he wanted to know what he should do.

Swayze advised him to testify that he knew nothing about the money. Apparently Turner satisfied the Federal authorities in Atlanta of the truth of his statement, for he was not held for further action. It was not difficult for the Atlanta authorities to be convinced, for advice had come out of Washington that it would be extremely unwise politically for so important a Negro Republican and officeholder as Turner to be convicted of counterfeiting.

When Turner returned and reported to Swayze, he was stunned

by Swayze's telling him that after thinking over Turner's confession, he felt that in his own defense and in the interests of justice he would have to make a case against him. Turner had delivered himself into the hands of his secret enemy, made so by Turner's having "stolen" the postmastership from Swayze! Could the devil himself ever have taken advantage of a better piece of luck! Before Swayze acted, Turner visited him several times and begged Swayze not to expose him. "Mr. Turner," said Swayze, "offered me everything he had, or expected to have."[76]

Swayze was not to be moved. With satanic glee he signed an affidavit charging that Turner had in his possession counterfeit money with intent to pass it. He brought the hearing before Federal Commissioner William C. Morrill, a native of Maine, who had settled in Georgia after the war. The defense objected that Turner had not attempted to pass it. Not to be outdone by this technicality, Swayze amended his affidavit, and the hearing was continued. In the meantime Turner had been placed under a $5,000 bond. A stream of witnesses was brought into court by the defense, almost entirely Negroes, including the Harris woman, who now denied that Turner had given her any money. The Turner lawyers offered no defense apart from the testimony of the Harris woman, but used their witnesses to prove that Swayze's character was bad and that he could not be believed under oath. With parrot-like regularity they repeated this judgment.

The trial was big news both in Georgia and over the nation, and it caused some consternation among the Radical leaders in Washington from the President on down. It was in fact only a hearing before the Federal Commissioner to determine probable guilt sufficient to remand Turner to the Federal Court to be tried. There were delays and adjournments in the hearing, caused by advice from higher up the political ladder; and it later came out that Commissioner Morrill had loaned the money to Turner to pay his lawyers—money which Turner never paid back. The result of the hearing was what many observers were beginning to expect while it was in progress: Turner was freed and his bond cancelled.[77] A reporter called it a "farcical proceeding, . . . a miserable farce from beginning to end."[78] John Milledge, the United States District Attorney, said that since Turner had returned from the North, he had every appearance of a person laboring under the consciousness of guilt; and that at a Commissioner's hearing the prosecution was not required to produce evidence sufficient to convict, but only to show probable cause of guilt. "This is no place to clear Turner," he said. "Let him appear in a regular Court of Justice before twelve good and true men." Let them decide his innocence "and then send him out of Court without a stain upon his character."[79] Swayze insisted on a court trial both to clear his own name of the slanders cast upon it in the Morrill hearing and to prove the guilt of Turner; but he was unsuccessful though he demanded it with vehemence. "We shall claim that Turner acknowledges that he is guilty of the crime of which we charge him," said Swayze, "unless he asserts his innocence by prosecuting us for libel. There's the point; does he see it?"[80]

Swayze was slow in letting the matter rest. He insisted that the United States must investigate the charges against Turner and not allow the serious crime of counterfeiting or forging names to money go unpunished. Swayze was no darling of the conservative Georgians, yet if his truthfulness should be discounted, said the editor of the *Greensboro Herald*, "circumstantial evidence, as strong as Holy Writ, confirms Swayze's statements."[81] He further insisted that the hearing was "a mockery of justice," and that as bad a character as Swayze might be, he deserved a hearing.[82] "Swayze's demands are fair and reasonable," commented the *Macon Telegraph*. "They ought to be heard; and if the people of the North are not entirely lost to public virtue, they *must be heard*."[83]

"We never entertained a doubt of his [Turner's] guilt from the first moment of his arrest;" remarked an Augusta editor, "but we had serious doubts of his conviction," because high-up authorities in Washington and Atlanta were bringing pressure on Commissioner Morrill.[84] It was generally believed that Turner's acquittal was "based on policy." "But," commented the Augusta editor, "if the policy be to save the black wing of the Republican party in Georgia, why *it is only another fraud* upon the people of the State and country."[85] Swayze declared that "the government means to shield its colored citizens from the rigors of the law, when in parallel cases it would leave no effort untried to hunt down a white man."[86] And some years later he asserted as his mature judgment that if "Turner had been a white man, he would to-day be ruminating over a pile of rocks in the Penitentiary."[87] Turner seemed not to have suffered much in the estimation of his black brethren, for he continued his preaching during the turmoil of these times. This fact led Swayze to exclaim, "Here this treacherous villain is blaspheming in the name of God—seeking with his false tongue, to stir the souls of those who desire to serve the Lord!"[88] It was said that Charles Sumner wrote a long letter to Swayze, urging him to cease his vendetta against Turner.[89]

The Negro Schurman was arrested and brought to trial in Washington and, after various delays caused by the absence of Turner, found guilty, but the sentence and its execution seems to have been lost to view "based on policy," the same "policy" which freed Turner.[90]

An amazing revelation of Turner's character was brought out in the hearing by Commissioner Morrill. In some way Swayze had got possession of a letter which Turner had written sometime in the fall of 1868 when he was a member of the legislature, addressed to a Negro preacher by the name of Jones, who lived in Marietta. The letter was probably in answer to a request Jones may have made for a pass over the Western & Atlantic Railroad, which was state-owned; for Turner, who was high in the counsels of the state administration, enclosed such a pass. The black mark against Turner was not that he had got a pass for a Negro preacher, but it was the text of the letter, which was described as containing "exceedingly lascivious and licentious remarks." It was so beastial, low, depraved, and filthy, that its contents could only be alluded to, never described, either in the Morrill hearing or in a proceeding two years later, when Turner's character was being a subject of comment. In the latter instance, Senator

Bayard of Delaware in trying to gain some idea of what was in the letter, asked Morrill if he would care to repeat the language of that letter. Morrill answered, "No, sir; I do not think I would." He added, "It was the most obscene language I ever saw written in my life." "Was it such language that any respectable religious man could have used under any circumstances?" asked Bayard. "No, sir; nor any other man," Morrill replied."[91]

Morrill said that Turner had not objected to have his character gone into at the hearing and had not denied that he had written the letter. "I felt that it was a disgrace to him," Morrill continued, "as it would have been a disgrace to anybody. I asked him why he wrote such an infamous document; he said that he could not give any explanation at all."[92] "It was pure Anglo-Saxon," he said, meaning, no doubt, that it was sprinkled with those famous four-letter words of that language.[93] Judge Cole said that Turner had admitted to him that he wrote the letter, "and gave as an excuse to me for writing it that he did it in fun." Senator Bayard in trying to get a slant of what was in the letter asked Judge Cole, "I do not ask you to soil your mouth by repeating the language, but what was the character of it?" Cole replied that it "was so obscene" that he did "not desire to repeat it."[94]

Again had Turner played into the hands of his arch-enemy Swayze, who was not to let anyone forget this infamous letter, as long as Turner remained in Georgia. He had thousands of copies of it printed and circulated privately, and when in 1872 Turner moved down to Savannah, Swayze announced that he had a few thousand copies left and would turn them over to any gentleman there who would "pledge himself to give them judicious circulation."[95] He commented, "If the colored people have not the elements of morality among them sufficiently to cry down such shameless characters, they should not expect to command the respect of decent people anywhere."[96]

The letter did not cause Turner to be turned out of his pastorship of his Macon congregation or to lose their support and respect, but it led to his dismissal from his postmastership, for this letter played into the hands of the citizens of Macon no less than it served Swayze. The campaign to get rid of Turner was now stepped up. Judge Cole, Commissioner Morrill, and others went to Washington and interviewed President Grant and showed a copy of the letter to him and to Postmaster General John A. J. Creswell. They also emphasized Turner's criminal "money business" (but Morrill had little to say about this, since he had dismissed these charges in his hearing). The Radical leadership in Washington was too wise to allow the Turner millstone to hang around the neck of the Radical Party in Georgia; Creswell soon dismissed Turner and restored to the postmastership J. H. Washington, who had been displaced to make way for Turner.[97] The *Macon Telegraph* had been much less interested in whether or not Turner was guilty of counterfeiting than it was in getting him out of the post office. While the question of Turner's dismissal was pending, the *Macon Telegraph* stated that the Post Office Department in Washington had "such evidence of hideous moral delinquency on the part of Turner in its possession, that it cannot retain him if it would—it *dare* not retain him, unless it dare make itself the scoff of the whole country."[98]

5. Conventions and "Rebel Atrocities"

Since Turner was able to maintain the steady support of the Negroes, come what come may, he decided that his day in politics was no more over than it could ever be in the church. All along he knew how to build up support and maintain it both in his faction in the party in Georgia and with the Radical regime in Washington. His most successful method was to call and attend conventions of Negroes in Georgia and the South and to play a conspicuous part in conventions of Negroes in the North— and especially under the eyes of government leaders in Washington, where, for example, in 1869, he was elected temporary chairman of the National Colored Convention, preceding the election of Frederick Douglass as permanent chairman.[99]

The favorite tune which Turner played, in season and out, was "rebel atrocities." No convention was considered completely organized or hardly worth-while, which did not appoint a committee to compile statistics on "murders and outrages." As president of the continuing "Georgia State Convention," in the summer of 1871 he called a convention of Negroes to meet in Columbia, South Carolina, in the following October, to be attended by delegates from all the Southern states. In reporting the work of that convention Turner said that "according to the best of our knowledge and belief it was estimated that since reconstruction between fifteen hundred and sixteen hundred murders had been perpetrated" in Georgia alone, and that there had been no fewer than 20,000 throughout the South. He added, "Of course it was only an estimate, to the best of our belief."[100]

In early 1869 Turner received a warning from someone whom he considered to be a member of the Ku Klux Klan, which he answered in flamboyant language, inviting him to "bring his clan of cut-throats, rogues, thieves, robbers, church and school-house burners, women ravishers, liars, scoundrels, hyenas, and incarnet [incarnate] devils with him, and if they don't meet the grandest reception ever given to a set of fiends (except when they enter hell), then I will give my head for a soap gourd."[101] He was soon in Washington testifying before the Committee on Reconstruction, telling how he had seen Negroes "with bullets in their legs, bullets in their sides, and bullets in their heads."[102] The only solution was the military occupation of Georgia, he felt, which later the Radicals carried out when General Terry was sent to take charge. Heartened by his visit to Washington, Turner reported that he could now "dispense with a keg of powder for a pillow at night, and a burning match to be ready to meet the execution of threats that rebels make."[103]

In a report which he made more than two years later, having had more time in which to observe "rebel atrocities," he said, "I have seen men who had their backs lacerated. I have seen other men who had bullets in them; I have seen others who had their arms shot off, shot so badly that they had to be amputated; I have seen others with legs shot off. I have heard of any quantity of horrible deeds." He said that he had "heard of so many outrages" in Washington County, "that I hesitate, really, to itemize the kind of outrages I have heard of."[104] In 1868 Turner said that every morning before he got out of bed "a crowd of colored persons are knocking at my door, some of whom come from more than one hundred miles, for the purpose of relating to me the outrages and murders daily perpetrated upon them. . . . I know there is a reign of terror in the land." He added that the only advice he could give them was to "slip, dodge, run, hold your mouths, and pray for God to send relief. I believe he will either bring this country to its senses or swallow it up in an earthquake."[105] As president of the Civil and Political Rights Association he issued a proclamation, asking God "to save our people from the brutal murders and fiendish outrages, that have hurried hundreds to unnatural and premature graves."[106]

Turner insisted that all the blame should be placed on the white people, that no Negro ever gave any provocation. "I challenge every white man in Georgia," he said, "to show an instance in which a negro ever attacked his person, or first commenced any sort or kind of quarrel with him."[107] He had seen Negroes in their meetings in numbers ranging from 100 to 5,000, but he had never yet seen or heard of a Negro who "inaugurated strife with the whites" and he had "rarely ever seen a drunken black man."[108] Yet, forgetful of these statements, he later said that in a certain disorder the Negroes had told the whites "to their faces that if one colored man was killed they would burn their town down."[109] In November, 1871, Turner said that the Negroes were about ready to leave Georgia, and "if the leading men were to give any encouragement to it at the present time the colored people would commence a regular exodus, and that thirty thousand people could be got out of Georgia between now and Christmas, if the leading men would give any encouragement to it."[110]

Carleton B. Cole, who was serving as judge of the Macon Circuit under the Radical regime, said that Negro testimony was "frequently of not much weight,"[111] and Commissioner Morrill, on being asked by Senator Bayard how reliable Negro testimony was, replied that some could be accepted and some not, and added,

"In fact you could hardly expect a clear legal opinion or decision or evidence from a colored man, taking everything into consideration, their lack of knowledge and education, and everything of that kind, with their peculiar views of things, their vivid imagination." He stated that a great many outrages were reported to him, "some true and some not, for I investigated them all."[112] A Greene County citizen answering Turner's charge of the mistreatment of Negroes, said, "We challenge the mention of one single instance in our county where a negro has been either, killed, whipped, or run off by a planter."[113]

The Radical "rebel atrocities" propaganda campaign, which sprang up all over the South, led Congress on April 7, 1871, to appoint a joint committee "to inquire into the conditions of the late insurrectionary States, so far as regards the execution of the laws and the safety of the lives and property of the citizens of the United States." Hearings began in Georgia in July, 1871, and about the end of the month were adjourned to October and were continued into early November.

Turner was one of the witnesses; and two other witnesses, Judge Cole and Commissioner Morrill, had much to say about Turner. Turner gave a lurid picture of conditions in Georgia in line with what he had been saying for the past few years. "I am satisfied, and every man in Georgia who has got any brains must be satisfied," said Turner, "that there are organized bands of night assassins, murderous villains, who have banded themselves together and roam about and kill republicans, kill any man who has got the name of radical attached to him, especially if he is a leader. . . . They will kill out all they can kill."[114] When asked about the Ku Klux, Turner admitted that he had never "seen any Ku-Klux, . . . as a band roaming about at night"; but he said that in his travels over the state his life had often been threatened and that he had hid in houses, in the woods, and "in a hollow log at another time." However, only once had he seen "men banded together," whom he thought meant violence to him. He and three associates were traveling in a wagon from Jasper County to Butts County and when they were about to cross the Ocmulgee River they saw a band of men, who acted strangely; "but one man in our party, being somewhat intoxicated, talked very big and cursed very loud, and they did not do anything. . . . I think that if I had been by myself, or if there had been but one or two with me, we would have been killed and thrown into the river; but as there were four of us, nothing was done."[115] When Turner had finished his testimony, the chairman asked him if he had any other facts to present. Senator Bayard exclaimed, "Facts!", and Turner replied, "I am telling nothing but facts, so far as I am concerned. All that I may say I am willing should appear in the papers to-morrow, if you choose."[116]

When Judge Cole was testifying, Senator Bayard asked him what Turner's reputation was among "respectable men." Cole replied that it was "very bad," adding, "To my knowledge, he is one of the most licentious rakes in our community; he is to-day the most profligate man almost that I have ever known in my life. I know now, from the statement of a colored woman that I raised from infancy, and who has lived with me and my daughter ever since she was free, who is living with me now, the nurse of my grand-children—she says she heard him say to some negro girls that there was no harm for the shepherds and the lambs to lie together."[117] Commissioner Morrill, in commenting on Turner's character, said that when he learned of the lewd letter Turner had written and of his other misbehaviors, and remembering that Turner considered himself a preacher of the Gospel, "I felt so indignant about it that I never had any confidence in him afterwards. As I said before, I think he is a scoundrel."[118]

6. The End of the Political Road in Georgia

The session of the legislature from which Turner and the other Negroes had been expelled in September, 1868, had been recalled in January, 1870, and through "Terry's Purge," the Negroes were reseated. This session after several adjournments continued until near the end of October, and on the third of that month, passed the so-called Akerman Election Law. This law was in preparation for the next election and applied only to it. The "charge was very generally made that it was so framed for the purpose of aiding fraudulent voting in the interest of the republican party." It provided that voting should be held over a period of three days, December 20th, 21st, and 22nd; that voting precincts might be changed; that Governor Bullock should appoint three of the five election officials for each precinct and that the ordinaries (who were generally Republican) should appoint the other two; and that no voter might be challenged.[119]

Turner now entered the campaign for re-election, confident that nothing that had been or could be said or revealed about him would shake the confidence his black brethren had in him. The Negroes were bold, determined, and armed "with very few exceptions." Turner was "very inflammatory" in his speeches, and the night before the first day of the election period, Turner and another Negro candidate made "incendiary" speeches and "denounced any negro who should vote the democratic ticket; they said they must be taken care of." And as reported by Judge Cole, "They did not hesitate to say that they would not allow any negro to vote the democratic ticket."

Cole testified further before the Ku Klux Committee that on one of the election days he saw a group of Negro men and women, "the women . . . more violent than the men," using "threatening, . . . very loud and noisy" language against an old Negro man who had a Democratic ticket in his hand and said that he was going to vote it. One of the women said that if he did, they would " 'burn his damned . . . off.' " Cole said that there were "some white ladies passing by, and I spoke to these women, and told them that such language could not be allowed in the streets. One of them replied to me that they had a right to use such language as they pleased."[120]

Turner did not refrain from giving a realistic account of the election in Macon. He said a Negro was going to the ballot box with two Democrats, who he believed had paid the Negroes to vote their ticket, and as "he was coming out the colored republican hollered, and jeered, and laughed at him." And then someone fired a pistol and the Negro crowd dropped back, and seeing a wagonload of wood, "they picked up the wood and commenced heaving it; the owner never saw his wood after that." The military forces were called in and prevented a riot or anyone getting hurt. Turner asserted that the Democrats voted everybody they could find, a circus crowd, people on cotton wagons from the country; and some people they voted two or three and even four times by disguising them slightly, putting a cloak or a high hat on them. He said there were only about 1,600 or 1,700 Democrats in Bibb County, yet they voted 2,700. Turner admitted that there "may have been some fraudulent votes on our part. We have some twenty-five hundred voters in that county that we know of, and we voted twenty-seven hundred votes at that election. . . . There may have been some repeating; they saw the democrats were doing it, and I dare say some of our men did the same."[121]

In this campaign Turner did not confine his speech-making to Bibb County; his oratorical ability led white Radicals in other parts of the state to call on him for help. He spoke in Greene County in aid of a white Radical there, trying "to prejudice the unsuspecting and ignorant colored voters against the white people." The editor of the Greensboro newspaper remarked, "The negroes are fast learning their relations to the white people, and the time is approaching when these insurrectionary demagogues will not be countenanced not even by the negro."[122]

The three Radical candidates in Bibb (James Fitzpatrick, an Irishman; Turner and Moses Pollock, Negroes) received respectively 2,768, 2,734, and 2,747 votes; while the Democratic candidates (J. B. Ross, C. A. Nutting, and A. O. Bacon, all white) received respectively 2,717, 2,713, and 2,705. The average Radical majority was 38.[123]

The Democrats entered their protest, contending that no fewer than 700 illegal votes had been cast by the Radicals, such as by Negroes, underage, non-residents, idiots, and lunatics. They contended further that the polls were closed when twenty legal voters were trying to cast their ballots, and that legal voters had their ballots rejected "when they stood ready to take the affidavit required by law." And there were other irregularities.[124] When the legislature convened the following year in November, it denied seats to Turner and his Radical colleagues from Bibb County and seated the Democrats.[125] This marked the end of Turner's political career in Georgia.

Before the contest had been settled when Turner stood elected on the face of the original returns, Swayze did not forget to offer his comments: "This vagabond has been elected, by a bare majority of 17. Instead of going to the Legislature, if he had received his deserts he would have gone to the Penitentiary." He was "a thief and a scoundrel, and yet they voted for him!"[126] Before Swayze departed Georgia to edit his newspaper in Topeka, Kansas, he took this parting shot at Turner and his Georgia Negro supporters: "a licentious villain, robber and counterfeiter, a vulgar blackguard, a sacrilegious profaner of God's name, and a most consummate hypocrite. . . . If the colored people have not the elements of morality among them sufficiently to cry down such shameless characters, they should not expect to command the respect of decent people anywhere."[127]

7. *Subsequent Career*

Charges of counterfeiting and forgery against Turner and his dismissal from the Macon postmastership did not destroy his reputation with the Radical regime in Washington. His exclusion from the legislature in 1871 was a recommendation to the Radicals to take care of him. This they did by appointing him United States custom inspector and government detective, with headquarters in Savannah.[128] On his departure in early 1872, Swayze's *American Union* newspaper speeded his going by announcing that he had "folded his tent and without the least demonstration, has quietly slipped off to Savannah, where, we understand he is to teach *morality*, so-called, for a season."[129] It is not known how long this "season" was, but in 1876 Turner was in Philadelphia, serving as manager of the A. M. E. Book Concern. In 1880 he was elected Bishop of Georgia with headquarters in Atlanta, and for a dozen years he was chancellor of Morris Brown College, a Negro institution in that city. In politics he deserted the Republican Party, joined the Prohibition Party, and in 1900 he voted for William J. Bryan.[130]

His fame as an orator never dimmed, and as a Prohibitionist he made a speech in Atlanta, in 1887, to a mixed audience of about 8,000 people, in his unrestrained and extravagant style of speaking. Referring to "King Alcohol," he said, "It has cursed man from the crown of his head to the sole of his feet: it has cursed his hair, his eyes, his lips, his tongue, his brain, his heart, his lungs, his flesh, his tissues and in his intellect; it alienates him from his God, shortens his life and damns his soul." He declared that it had "wrung tears enough from mothers, wives, daughters and sisters to float the British navy, and if collected together in one place and descending on Atlanta would drown every living thing and sweep away every building."[131]

His racial attitudes grew stronger as the years passed. One of his last acts in Macon, before going to Savannah, was to make a speech on January 1, 1872, at a Negro meeting to celebrate the Emancipation Proclamation. During his speech he introduced resolutions calling on Congress to pass the Civil Rights Bill, which was then before that body.[132] Three years later it became law, but in a decision in 1883 the United States Supreme Court declared it unconstitutional. This decision so enraged Turner that he denounced the judges in unmeasured language and deserted the Republican Party.

An "ungodly tribunal" had made an "abominable," "a horrible" decision.[133] "Now, before the God of nations and civilized man," said Turner, "we hold that the action of the Supreme Court is nothing less than a public outrage, and an invitation to murder all colored persons who possess the elements of true manhood."[134] In a great display of words to show his deep learning he offered this apostrophe to Liberty: "The giant form of liberty bows and weeps at the shrine of injustice. Her polychromatic robes of honor have been rent and tattered by the ruthless hand of the Supreme Court of the nation. Where equity should be enthroned, robed with azure hues, tressed with glittering gems, balustered with sapphires, crowned with vermillioned gold, bearing the armlets of divinity and defended by the trident of Omnific power, injustice, desecration and human vampirage now hold sway."[135]

As for the judges (all but John M. Harlan, who dissented), they "made their names odious to every colored man and woman now living, as well as to every human being who is not dead to all the impulses of justice."[136] "The eight million of my race and their posterity," said Turner, "will stand horror-frozen at the very mention of their names."[137] He called on the Negroes to rise up and organize or leave for a better land, and any Negro who failed to do this was "evidently of the lowest type of human existence, and slavery would be a more befitting sphere for the exercise of his dwarfed and servile powers than freedom."[138]

The better land which Turner had in mind was Africa. He listed himself as "one of principal agitators of return of his race to Africa."[139] He did not have in mind Liberia, which the American Colonization Society had set going more than a half century previously. He wanted a new start to be made in another part of Africa and felt that the United States Government should appropriate money to help get his new nation established; and when Senator M. C. Butler of South Carolina in 1890 was promoting his bill in Congress to appropriate $5,000,000 for this purpose, Turner listed him as one of the greatest men in America.[140]

In a conference with President Benjamin Harrison, Turner hoped to convert the President to this plan, and among the speeches he made in promoting his African black nation, was one in Boston where he advocated sending out a vanguard of 100,000 or 150,000 Negroes.[141] He believed that Negroes had no future in the United States, but if they could go back to Africa they would show the world what the Negro race could do. Africa was a rich land, and these American Negroes would develop its natural resources and make the land bloom like a rose.

This was only part of Turner's plan for his African nation; by setting up this nation the returning Negroes would be working as the hand of God in bringing the native Africans to Christianity. And here Turner paid a tribute to the institution of slavery which had existed in the United States. He believed it had been God's plan to bring Negroes to America where as slaves they were Christianized and civilized so that they might go back to Africa and carry Christianity and civilization to their black brothers.[142] The *Atlanta Constitution*, commenting on Turner's plan, said, "Slavery was a university in which he [the Negro] was both Christianized and civilized, as even the more thoughtful abolitionists now admit, but he is still too young in the business to be thrown wholly on his own resources in the jungles."[143]

Turner became so interested in Africa that he made one or more trips there and traveled widely over the continent, viewing the land and carrying Christianity to the people. He organized conferences of the African Methodist Episcopal Church in Sierra Leone, Liberia, the Transvaal, and in South Africa. In 1894 the College of Liberia honored him with the degree of Doctor of Canonical Law.[144]

Turner, like other Negro leaders before, during, and after his time, saw the African dream go glimmering; and his bitterness against the United States increased with his years. He called the United States flag "a dirty contemptible rag," and said that hell was an improvement over the United States for Negroes. He hoped that he would not die in a land over which that flag flew.[145]

On May 8, 1915, in Windsor, Ontario, Canada, Turner died— his flag wish had come true. He was buried in Atlanta. He was married four times, first in 1856 and last in 1907.[146] Indeed, the elements were mixed in Henry McNeal Turner. If he was the greatest man the Negro race ever produced, then that race had not reached the stage in civilization which has generally been accorded it.

CHAPTER VIII

The Woolfolk Murder

1. The Woolfolks

THOMAS W. Woolfolk, of a prominent North Carolina family, migrated to Macon during its early history and bought in 1828 a hundred-acre tract, including old Fort Hawkins, in what was incorporated the next year as East Macon.[1] Coming from a family famed in war and peace,[2] he played a prominent part in Macon's growth. Being well-to-do, he sent one of his four sons, Richard F., to the University of Georgia in Athens. Here Richard was graduated in 1854, and during this year he married Susan, a daughter of Thomas Moore, who was superintendent of the Georgia Factory in that town.[3] A sister of Susan's married John Ross Crane, an Athens architect and builder.

In the Civil War, Richard was captain of a Georgia militia unit,[4] and thereafter he was known as Captain Woolfolk. Following the war he first went into the hardware business in Macon under the firm name of Woolfolk & Company. Having bought out the other members he soon found himself in financial straits with the falling of prices; but he was able to save most of his property, including a plantation in the Hazzard District, about ten miles west of Macon, where he moved. Here on his 867 acres, said by some to be worth $25,000, he had his Negro tenants and ran his ten plows.[5] He lived on a commanding hill surrounded by his level farming lands, with two natural terraces, one a few hundred yards below, and the other slightly lower, on both of which were tenant houses. Woolfolk's house was of tasteful architecture, one story, with a porch of six columns. He was the leading citizen of this section of Bibb County and was popular with his neighbors.[6]

Richard Woolfolk and his wife Susan had three children, two girls and, the last, a boy. The boy was born on June 18, 1860, and was named Thomas G., the Thomas for his grandfather Woolfolk. Tom's mother died soon after his birth. She was buried in the yard of the Woolfolk plantation home, and a holly bush was set out to mark the spot.[7] Tom was then sent to Athens to be cared for by his Aunt Crane, who kept him until he was seven.[8]

At this time Richard Woolfolk was able to get his family together again, for now he married Mattie E., daughter of Benjamin F. Howard, of a cultured family. Mattie was a graduate of Forsyth Female Collegiate Institute, in Monroe County. Soon after their marriage, Richard "in consideration of the natural love and affection" he had for Mattie, deeded to her considerable property in East Macon,[9] which may have been a method of saving it from his creditors; and in 1873 Mattie's father gave her fifty acres of land in the Hazzard District, "including the house and improvements of what is known as the Woolfolk Homestead Place,"[10] which he had saved from being sold out of the family. Also this same year Mattie bought at a sheriff's sale some of Richard Woolfolk's property in East Macon, which was being levied on.[11] Thus the old Woolfolk plantation homestead and other Woolfolk property was saved for the Woolfolks.

With the three children by his first wife, Richard and Mattie now began a family, which by 1887 included six children, two boys and four girls. The boys were Richard F., Jr., twenty years old and Charles, five. The girls were Pearl, seventeen, who had attended Wesleyan Female College; Annie, ten; Rosebud, seven; and Mattie, eighteen months old.[12] In the meantime Richard's two daughters by his first wife had married: one, to H. P. Cowan, and was living in Hawkinsville; the other, to a Mr. Edwards, and was living in East Macon.

Tom became the problem child. Although it seems that he could not have had a clear recollection of his mother, he never learned to like his stepmother and he resented her being around. Probably he visited the holly bush frequently. He became wayward and wilful, and dissolute, too, using "bad language" and liking strong drink. He was later referred to "as a sharp, cunning, dissipated, unscrupulous fellow";[13] and also as being "a very perverse, obstinate, eccentric and . . . a crazy sort of a person."[14]

He soon left home to go into business for himself. First, he leased a plantation and tried unsuccessfully to run it for a year or two, living alone in squalor. Next he ran a store in Macon, selling groceries and liquor, moving several times; and when he failed, he went to Texas. No one seemed to know for just what purpose he went or what he did out there. He was gone only a few months.[15] It was stated that he went to buy horses and bring them back to the Macon market; and a rumor had it that he might have killed someone there, that he went with $50 and came back with $500.[16] Tom said that he worked as a cowboy.[17] When he returned, he became a streetcar driver in Macon for a few days until dismissed—so it was reported.[18] He then opened a little grocery store between Macon and Vineville; but failed as usual.[19]

Tom visited his Aunt Crane in Athens, on frequent occasions, and began in later times to attract attention there by his strange conduct. When not sleeping he was likely to be pacing the floor. Mrs. Crane said, "He seemed to be a creature of wild unrest. He paced the floor the whole time he was in the house. He kept his lamp burning all the night, and his talk at times was incoherent." He would start out on a subject and suddenly change to something different. He seemed to think that everyone was against him, and when he would see two people talking he thought they were plotting against him. He carried a pistol, even when visiting his aunt. On one occasion when in Athens, although he had no money he wanted to buy an interest in a mill there. Mrs. Crane and Tom's sister, Mrs. Floride Edwards, discussed Tom's strange behaviour and agreed that he must be losing his mind. Mrs. Edwards told her father the same thing, but Captain Woolfolk did not think so.[20]

Money and property were an obsession with Tom. His father had helped him on several occasions, but Tom had always made a failure of all his business ventures. He had had hopes of getting most of his father's estate in the course of time; but as he viewed the situation, his stepmother and her children came between him and this good fortune. He was heard to say that she would never get it and that she would be sorry that she had ever married his father.[21] Tom had the mistaken notion that his father had deeded the home-place and other property over to his second wife on condition that she would marry him. He grew up imagining that she looked upon him as an intruder, and he looked upon her as having deprived him of his property. It was said that she upbraided him on one occasion for having ridden off on one of "her horses."[22] In 1885 when Tom was paying the rent to J. Dannenburg in Macon from whom he had rented a storehouse, he asked Dannenburg what the law was on the inheritance of property, the assumption being that he was afraid that his stepmother might get it.[23]

Also Tom's father came in for resentment. Tom believed that he himself had a right to an inheritance from his mother, which he never got on account of the re-marriage, that his father quit giving him money because the other children must have it. Tom was always wanting money, and never having any; and if he got what was due him he thought he would have plenty and would never have to work.[24]

In the summer of 1887 Tom decided to get married—he was now twenty-seven years old, and it seemed to him that it was about time. Also, by doing so, his father might set him up in business again. He had become acquainted with Georgia Bird (or Byrd), the daughter of a well-to-do farmer near Holton, in the adjoining county of Jones. Objection was raised by Georgia's parents and by some acquaintances, but willing to take a chance, she conformed to a bizarre scheme which Tom had concocted. She boarded a train passing south to Macon, on which Tom was a passenger and also a minister whom Tom had engaged, and with the train going at full speed Tom and Georgia were married standing in the aisle. Tom had told her that he had a fine mansion in Macon, where they would live; but when they arrived, he took her to the home of his sister, Mrs. Edwards.

Like all of his other businesses this marriage was a failure from the start.[25]

After three weeks of a miserable existence, Georgia was rescued by her mother and taken back to her old home. Georgia said that she wanted to leave Tom after the first day. In an interview with a newspaper reporter, she said that Tom told her that he thought his father was going "to set him up again" after he should marry. Later he said, "Georgia, father has not fixed me up, and I'm going to burn the family; father's rich and got plenty; if I can't get any of it none of the others shall get it." When asked if she thought that Tom was crazy, she replied, "No, he is not crazy. It is simple meanness. He is the meanest man I ever saw, and there is nothing too mean for him to do."[26]

After Georgia had left him, Tom in lamenting his woes to an acquaintance, said that everybody's hand was raised against him, that he had no friends and nothing, that he was a fool for ever marrying Georgia, that she was no good and that he might have "to frail [flail] her out." Tom seemed much depressed, but remarked that he would be up in the world sometime and have more friends than he needed.[27] Having reached the end of his road, like the prodigal son, Tom returned to his father's house, and agreed to work on the plantation for $9.00 a month.[28]

2. *The Murder*

During the dark hours early Saturday, August 6, 1887, sometime between 2 a.m. and 4 a.m., one of the most ghastly slaughters in the annals of crime took place. Captain Richard F. Woolfolk, his wife Mattie, their six children, and Mrs. Temperance (Tempe) West, the 84-year-old aunt of Mrs. Woolfolk, were slain by being smashed in the head with an axe. All were left dead and no one to tell the tale, except Thomas G. Woolfolk, who about daybreak scurried down the hill to Negro Green Lockett's cabin to summons him to go with him up to the house, saying that all the family had been slain and that only he had been able to save his life by jumping across his bed and out of the window. Lockett, true to his Negro nature, demurred; but with other

Negroes in the vicinity and aided by boy runners he spread the alarm through the neighborhood. In the meantime Tom went back to the house, did some arranging of the bodies, noting that they were all dead, and got some blood on his clothes, and on his body. There was blood on the floor and smattered over the walls, and some of the blood on the floor Tom had tried to wash away with soap.

The news spread like wildfire to Macon and all the surrounding country; and before the day was out between 2,000 and 3,000 people had gathered. In the meantime Tom, unemotional and unperturbed, had sat down under a tree. Not a tear and "not a muscle quivered in agitation," it was reported. The evidence seemed to the early arrivals to point to Tom as the murderer, and he was penned up in one of the rooms awaiting the arrival of a coroner's jury and the sheriff. He was then hurried off to the Macon jail and to safety from a gathering storm of vengeance which was sweeping over the crowd. Tom had been using the axe the day before, to cut white oak saplings to make splints for baskets and it was not now in its accustomed place. The blood on him, and the fact that he had changed his shirt and underwear and thrown them into the well, heightened the suspicion. Of course, Tom did not say that he had done this; only later these objects were fished from the well.[29]

Newspaper reporters and others pictured in their imagination how the terrible crime had been committed. The murderer went first to Captain Woolfolk's room and slew him and his wife, then into Pearl's room, and on and on until all were dead. Before making his departure, Tom said that hearing screams in his father's room, he rushed there following his twenty-year old half-brother Richard, and in that way Richard was killed, and he himself providentially spared.

It was probably the *Atlanta Constitution* that played up the news to the highest pitch, with its reporter using his imagination in great detail of what took place that bloody night. But he was reporting what he saw when he wrote that the Woolfolk house was a typical plantation home situated on an eminence

overlooking "the spreading fields of the plantation," with the
approach through "a grove of ancient oaks, that seemed to droop
their branches in a solemn hush in sympathy with the dreadful
tragedy that had been enacted within." The first story carried
by this newspaper filled its whole first and second pages; and
when this edition was soon sold out, the story was repeated the
next day.[30]

There was no need for those who saw the sight to use their
imagination. "Opening the door [of the Captain's room]," said
the *Atlanta Constitution* reporter, "we beheld a scene that the
stoutest-hearted among us will not forget to his dying day."
Blood and brains splattered over the floor and walls throughout
the house with bodies scattered on floors and beds: "The heart
grew sick and imagination refused to credit itself with what it
saw."[31]

The editor of the Greensboro *Herald and Journal* was deeply
moved in reporting the news in his paper: A family of nine,
butchered in cold blood while they slept, from a "babe in the
cradle to helpless old age . . . almost beyond human conception
. . . the blood chills in the veins and the heart sickens at the
ghastly revelation. . . . Never before has the history of Georgia
been stained by a record so bloody, and we trust the public
prints will never again be called on to chronicle the details of a
crime so heinous." Continuing he said, "The dreadful picture
will not soon fade from the imagination, even of those who only
read the account in the public prints"; and "We doubt if the
world's criminal calendar contains a crime more bloody, more
fiendish, or one showing in all of its horrid details a deeper
depravity."[32] And the editor of the *Calhoun Times* echoing
the Greensboro editor said that the deed stood "without a parellel
in the annals of crime," and that none "but an incarnate fiend
could have done the bloody work."[33]

Catering to that low human instinct of enjoying horror thrills
which was to be capitalized on a half century later by the
moving picture industry, a Macon photographer hurried down
to the Woolfolk house the morning after the murder before

any part of the bloody scene had been disturbed and made pictures of the mangled corpses and the blood-stained walls and furniture. These pictures were hawked on the streets of Macon and other cities, sent to newspapers, and sold on trains. When later, one was shown to Tom, he furtively glanced at it several times, then gazed at it for a moment and exclaimed, "Oh, my God, that is horrible!"[34]

A judicial attitude toward Tom was impossible in such an atmosphere; it was assumed without further consideration that Tom did the bloody deed; and it was asserted that not a person in Bibb County believed Tom innocent and that if the sheriff had not arrived when he did, Tom would have been hanged by the enraged crowd.[35] Tom was to be tried by the people and by the newspapers and found guilty long before he reached the courts of justice. The *Macon Telegraph* without mentioning Tom by name but intimating that he was the criminal, said that the person who did it was "a brute of the lowest form, acting under the impulses of a person whose baseness is unfathomable and with a deliberation rendered possible by an inherent and complete depravity."[36] Pinning the crime on Tom, a correspondent of the *Atlanta Constitution*, signing himself "Nemesis," wrote, "No punishment could be devised commensurate with his crime—the fiery stake, the rack, the tearing asunder of his vile body by wild horses would be wholly inadequate."[37] The editor of the Athens *Banner-Watchman*, while not ruling Tom out, observed that "Tom Woolfolk, if a murderer, is a madman," and recommended that before he should be turned over to the courts he should be examined by "a medical commission" to determine his sanity.[38] He quoted and agreed with a newspaper dispatch which stated that a plan "so accurately arranged and so thoroughly carried out as to leave scarcely a single witness to the bloody affair transcends the wildest imagination."[39]

The crime was heralded throughout the country, the *Cincinnati Enquirer* declaring that this murder was "without a parallel in the annals of crime in America," and that the criminal was "the greatest monster of the age . . . the cruelest and [most] bloodthirsty brute on record."[40]

The lot now fell to a Macon undertaker to go to the scene of the tragedy to prepare the bodies for burial. He had hoped to bring them back Saturday night to Macon, where they were to be buried in Rose Hill Cemetery, on Sunday; but his ghastly task took longer than he had expected, and not until 6 a.m. did the procession leave—five hearses carrying the nine coffins, with wagons and carriages bearing other equipment and people. As it proceeded the twelve miles to Macon, it was joined by car-

Thomas G. Woolfolk.

From an illustration in the *Oglethorpe Echo* (Lexington, Ga.), November 7 (8, 3), 1890. adapted from a photograph taken while Woolfolk was in the Macon jail.

riages, buggies, wagons, carts, men on horseback and people on foot, until the line of mourners had become a mile long by the time it reached Macon. Many who did not join the procession, especially Negroes, lined up along the roadway. The Negroes demonstrated with prayers and shouts, and one old Negro woman said, as the hearses passed by, "Dar goes Miss Mattie now. I nussed her, an' tuck keer on her when she was sick. She was always a good woman. Lord bless you, Miss Mattie, I'll meet you in heaven, but dat boy what kill you he will roast in hell."[41]

Two thousand people crowded on the side of the cemetery hill above the nine graves, near which were arranged nine coffins, five of which were in black for the adults, and four in white for the children. The minister conducting the ceremonies, the Rev. I. R. Branham, read from the 25th chapter of St. Matthews, "Watch therefore, for ye know neither the day nor the hour wherein the Son of man cometh," and he prayed for Tom, "whatever may be his destiny, O, Lord, prepare him for it."[42]

From now on, Tom was the center of attention. He was not to stay in the Macon jail long, but while he was there he impressed a Negro prisoner with his calm unruffled demeanor. "Dat's de coolest man I ever seed," remarked the Negro.[43] It was not a cool atmosphere outside, for within less than twenty-four hours Tom was safely in the Atlanta jail, whisked there Saturday night to escape possible violence in Macon.[44] On the train going up, he remarked to Jailer Nat Birdsong, who had him in charge, "Well, nine of them are gone, and the tenth will soon go, I reckon."[45] This statement was interpreted by some people as a sort of half-confession.

For the next few weeks, Tom was the greatest attraction in Atlanta. Unprotected from streams of the curious and also from the newspaper reporters, Tom became morose and sullen. He finally refused to talk to any of them, and asked the jailer to let no one come to his cell. A visitor in noting the constant crowds of people who had come to gaze on Tom and ask him questions, remarked, "They look at him with the same morbid interest with which they would gaze upon some physiological monstrosity. . . . The same feeling which would prompt a man to pay fifty cents to look at Jesse James or an eight legged dog."[46] He had been there less than a week when it was reported, "He is glum and reticent. He seems to be worried nearly to death."[47] He talked in his sleep and began to show a special dislike for newspaper reporters, whose comments on him he read in the papers. One of the most frequent speculations was whether Tom was crazy. One gazer remarked, "That fellow is perfectly sane. He is no more crazy than I am."[48] Tom was visited by an Atlanta physician, whose interest may have touched on psychiatry, who concluded that Tom was not entirely sane, but not too insane to escape hanging, for he knew what he was doing.[49]

While Tom was in the Atlanta jail, his two sisters and his Aunt Crane visited him to comfort him, for they stood by him to the end, believing him to be innocent. He exclaimed to them, "Great God! what a terrible crime they charge me with. But look at me, before God and man I am an innocent man."[50]

3. The First Conviction

Pending a setting of a date for Tom's trial, which would be held in Macon, he began immediately on arrival in Atlanta to bestir himself for a lawyer—it having been erroneously stated that no lawyer in Macon would take his case. Judge James T. Nisbet, a Maconian, who knew Tom personally and who was now private secretary to Governor John B. Gordon, visited Tom in jail. Tom wanted him to be his lawyer, saying that that all the members of his family were now dead (excepting his two sisters) and he could, therefore, pay a big fee. Nisbet told him that it would be impossible for him to take the case since he had to give all of his time to his secretaryship. Also he informed Tom that his chances for coming clear were slim. Tom replied, "Well, I am innocent, but I don't care much about living, and yet, I don't want to hang. But if I have got to die, I'll die like a man."[51]

Soon, without any expectation of receiving a fee and not asking for one, Frank R. Walker, a young lawyer, who had graduated at Washington and Lee University in 1883, agreed to defend Tom. And a few months later, Tom was able to add another lawyer to his counsel, John C. Rutherford of the law firm of Bacon & Rutherford. Augustus O. Bacon, the Bacon of this firm, was later to represent Georgia in the United States Senate for almost twenty years; Rutherford was a son of Williams Rutherford, who for many years was a professor in the University of Georgia. One of John's sisters was Mildred ("Miss Milly"), who at this time was principal of The Lucy Cobb Institute, and who was ever the quintessence of the Old South and a defender of the good name of the Confederacy. Rutherford became thoroughly convinced of Tom's innocence and put forth such superhuman efforts as practically to give his life in his attempt to clear Tom, for he died soon after the conclusion of the last of the trials.[52]

Although probably none of Tom's lawyers ever received recompense for their services, Tom turned over to them every right he had to all the Woolfolk property which he thought he could lay claim to. On November 9 (1887) he executed to Rutherford and Walker "in consideration of the sum of" $2,000 a deed to all his "interest of what kind whatsoever" in 867 acres of the Woolfolk plantation.[53] And on the same day, taking advantage of any legal technicalities incident to the question of whether his stepmother died before his father, he deeded to the same lawyers all his "interest" in the property of his stepmother, which included the 50-acre Woolfolk home-place and her various Macon properties—all in consideration of $2,000.[54] Then on December 11, 1888, after Walker had dropped out on account of ill health, and in recognition of the fact that his two sisters would have the same interest in all Woolfolk property which he had, Tom now executed to Rutherford (in the name of his firm Bacon & Rutherford) a deed to his one-third interest in the selfsame property described in his previous deeds. This was in consideration of $3,000.[55]

Tom's lawyers had a terrific task before them to clear him, for he had already been convicted in the minds of almost everyone in Bibb County. What could their defense be? There were two lines of procedure: Deny that Tom committed the crime and prove that others did it or rest the case on the evident fact that if Tom did it he was crazy, and, therefore, not responsible for his acts. In the early stages of the defense work before the trial started and before Rutherford had been engaged, Walker said, "I shall prove first, and above all, that Thomas Woolfolk is insane; that rational as he may appear at times, and on some subjects, he is a monomaniac and devoid of all reason when it comes to weighing right and wrong, good and evil, and is no more responsible for dyeing his hands in human blood than is the lion of the jungle or the mad dog."[56] Tom realized that it would be very difficult for him to get a fair trial, and in one of those mental abberations while in the Atlanta jail he tried to bribe the solicitor-general, J. L. Hardeman, by saying that he would give him $1,000 for a fair trial.[57]

Also, the defense counsel knew that the longer they could put off the trial the better their chances would be, for they expected the extreme passions of the multitudes to subside; but the people were crying for a quick trial, and it was set by Judge George W. Gustin for November 21. Rutherford and Walker were able to secure a postponement of two weeks, which set the trial for early December (1887).[58]

The trial began with Judge Gustin presiding, Solicitor-General Hardeman assisted by Dupont Guerry and Joseph Hall for the prosecution, and Rutherford and Walker for the defense. The courtroom was packed long before the hour for the trial to begin. Tom's two sisters, Mrs. Cowan and Mrs. Edwards, and his Aunt Crane and a cousin Mr. Shackelford were all seated with Tom and his lawyers, and these stood by Tom through his various trials to the end—his sisters greeting him with a kiss on the cheek and bringing him bouquets and fruit. It took two days to get a jury, after 163 names had been called. The total number of witnesses announced to be called by both sides was 165 whites and Negroes, and at least 70 were used. Although there were nine indictments against Tom, he was tried on the murder only of his father.[59]

Throughout the trial Tom was the object of every eye at one time or another, and a puzzle and an enigma to everyone. Almost at all times perfectly composed, yet he was alert, watching everything going on and noting every word spoken; but there was an "occasional flush of his face and forced compression of his lips."[60] He had a collosal will power and composure and an iron nerve. To one observer his iron countenance appeared "so fixed that it might have been moulded in iron—no nervousness, no anxiety, no alarm; his face in its rigid cast has been as calm and unspeaking as that of the immemorial Sphinx."[61]

The prosecution in charging Tom with the murder, sought to establish his motives; and although no one lived to testify to the murder, the state assumed the old axiom: "Witnesses may lie, circumstances cannot." The controlling motive which the state sought to establish was Tom's consuming passion for the Woolfolk property, and incidentally his profligate life and hostile feelings toward his stepmother, and even toward his father. And, of course, Tom's movements on the morning of the murder had to be established.

The first witness was Sam Chambliss, a neighbor, who had been early on the scene. He described in lurid detail what he saw in the house. The prosecution handed him a bloody axe with some long hair still matted on it, which he identified as the weapon he saw on the spot. Next he was handed a package and asked to open it. In it he identified the bloody socks and other clothing which had been fished out of the well. Before the end of the first day a young man in the gallery fainted and was carried out. Day after day witnesses, white and black, testified. Two Negro women told how they had heard screaming up at the Woolfolk house the night of the murder, how the dog was barking and the cattle bellowing[62]—much of the Negro testimony was highly imaginary and contradictory and almost valueless.

J. Dannenberg, who owned store property in Macon and who had rented Tom a storehouse in 1885, told how Tom had asked him one day, "Dannenberg, you know a good deal about law, and you are a pretty smart man, tell me something in regard to property." Dannenberg replied that he knew nothing about the law of property, and Tom then observed, "I am going to have money before I die."[63] Pursuing the property line, the state introduced John Owens, a Negro, who told that while he was whitewashing Captain Woolfolk's house, Tom remarked, "Do you see all this property lying around here? It all belongs to me and my sisters. Some day I will own every bit of it."[64]

To prove Tom's hostility toward his stepmother, the state introduced Benjamin F. Howard, the 76-year-old father of Mrs. Woolfolk, who testified that his daughter came to him a few days before the murder and "said her visit was to see me and to know what to do; that her life was in danger from Tom Wolfolk— the way he treated her she expected to be killed."[65] She said that Tom "ordered her about and spoke roughly to her," that he grumbled at breakfast and said that he would not eat such food, and also, that he was cross to the children.[66] F. P. Davis testified that Tom was also critical of his father, that while Tom was riding with Davis in his buggy one day, Tom said, "Most boys can drink and spend a little, but I can't. Father won't let me stay at home unless I work. He calls it loafing. I'll see the last one of them in hell before I'll stand for it."[67]

Tom's lawyers never used the insanity plea in their defense, which some people thought might have been their "best bet," and which Walker had originally suggested. Rather, they decided to show that no one person could have performed such a gigantic labor of slaying nine persons, of whom, five were adults, or nearly so, and that there was a conspiracy of Negroes who committed the terrible act. Also, they would incidentally attempt to prove that Tom was always on good terms with his father, stepmother, and the children, and to do so they introduced Tom's two sisters and his Aunt Crane, who testified to Tom's affection for the whole family.[68]

The defense lawyers charged several Negroes with the probability of having slain the Woolfolk family. They brought in one

Pennington, who testified that he was taking a lunatic from the Macon jail to the train and got a by-standing Negro to help him and when he offered the Negro 25¢ an hour for his work he became abusive and said, "You have treated me like the damned Woolfolks. I have been chopping cotton for them, and I intend to kill the last damned one of them." The Negro elaborated by saying that he had worked for thirty days for the Captain and he would not pay him. Pennington did not at the time know the name of the Negro, but he was later identified as John Jeff.[69]

Another Negro suspect on whom the defense sought to pin the crime was George Cadwell (sometimes called Caldwell). They brought out the fact that Cadwell had stolen an ax (sometimes reported as an ox, but probably a typographical error) from Captain Woolfolk and that Cadwell had served a term on the chaingang. He was said to have threatened the Captain with death.[70] But the Negro suspect who was to be a key figure was Jack Du Bose, whose flighty nature was to inject an element of levity into an otherwise sombre situation; however his importance was to come in later proceedings.[71]

As their trump card the defense put Tom on the stand. There was the hush of the tomb as he ascended the stand holding a sheet of paper with notes on it and began in a "calm, low, but earnest voice." He said in the beginning that he was innocent of "this terrible calamity." Then in a long and at times involved statement he continued, saying that he "slept until about two hours before day, when I was awakened by a groan and a blow and a scream. I jumped up to go to my father's assistance—into the room where I heard the noise. My brother Richard was quicker than I was, and he rushed in ahead and was knocked down. I could not see what happened. The light had been blown out. I could not see him, but I heard him fall. I knew that my life was in danger. I was greatly excited. I turned round and jumped over my bed and out of the window on to the front porch and ran down to Green Lockett's house, the nearest negro house on the plantation. When I was going out of the front yard I heard screams from the children. I called Green and called him.

He came after calling him for several times, and sat down on the steps as if he was very much disturbed. I begged him and begged him to return to the house with me, to help me to protect the family. He said he was afraid to go up."

Then in great detail Tom told of hearing voices of the killers in the house and the dog barking and of following them to the back gate and hearing the gate slam as they ran down the hill. "Then I approached the house very cautiously," and entered it and found all dead. Then he told how he was immediately accused by the crowd that collected. Next he switched to the testimony that had been given against him in the trial. He said that Owens was a "bad character," and that he was put on the chaingang "for stealing corn in the swamp, and he also cut a white man." Tom said that he had no recollection of telling him anything about expecting to own all the Woolfolk property, but he did remember Owens saying that he was painting the walls "white now, but he would paint them red before long; he hadn't forgot about the chaingang business." Also, Tom remembered no conversation with Dannenberg, but "If I said anything, it was not a threat towards my father, or parents, or anything of the kind." He ended his statement by saying to the jury, "Now, gentlemen, if you think I am guilty, I hope this crowd will take me and cut me all to pieces, and I won't flinch from it."[72]

Soon the rumor spread that Tom had confessed, and some of the newspapers published it. Later, when Tom was back in his cell and he was asked about it, he replied, "Confessed? Confessed what?"[73]

After more than a week the testimony was closed and Solicitor-General Hardeman began to address the jury before a packed courtroom. When he was reaching the peak of his eloquent emotionalism, a cry burst forth from someone in the audience "Hang him, hang him." Excitement swept the audience and for a time there appeared to be a panic in the making. Tom's sisters threw their arms around him, as if to protect him from a mob. Judge Gustin rapped for order, the disturber was removed, and Hardeman toned down his oratory. The Athens *Weekly Banner-*

Watchman used these headlines for its story: "SOLICITOR
GENERAL HARDEMAN'S VIVID RECITAL OF THE
TERRIBLE TRAGEDY CAUSES STRONG MEN TO
TURN PALE AND WOMEN TO TREMBLE WITH TER-
ROR—CRIES OF 'HANG HIM, HANG HIM!' COME IN-
VOLUNTARILY FROM DIFFERENT PARTS OF THE
HOUSE."[74] Hardeman was followed by the other members of
the prosecution.

Both Walker and Rutherford, for the defense, addressed the
jury. Rutherford made the principal speech and talked in all for
thirteen hours. It created almost a sensation, but not for the
same reasons as Hardeman's speech. Both the bench and the bar
highly complimented him for his masterful presentation, Judge
Gustin saying that it was the ablest argument he had ever heard.[75]

The jury retired and was out twelve minutes "to the second"
(some accounts said only ten minutes) and brought back the
verdict, "Guilty." Judge Gustin complimented the jury and
declared it was the most distinguished one he had ever known.
He sentenced Tom to be hanged on February 10, 1888. The
hanging was to be in private with only those present whom Tom
wanted, the officers of the court, the physician to pronounce
death, and such persons as Sheriff Wescott might see fit to
invite.[76]

Tom heard the verdict without a flinch. As an observer reported, "Not a muscle in Woolfolk's face changed. He seemed
to be about the coolest man in the court room."[77] Apart from
Tom's fixed characteristics, there was another reason why he
showed no agitation at the verdict: He had perfect confidence in
Rutherford, such as a small child might have in its father; and
he most probably expected the verdict.

Of course, Tom and his lawyers felt that he had not had a
fair trial, and there were many others who had the same feeling,
although they believed he was guilty. A country editor remarked
that the evidence was circumstantial "and it is not always safe
to hang on circumstantial evidence."[78] Another editor wrote,
"The Woolfolk trial could have had but one conclusion. The

man was clearly guilty. There was never any doubt about it from the morning the murdered people were found in their beds. The argument of his counsel was faithful and full, but after all, the defense could only be a tissue of plausible and ingenious suggestions, skillfully avoiding the protruding evidences of guilt. No one saw the crime committed, but the conduct of Tom Woolfolk after the tragedy, the blood marks and the threats of the prisoner against his family, were points too conclusive to be over borne." However, continuing, he said that Tom did not get a fair trial; he was convicted in the newspapers all over the state; everybody in Macon and Bibb County said he was guilty; hence a fair trial was impossible; and there must be a new trial. "It will be a black day in Georgia," he said, "when passion, however biased, or indignation however natural shall drive juries into their decisions."[79]

Dr. Henry H. Tucker, an eminent Baptist divine, former president of Mercer University and later chancellor of the University of Georgia, remarked that if he had been on the jury "I might have brought in a different verdict." "Woolfolk," he continued, "was tried by the newspapers and public opinion. Morally, however, I think he did it. He had a motive for it, and it is just like him."[80]

Tom was not to hear the hammers of the carpenters as they began to build the gallows in the jail yard, for immediately after the trial he was secretly hurried back to Atlanta to escape possible mob violence. He was glad to be back, and he immediately asked for his old cell and even the old mattress on which he had previously slept.[81] His residence in Atlanta was to be short, however, for the Macon authorities believed he would be perfectly safe in their jail. When Jailer Birdsong came for him Tom jokingly remarked that he did not think they would want him until February (when he was to hang). He liked the Atlanta jail much better, for he said that he was treated better there and did not have to wear chains.[82] But Tom was not in favor of being in either jail, for on the train going to Atlanta he kept insisting that the window be raised, which Birdsong refused to do, and in the Atlanta jail he tried unsuccessfully to get a rope smuggled in on which he hoped to slide to freedom.[83]

4. Appeal to the Georgia Supreme Court

Tom could joke about hanging, for he never expected it; Rutherford visited him on various occasions and kept him posted on what was going on—and Tom constantly read the newspapers. Immediately after the verdict Rutherford asked for a new trial. In preparing his motion for a new trial he compiled an impressive list of twenty-three exceptions and added that new evidence had been found. He said that manifestly it had not been a fair trial, and in listing the exceptions he stated that the jurors had been prejudiced; that they feared to acquit Tom, for such a verdict would have imperilled their own lives by mob violence; that evidence had been admitted which should have been excluded and conversely that evidence was excluded that should have been admitted; and most of all, that the outrageous outburst in the courtroom should have led the judge to declare a mistrial.[84]

Judge Gustin granted a supersedeas (a stay of execution) to allow Rutherford time to compose his brief and for himself to consider it; and in keeping with the slow deliberations and the law's delay characteristic of court procedures, Gustin did not reach a decision until mid-summer (1888). He refused a new trial.[85]

Rutherford now appealed to the Georgia Supreme Court, which heard the case in early 1889. Indefatigably to the extreme he began his arguments before the highest court, insisting that the verdict was contrary to fact, for one man could not have committed the crime; that it had been proved that there was bad blood between three Negroes and the Captain; that a mistrial should have been ordered on the outburst in court; that Howard's testimony about what his daughter had said was absolute hearsay and should not have been admitted—and various other points he argued.[86]

The court considered the Howard testimony extremely damaging and held that it was inadmissible, and the judges were equally

upset over Judge Gustin's handling of the outburst in court. De-
livering the opinion of the court, Associate Justice T. J. Simmons
wrote that the trial judge sounding his gavel and ordering the
sheriff to remove the disturber and merely removing another
disturber was not enough; he should have punished to the fullest
extent of the law these disturbers and should have ordered the
solicitor-general to discontinue his speech. And it was not enough
for all of the jurors, as distinguished men as they might have been,
to say that this disturbance had no effect on their decision. "But
can any man say with certainty," continued Justice Simmons, "that
such things have no influence upon him? Can any of us know
how far our minds are influenced by applause or excitement of a
crowd which surrounds us?" The court reversed the judgment and
ordered a new trial.[87]

When Tom was given the news that a new trial had been
ordered, he appeared as stoical as ever, but he said that it should
be held somewhere else than in Bibb County. Judge Gustin remarked that if Tom should be cleared in the present case, there
were eight other indictments on which he could be tried.[88]

5. The Second Conviction

Always resourceful, Rutherford used every device to postpone
or slow up the new trial. He insisted on what was evident, that
Tom could not get a fair trial in Bibb County, for opinion was so
inflamed against him that it would be almost impossible to get
an unbiased jury. Rutherford, therefore, argued for a change of
venue, to take the trial to some other county, preferably as far
away as possible. He also argued for a postponement, as he found
it difficult to get his witnesses to come to Macon on account of
their fear of violence.[89]

None of these arguments stayed Judge Gustin. He set the new
trial to begin in Macon on March 4 (1889). When court convened,
Tom's two sisters and his Aunt Crane were on hand as usual, and
his aunt pinned a bouquet of violets on him.[90] The first order
of business was the herculean task of securing a jury, and Rutherford made this his first line of defense. He now began a fight

which was the admiration of almost everyone, and especially of the newspaper reporters, one of whom saying that "Attorney Rutherford is making the greatest legal fight for Woolfolk ever seen in the south,"[91] and another writing, "It is the most remarkable legal battle ever witnessed in Georgia."[92]

Rutherford objected to every name that was called, either because the panel had not been legally constituted or that the name was not even on the panel. Next he demanded of Judge Gustin the opportunity to question every prospective juror as to his understanding of the words "bias," "prejudice," and "perfectly impartial." In every instance Judge Gustin refused to allow any questions beyond those provided for in regular court procedure, and consistently overruled Rutherford. At the end of the first day, 96 names had been called and only one juror had been accepted.

There was an average of about one juror a day, and after five days when six jurors had been obtained, one of them (W. E. Hill) was heard to say that before he would turn Tom loose he would make it a mistrial. Rutherford immediately demanded that this be so declared.[93] Gustin rather than rule it a mistrial, decided to dismiss all six jurors and start anew as a continuation of the same trial.[94]

Rutherford again demanded a change of venue, but Gustin refused to be moved and began again the laborious task of securing a jury. On one day no juror was obtained out of 68 names called, and soon almost all names on the jury lists were used up and the sheriff and his deputies went scurrying all over Bibb County to secure the few men whose names were still in the jury box. Finally the name of a Negro was reached (for Negroes frequently served on juries, but never where a white person was being tried for his life), however, the defense forced the state to strike him "for cause."[95] After nine days, ten jurors had been secured, but by that time "the bottom of the barrel had been reached," and Judge Gustin, unable to secure in all Bibb County "a jury of twelve good men and true," was forced to move the trial to some other county.

At last Rutherford had won a point. He wanted the trial to be moved away from Bibb County as far as possible, preferably to some city such as Atlanta, Savannah, or Augusta, feeling that rural people might be more prejudiced. Judge Gustin argued the very opposite point of view, saying that city people read the newspapers much more than country people and, therefore, made up their minds more quickly. The rule was that the prosecution and the defense lawyers agree on the place, if possible; otherwise, the judge would make the selection. In the Macon Circuit there were the three counties of Bibb, Crawford, and Houston. Judge Gustin chose Houston County and set the new trial to begin in Perry on the first Monday in May (1889).[96]

The trial was postponed, and actually began on June 3. In the meantime efforts had been made to take the case back to Macon and add some of the other indictments against Tom, for it was now believed that a Bibb jury could be obtained since the jury lists were being revised and new names added.[97] These moves were probably the result of a feeling that Tom might be cleared in a trial in Perry.

Walker had now dropped out, and Rutherford was able to secure other help. Also, Hardeman had been succeeded as solicitor-general by W. H. Felton, Jr. Perry was crowded; every boarding house and hotel was filled, and special trains were to run from Macon. Tom was secretly brought down a few days before the trial began and with the same cast-iron countenance he was to sit through the trial. As usual his sisters, Mrs. Edwards and Mrs. Cowan, and his Aunt Crane were to sit by his side and bring him flowers and fruit; and he was to spend much of his time reading Joel Tyler Headley's *Napoleon and his Marshals* when trivial details in the trial were of no interest. At least 125 witnesses were to be summoned.[98]

Ever alert, Rutherford used every tactic which he had previously employed, and at least one new one. He sought to disqualify Judge Gustin on the grounds that he could not be impartial, because before he became judge his law firm of Gustin & Hall had given advice to C. W. Howard, Mrs. Mattie Woolfolk's brother, on the law relating to the descent of her property—Gustin having become judge after Mrs. Woolfolk's murder. And, furthermore, Hall had become one of the lawyers to assist the prosecution. Gustin refused to disqualify himself. Rutherford renewed with great determination his fight over the selection of jurors, challenging the right of the court to bring up every name and insisting on asking the prospective juror his understanding of the meaning of "bias," "prejudice," and "perfect impartiality." Also, he argued for a change of venue since a fair trial could not be had in Houston County, and he called for delay because he had absent witnesses whom he either had not been able to locate or who were in other states and could not be summoned because he was unable to get the necessary legal papers.[99]

Again, this trial was plagued by jurors talking too much and by other jury trouble. Before the jury had been completed it was learned that one juror had said that he would not convict on circumstantial evidence, and there was a mix-up in names whereby a person was chosen whose name was not in the jury box. A mistrial was declared, but immediately the next day a new trial began and soon a jury was completed, and for the next nineteen days the trial went on. Much of the testimony was, of course, a repetition of what had been offered in the first trial.[100] Tom took the stand again and gave about the same statement he had previously made.[101]

But there was some new evidence, if it might be so called. A number of Negro witnesses so confused themselves and the court with their contradictions as to lead an impartial observer to consider the whole thing a travesty. Of a low mentality, they hardly knew what they were saying and were undoubtedly "skeered" as one Negro woman admitted when at one time she said that she was in Green Lockett's house the night of the murder, and at another time, that she was at home in Monroe County. This testimony was in connection with what the defense had called newly-discovered evidence—that there had been found in Lockett's house a trunk with some of Pearl's clothes in it and that the axe had been found in his house. But all of this "evidence" soon disappeared into thin air.[102]

The most amazing of these Negroes was Jack Du Bose, one that

Rutherford had planned from the first trial to find and put on the witness stand. A month or two before the first trial took place, Jack had been arrested by the sheriff of Cherokee County and placed in the Canton jail. While in jail Jack began to talk about the Woolfolk murder and seemed to know more about it than he could have got from the newspapers, even if he were able to read. Walker hurried up there and after talking with Jack, came away with the opinion that Jack committed the murder in connection with three other Negroes who robbed the house. He got the impression from Jack that he had stole an axe from Captain Woolfolk and had been sent to the chaingang, and that he was now an escaped convict.[103]

When Walker went back to Atlanta he was soon to find out more about Jack. It appeared that Jack was a half crazy idiot, who went around the state confessing to every crime he could think of—stealing watermelons, chickens, horses, burning down houses, burgarlizing houses, and being an escaped convict. As far back as when Alexander H. Stephens was governor of Georgia (1882-1883), Jack went to him and confessed to burning down six houses. The chief of police in Atlanta had arrested Jack shortly before the Cherokee County sheriff jailed him, and soon guessing that Jack might have hallucinations of grandeur in the field of crime, he decided to test Jack. He asked Jack if he was not the one who stole some chickens from John Broomhead down on Whitehall Street, and whether the chickens were not in a coop on the left hand side of the street, and whether he did not climb a fence to get to them. To every one of the questions, Jack answered "yassir." The chief had made up this story from start to finish.[104]

Although Jack had confessed to the Cherokee County sheriff that he saw some Negroes commit the murder while he hid behind a rosebush in the yard, the sheriff, realizing that Jack was an idiot, turned him loose, and Jack was supposed to have made his way into Alabama. And although some effort had been made by Rutherford to secure Jack as a witness in the first trial he was unable to find him. Now, in this Perry trial, grasping at every straw of evidence to pin the crimes on Negroes, Rutherford had Tom's name signed to a warrant for the arrest of Jack, and sent out handbills with his picture far and wide offering a reward for Jack's arrest. Finally he was found in Alabama and brought back to Macon and put in jail.[105]

Newspaper reporters soon made a field day interviewing Jack. To one of the reporters he said that Tom did the killing, with the help of Green Lockett, Lockett's wife, and another Negro. On being asked how they did it, Jack said that they blew the Woolfolks up with dynamite.[106] To another interviewer, Jack said that he was 150 years old, that he knew nothing about the murder, and that an attempt was being made to pin it on him because his hair was short and kinky.[107] At other times Jack would say that he was in the Woolfolk yard and saw Negroes do the killing and then that he was not there and knew nothing about it. He talked violently sometimes, threatening anyone, including the judge, if he was accused of the murder. Rutherford soon saw that it would be foolhardy in the extreme to bring Jack into court and put him on the stand.

The prosecution continued to push the property motive for Tom's act. They produced Crawford Wilson, who testified that Tom had said to him, "They are using my dead mother's property, and before I will stand for it, I will see them all dead and in hell, and I will wade knee deep in their blood."[108]

The trial had been going on for only eleven days, which produced more than 380,000 words for the record; but finally the testimony of the witnesses was brought to an end, and then the summing up speeches before the jury began. Rutherford spoke on three days in succession and consumed a total of 13 hours and 34 minutes. The other lawyers for the defense brought the total to 18 hours and 6 minutes; the prosecution took up 13 hours and 29 minutes. When all had spoken, the case went to the jury; and after forty-five minutes, the jury filed back into the courtroom and announced its verdict—"Guilty." There was no demonstration, but a smile of satisfaction appeared to pass over the audience.[109]

Rutherford turned to Tom, who had become a shade paler, his eyes twitching rapidly, and assured him that he could sleep peacefully as far as the verdict mattered. Tom replied, "Oh, I am not afraid." It was a foregone conclusion that Rutherford would again appeal the case to the Georgia Supreme Court. Judge Gustin sentenced Tom to hang on August 16, to be privately carried out, with only Tom's relatives and friends, the physician, and officials present. Replying to the sentence to hang, Tom said, "I will never hang; you can rest assured of that fact."[110] Tom was sent back to the Macon jail, where some of the ladies of the town, who thought him innocent, sent him flowers, fruits, and delicacies.[111] It is probable that Tom's wife never visited him more than once or twice and she never attended the trials. After the second verdict of guilty, she started divorce proceedings, on the grounds of cruelty and Tom's conviction. The divorce was granted in 1890 and she was given back her maiden name, Georgia Anne Bird.[112]

Jack Du Bose was still in jail and had to be disposed of in some way. In July, following Tom's conviction, Jack was brought to trial, which produced this comment from a newspaper correspondent: "It seems that the Woolfolk murder with its attending sequences will never come to an end and will forever live in the annals of time." When produced in court, Jack had no lawyer, and what was more remarkable, no one was present to prosecute him—he was being tried for the murder of the Woolfolks, which was on its face an absurdity both in law and fact. His case was sent to the court of ordinary, where he was adjudged a lunatic.[113]

A rumor which came to light soon after Tom's conviction had it that on the morning after the murder twenty-seven men formed an oath-bound group sworn to hang Tom if the law did not. They met at the first trial, and if Tom had not been convicted, twenty-seven bullets would have carried him off. They met again at the Perry trial, bent on the same mission. And now they swore that they would see that he paid the penalty, sooner or later.[114]

6. Second Appeal to the Georgia Supreme Court

As was expected, Rutherford filed a motion for a new trial, and Judge Gustin stayed his sentence for the hanging until he could consider the motion; and again as was expected he denied a new trial. Thereupon, Rutherford appealed to the Georgia Supreme Court, and it was rumored that if he should lose there he stood ready to appeal on to the United States Supreme Court, even though it would cost from $700 to $1,000 to do so.[115] Rutherford delayed the hearing of his appeal as much as possible, because he was getting together a very full brief and transcript of the case, which ultimately amounted to 1,200 printed pages; because he was hunting new evidence; because for a time he was not well; and because delay, he hoped, would cause sentiment against Tom to simmer down. When in May, 1890, the court had granted a delay of about a month, Jailer Birdsong hurried in to Tom's cell to rouse him and give him the news, in response to which, Tom said, "Is that all you woke me up for? I am going back to sleep."[116]

The Supreme Court began hearing arguments in June, 1890. Again Rutherford, putting his whole heart and soul into the case, presented his reasons for objecting to various rulings of Judge Gustin. Some of these exceptions the Court had previouly heard. Answering Rutherford's contention regarding Judge Gustin's refusal to let him question prospective jurors on the meaning of "bias," "prejudice," and "perfect impartiality," the Court said that these questions went beyond what the law required, and that Judge Gustin was within his right in refusing to let these further questions be propounded. Rutherford contended that both the state and Federal constitution provided for an *impartial* jury, and that asking these further questions was the safest way to get such a jury. Regarding disqualifying Gustin because his law firm had given to Mrs. Woolfolk's brother information on the rules relating to the descent of property, the Court said that this did not necessarily have a bearing on the murder case.[117]

In answering the defense's attempt to involve John Jeff in the murder, the Court answered that it saw no evidence "to indicate that Jeff was connected with the killing"; and as for relating any Negroes to the murder, the Court said, "It may have been the theory of the defendant that his father and his family were killed by the negroes on the place, but it has been his misfortune that he has been unable to show it, or by any proper evidence connect any of them with the killing."[118]

An unusual point came up in the matter of admitting a prayer that Tom was overheard to make, "Lord, have mercy upon me for what I have done; the only thing I regret is killing my father." The Court said that this evidence was admissible, although as far as it knew this question had never before come up in either the United States or England, but confessions to a priest had and had been admitted as evidence—however, never a prayer.[119] The Court also said that Judge Gustin was correct in admitting as evidence the testimony of two witnesses relating to Mrs. Woolfolk to the effect that Tom "had said, in substance, that she was the meanest woman in the world, the damnest meanest woman in the world, and that he hated her."[120]

The Court referred to Rutherford as "the able and indefatigable counsel,"[121] but it upheld the second conviction of Tom Woolfolk and refused to order another trial.[122]

7. Life in Jail

Tom spent more than three years in jail, nearly all the time in the shadow of the gallows. He was first sent to Macon after the murder, but was immediately transferred to Atlanta, where he spent about four months. Brought back to Macon for the trial in November (1887), he was returned to Atlanta for a short time, and then transferred to Macon again, where he spent the next two and a half years, before being sent to Perry for his second trial, and after that, back to Macon again, and finally to Perry again.

In Macon his jailer was Nat Birdsong, and there he and Birdsong had a long and not too pleasant acquaintanceship. In sizing up Birdsong, Tom said, "He is the most wicked man I ever saw."[123] Tom's dislike for Birdsong grew out of the close watch Birdsong kept over him, and the fact that he kept Tom in chains for a great deal of the time. Tom was the most resourceful prisoner the Macon jail had housed for many years, and his schemes for escape and attempts to bribe people to aid him almost drove Birdsong into losing his health. Tom could make a saw out of a case knife and keep it hidden in such unusual places as to drive Birdsong mad in continually searching Tom's cell for such instruments. At least twice, Tom sawed himself loose from his shackles; and he delighted in dragging his chains over the floor to annoy Birdsong.[124] The amount of escape material which Birdsong took away from Tom filled a small trunk: knives, awls, files, ropes, and other objects.

Birdsong used every strategy he could think of to guard Tom, and he felt the greatest tragedy that could happen in his life would be to find that Tom had escaped. He would hide himself and spy on Tom and slip up on him at the most unusual times. One time, in hiding, Birdsong saw a candle burning in Tom's cell, and heard him laughing loud and talking to the candle, and then saying to another prisoner, "Burnett, what do you reckon old Birdsong would say if he knew I took that butter I got him to get for me to-day and made this candle with it? He'd rip me up the back about it."[125]

In his early days of imprisonment, before he had learned to hate Birdsong, Tom offered him $1,000 to let him escape. Later he offered $500 to a workman repairing a nearby cell, for a chisel and a saw. Once he offered Sheriff Wescott $5,000 to place him in a certain cell where he could escape; and during his second trial, in March, 1889, when the sheriff was taking him from the courtroom to the jail, Tom cursed him and tried to make his escape.[126] When Tom had been in jail less than a year, a rumor was stated that he had broken out. It created consternation among the Negroes, who until they learned better refused to leave their houses after dark.[127]

People made special trips to Macon to see Tom and to talk to him, some coming from distant states; and newspaper reporters particularly annoyed Tom to the point that the judge ordered them excluded. One resourceful reporter was able to get by Birdsong by posing as a liquor salesman from Kentucky, and fooling Tom in a like manner. Tom talked freely with him, declaring his innocence and berating Birdsong. Tom said that he would rather be hanged than spend another year in jail, though he was not anxious to be hanged. He thought drowning would be an easier way to leave this life, and as for electricity (electrocution was now being talked about) he thought that might be too hot. This reporter described Tom as being five feet and seven inches tall, weighing about 160 pounds, and wearing a black mustache.[128] In May, 1889, Tom sat for his picture.[129]

Tom never learned to like jail fare; but a few months after his imprisonment a jail official remarked, "Woolfolk's as fat as a guinea pig"; but it turned out that Tom had mumps. Finally Tom wrote Judge Gustin informing him that he did not like the meals which he got in jail and asking him to have the county give him a dollar a day for his meals to be brought in from a restaurant, and that if this was not done he would never eat another bite. But one day when Birdsong brought him a plate of ham and rice, Tom ate it with great relish. But soon he went on a hunger strike which lasted for six days, until he was brought some light bread and syrup, which made him sick. Still holding out for restaurant food, which he never got, he said he would as soon die of starvation as in any other way, and that he would as soon die as live, anyway.[130]

It was difficult to determine just what Tom's mentality was. Birdsong heard him praying the prayer which was introduced in the trial and which the Georgia Supreme Court ruled admissible. After about three months in jail Tom said, "I am actually happier than I ever was in my life before, because I have put my trust in God." A year or two later, people walking by his cell could hear him praying fervently and then start shouting and raving like a madman.[131] After Tom had been in jail for more than two years, it was reported that he was "seeing things." He saw women dressed in black and strange figures moving about and heard the cries of people being beaten. In February, 1890, he wrote a long rambling letter to Governor John B. Gordon asking to be removed to the Atlanta jail. There were horrible things going on in the Macon jail, he said. The jailer and his gang were killing people: "They are first arrested, tied, gagged, thrown into a bath tub, while one of the assailants sits on him till he drowns." Tom said that he feared that he would be next. Yet there was fear that Tom would commit suicide, and Birdsong was careful to keep from him all sharp instruments and cords. Tom told the sheriff that there were a hundred ways he could kill himself.[132]

8. *The Hanging*

When Tom was told that the Georgia Supreme Court had refused to order a new trial he did not seem to be upset in the slightest. He remarked, "Colonel Rutherford is here yet. I don't believe I will ever hang."[133] He said further that he had never had a fair trial and that his case would be taken to the United States Supreme Court. He then began pacing his cell, "where he has already walked so many thousands of miles."[134]

The question was often asked: Will Tom confess? And this was one answer that was given, "Those who know him best are inclined to doubt that he will ever confess." He was "of a cranky nature," and when he made up his mind he stuck to it; and, furthermore, there was no one close enough to him to whom he would confess.[135] Now and then he became moody and silent and no longer sang love songs and Sunday School hymns with which he had beguiled his time. He told Birdsong that he would as soon be dead as to continue in suspense. "But I want to tell you right now," he added, "that I ain't going to confess nothing, because I ain't done nothing to confess about, because I am innocent. I'll stick to that. I tell you, I didn't do that killing. If I was guilty, I would have been crazy long before this, with all I have had to go through. I have prayed God Almighty to give me strength to bear it, and that is all that has carried me through."[136] He was transferred to another cell, and two men were appointed to watch him, one by day and the other by night. And again Tom had outwitted the enemy he had contested with so long, for when he was being transferred Birdsong saw a knife fall from his sleeve.[137]

About six months before the Supreme Court heard Rutherford's appeal from the second conviction, Judge Gustin resigned, and Governor Gordon appointed A. L. Miller of Houston County to fill the unexpired term. Miller had been one of the lawyers aiding Rutherford in the Perry trial, and if the Supreme Court had granted a new trial Judge Miller would have been forced to disqualify himself; but even as it was, it would seem highly improper for Judge Miller to sentence Tom. To solve the problem, Judge George F. Gober of the Blue Ridge Circuit swapped places with Judge Miller, and at the next term of court, which was in October (1890), Judge Gober sentenced Tom to the gallows.[138]

Rutherford had become too ill to handle Tom's case any further and was not now present in court, and the other defense lawyers made no move. It was often said that if Rutherford had not practically given his life to save Tom, he would have appealed to the United States Supreme Court and Tom might never have hanged. Rutherford died the next year. When Judge Gober asked Tom if he had anything to say before being sentenced, Tom replied, "I didn't do it, but I would rather be in my grave than to be alive under the circumstances that surround me."[139] The date set for the hanging was October 29. This was the third time Tom had been sentenced to hang, and there were many people who were saying that Tom would never hang. There were others who were saying that at the last minute he would confess.

Tom had several visitors during his last night on earth; and it was not a lugubrious occasion. Tom Collins, a Macon real estate dealer who had formerly sold wagons and had sold Tom three for which he had never paid, was one of the visitors. After pleasantly reminiscing, one of them mentioned the wagons, and Collins in a bantering spirit told Tom Woolfolk that he would tear up the wagon note if Tom would let him be the last man to shake hands with him on the gallows. Tom laughed loudly and said, "Collins, I'll do it."[140] Another visitor from Macon had a long and light conversation with Tom, in which the latter engaged in various witticisms and reminisced of his horse-trading days, telling how he got the best of the other fellows.

In talking to others in a more serious vein, Tom said that he had no statement to make. "I am an innocent man," he said, "and will protest my innocence to the last." He continued, "Life in prison is a life of torture, and I am ready to die. I would rather die now than to remain in prison another year." Tom read his Bible every day and night and prayed regularly. He said, "If I were a free man I would join the church and be baptized, but as it is I don't think it is necessary to do so." It was being remarked that he no longer used profane language, which was his custom until a few months back.[141] On this last night, Tom made one more effort at bribery. He offered the deathwatchman $500 and a history of his life if he would let him escape; later he offered him $100 and a history of his life for a bottle of morphine.[142] This last night was a mixture of levity and of solemnity. After going to bed Tom was slow in going to sleep and did not make it until 2 a.m.—and it was now his last day on earth.

THOMAS G. WOOLFOLK
From an illustration in the *Athens* (Ga.) *Weekly Banner*, November 4 (p. 5), 1890, to represent him at the time of his execution.

Tom slept well when once he went to sleep, and the sheriff had difficulty waking him the next morning. Before breakfast he took a drink of whiskey, saved from the night before, and smoked a cigar presented to him. His last breakfast was sumptuous and he enjoyed it: ham and eggs, batter cakes, waffles, rice, grits, syrup, hot biscuits, and a pot of coffee.[143] (This did not remind him of Birdsong's jail fare.)

After breakfast Tom was visited by three preachers, two Baptists and a Methodist, who remained with him for about an hour. He let it be known that he did not want to be buried in Macon with the other members of his family (except his mother, who rested under that lonely holly tree, near the house where the terrible crime had been committed); he chose to be buried in Hawkinsville where his sister Mrs. Cowan lived. He did not want his body to be taken by train, but by hearse, which was twenty miles to the southward, and he did not want his sister to see his face, but her husband might. Tom talked about his burial "with as little show of emotion as he might have displayed in selling a bale of cotton."[144]

Tom would have chosen almost any other way of dying than by hanging, but still he was interested in seeing the gallows ahead of time, and he asked Sheriff Cooper to show it to him—it was in the jail yard and had been used before. When he saw it he asked, "Is that what you are going to hang me on, Mr. Cooper?" When told that it was, he replied, "Well, I don't like the looks of it," and requested that it be whitewashed. Sheriff Cooper had it done.[145]

The place of the hanging was to be in a valley in the southwestern part of Perry, near where the Fanny Gresham Branch joined the Big Indian Creek, with the railroad nearby and the town cemetery on the hill in clear view.[146] Early in the morning all roads led to Perry and they were crowded with wagons, buggies, and people on horseback and on foot. A special train of five cars packed to standing room arrived at 11 a.m. and the regular train came in at 12:30 p.m. Soon the streets were crowded with men, women, and children, ready to make their way to the valley, where there was room for 10,000 spectators, and where there assembled a near capacity crowd. The majority were Negroes, who loved a hanging equally as much as a funeral, "the solemnity of the occasion seemingly having repressed the loud mouthed propensities of the African excursionists."[147]

The gallows, which had been whitewashed and moved to the place of hanging, was a square structure resting on four posts with the trapdoor in the center, providing for a drop of six-and-a-half feet. Shortly before the hour of the hanging, which was to be at 1:30 p.m., Sheriff Cooper with Tom entered a carriage, escorted by the Perry Rifles, and drove to the valley, with a great crowd following. Dressed in black and handcuffed to Sheriff Cooper, Tom ascended the gallows. At Tom's request, the sheriff removed the handcuffs. The three ministers offered short prayers, Tom in the meanwhile showing no signs "of emotion or excitement." Then one of the ministers stepped forward and read a statement which Tom had prepared that morning: "I, Thomas Woolfolk, recognizing that the infinitely wise and Holy God sees my heart and knows all that I have ever done, and fully understanding that I must stand before His judgment bar, and that to-day in a few hours, I shall be called into His presence, do, in view of the solemnity of the occasion, declare my innocence and leave as my last declaration that I did not take the life of my father or of any member of his family, or have I any knowledge of the person or persons who did the murderous deed."

Next a great sensation was created when Tom unexpectedly stepped forward and offered this prayer, into which might possibly be read an element of confession of guilt: "Most omnipotent father, in the name of thy beloved son Jesus Christ I ask thee to take me now and wash my heart and make it as white as snow. I ask thee, oh father, what I have asked no man, for mercy. Bless my sisters. Bless these good people who have done so much for me. And bless those who are not good, too, oh father, and may all stand around me in heaven. And for Jesus sake have mercy on my soul."

The trap was sprung at 1:30, after Tom had in vain begged the sheriff for five more minutes of life. The noose not having been properly adjusted, Tom's neck was not broken, and his pulse continued to beat for eleven minutes. He was pronounced dead at 1:58, and at 2:05 his body was cut down, placed in a hearse, and taken to Hawkinsville, where he was buried in Orange Hill Cemetery. About a hundred people attended his funeral.[148]

*   *   *   *

Was Tom guilty? Despite the fact that in the beginning almost everybody who had ever heard of the murder had concluded that Tom was guilty, yet as time dragged on and Tom underwent more than three years of suspense in jail and consistently affirmed his innocence, and nothing but circumstantial evidence could ever be found with which to convict him—in the light of all this there began to develop in the minds of some people a feeling of sympathy for Tom and a suspicion that he might not be guilty. One newspaper reporter wrote that Tom's protestations of innocence had "convinced hundreds that an innocent man was hanged."[149] One of the ministers who had attended Tom in his last hours believed that he was innocent.[150]

Yet witnesses may lie, but circumstances, never—this old axiom seemed to have left no other conclusion than that Tom was guilty. The defense was never able to connect any one else with the murder, although they attempted to involve Negroes in the neighborhood. The Georgia Supreme Court denied that any such evidence had been found. Whether insane in spells or not, Tom was abnormal. He had an amazing determination of will power and an absolute control of his feelings. Having announced his innocence, it is not difficult to see how he could hold out to the last. This comfort he could give to his sisters and other relatives who had never swerved in their support of him. And it was a final fling at those who thought he was guilty and had predicted that he would at last confess.

"The Last of Woolfolk" was the heading the *Atlanta Constitution* gave its editorial comment on "the most brutal murder that ever figured in the annals of our State." Tom "was convicted and executed because the evidence against him was so overwhelming

that impartial and clear-headed men found it impossible to entertain a reasonable doubt of his guilt."[151]

An event so utterly beyond comprehension and so filled with
such deep emotion as the Woolfolk murder, was bound to find
its way into folklore, just as had the deeds of John Wilkes Booth,
Charles Guiteau, and Jesse James. For fifty years after Tom was
gone, people went about their work or sat around singing

> Woolfolk, Woolfolk, see what you've done,
> You've murdered your whole family, and never fired a gun.

For years afterwards, Negroes who at the time of the murder
had been bewildered and consumed with fear, occasionally enacted
in their churches the murder and hanging to attract a crowd and
hope to increase their membership.[152] And the legend grew up
among the uninformed which it seems impossible that even they
could have believed, that Tom was never hanged after all—that
like John Wilkes Booth, he was later seen in Texas.

CHAPTER IX

The Acadians in Georgia

NOVA Scotia, a province of Canada, jutting out into the Atlantic Ocean east of the State of Maine, was first successfully colonized by the French, beginning in 1604. The English made several descents upon the region and held it for a time but they always restored it to the French until 1713, when by the Treaty of Utrecht they were awarded final possession of it. The French had called it Acadie (Acadia), but the English now changed its name to Nova Scotia and required the inhabitants to swear allegiance to England.

These Acadians were intensely French and, therefore, they could hardly suppress their feelings for their mother country despite all oaths they had taken. In 1754 hostilities flared up on the western frontiers between the French and Indians on the one side and the English on the other, signalized by General Edward Braddock's defeat in western Pennsylvania, in a war known in America as the French and Indian War but soon merging with the Seven Years War, which two years later broke out in Europe.

Fearful that the Acadians might aid the French, Charles Lawrence, the governor of Novia Scotia, took it upon himself in 1755 to expel most of them, sending those who did not escape into the wilderness to the various English colonies from Massachusetts to Georgia. From these places many of them were forcibly removed or made their way voluntarily to England, France, the West Indies, and to the Spanish province of Louisiana. Henry Wadsworth Longfellow in his long narrative poem "Evangeline," published in 1847, so popularized those who went to Louisiana, that sight of those who went elsewhere has remained dim. And it should be noted that most of those who went to Louisiana did not go until 1785, taken there from France by the Spaniards, having arrived in France from English prisons and originally from

Virginia, where the authorities had refused to receive them from Nova Scotia.[1]

About 2,000 Acadians were sent each to Massachusetts (Boston) and to Maryland; 1,500 to Virginia, who were refused and sent to England; 700 to Connecticut; 250 to New York; 754 to Pennsylvania (Philadelphia); 500 to North Carolina; 1,500 to South Carolina; and 400 to Georgia. Everywhere they were received with misgivings or open hostility, except in Virginia where, as previously stated, they were not received at all, and in Connecticut, where they were given greater consideration than anywhere else.[2]

There was almost consternation in Savannah when late in December, 1755, two ships appeared off Tybee at the mouth of the Savannah River, laden with Acadians, one with 120 passengers, mostly women and children, and the other with 280, mostly men. Governor John Reynolds was then in Augusta, having gone there to deliver presents to about 300 Indian chiefs and headmen, who were expected shortly. On learning of the arrival of the ships Governor Reynolds, though much disturbed, allowed the ship with the women and children on board to be brought to Savannah, but he ordered the other to remain at Tybee. Reynolds might well have been disturbed, for Georgia was extremely weak as a colony, having only about 3,000 people (one half being Negro slaves). Furthermore, on its western frontiers was a large Indian population, which was subject to the intrigues of the French, who had penetrated far to the eastward of their own Louisiana. With a war now being fought against France and the Indians, it was the part of wisdom for Reynolds "to brighten the chain of friendship" with the Creeks and Cherokees, for the Acadians could be as big a danger to Georgia, as Lawrence thought they would be to Nova Scotia.

The Indians were so slow in gathering at Augusta that Reynolds, now worried with the problem of what to do about the Acadians, decided to wait no longer. Turning over the distribution of presents to his lieutenants, he hurried back to Savannah, only to find that the second ship had come up the river and was at the Savannah landing.[3]

Governor Reynolds at first refused to let William Trattles, the master of this ship, the *Prince Frederick*, land his passengers, and ordered him to depart the province. Trattles stood firm and declined unless his ship was "Victualled and Indemnified." In view of this difficulty the Governor and Council agreed to let the passengers be landed and to give each of them a pound of rice for a period of ten days. To prevent Savannah from being burdened with this large group of potentially hostile people, the Council ordered boats to be provided to take them to various outlying parts of the colony—to Frederica, Midway, to Great Ogeechee and to Little Ogeechee, and to Joseph's Town. Also it recommended these people to the care of the magistrates of these places. Although the record is silent, it should be inferred that the women and children from the first ship were included in this dispersal.[4] Apparently there was much delay in carrying out this scattering of the Acadians, if indeed it was ever done on a large scale, for more than two weeks after they had been landed, they sent a petition to the Council, stating that many of them were in "a Sick and Languishing Condition and incapable of Supporting themselves and families and must (if not assisted) perish." The Council ordered the Commissary to provide a "Weeks Provision" to those who were "sick and in Necessity."[5]

Governor Reynolds was glad to have any of them who wanted to build boats to do so and to use them in leaving Georgia, judging "it best to let them go as they were all Papists & consequently enemies to our Religion & Government & unfit to be suffered to remain in such a very weak & defenceless Colony as Georgia then was."[6]

The Lords Commissioners of Trade and Plantations (popularly called the Board of Trade), the authority in England directly concerned with the management of the colonies, commended Reynolds for the way in which he had dealt with the Acadian problem: "It gave us great uneasiness to find, that so large a

Number of the French from Nova Scotia were sent to your Province; and We approve the measures you took for providing for their reception and accomodation, But We hope that you will have been able to have fallen upon some method of settling and disposing them in such a manner as that they may become as little a burden and expence to the public as possible."[7] But later when Reynolds had through dictatorial methods lost favor in Georgia and had been brought to taw by the Board, it chided him for having gone on to Augusta when he should have stayed in Savannah to meet the Acadian problem—probably intimating that he should have refused to let the passengers land.[8] The Board also accused him of not keeping it informed of the situation. For this reason, but principally for others, it supplanted him in 1756 with a new governor, Henry Ellis.

Governor Ellis was more sympathetic with the Acadians than Reynolds had been. The economy of the colony was increasing with the developing of more and larger rice plantations, herds of cattle and swine, and the exploitation of the forests for such supplies as lumber, shingles, staves, and shipbuilding requirements. Although slavery had now been introduced into the colony, still labor was scarce, and the Acadians might well help to supply this need. The Commons House of Assembly and the Council were considering some legislation relative to the Acadians a few weeks after they had arrived, and finally a year later (February 8, 1757) they passed an act entitled "For the providing for & disposing of the Acadians now in this Province." After reciting the fact that most of them were still living in and about Savannah and were cutting down valuable timber belonging to private individuals, it was now deemed wise both for the good of the Acadians themselves as well as for the public benefit to distribute them to different parts of the province. They were to labor for anyone offering them work and to receive for such service their upkeep only, meaning food, clothing, and lodging; but no families were to be separated. Anyone refusing such offer might be bound out according to the regulations governing white indented servants.

Such person was not allowed to have or use any firearms or other dangerous weapons except on his master's plantation and under the master's inspection and observation. No one over eighteen years of age should be bound for more than three years, and no one under that age should be held beyond his twenty-first year.[9]

The next month Governor Ellis reported to the Board of Trade that some of the Acadians had "built themselves huts" near Savannah "and are very useful to the Colony." They were employing themselves in making oars, hand spikes, "and other implements for Sea Craft," for which they found a ready market in the West Indies.[10] He was desirous of keeping them and making them a part of the colonial population. But the picture of these "French Neutrals," as Ellis called them, was not wholly a pleasant one, in his eyes. Soon he was out visiting among them and he reported to the Council that he "was very much affected to see such a Number of distressed People surrounded with large Families of helpless Infants," and he proposed to the Council that it allot land to them, where they might cultivate the ground and raise sufficient food not only to feed themselves but by marketing the remainder, secure money for themselves. The Council agreed that those asking for land should receive it. Ellis promised the Council that he himself would "supply them with all Manner of Garden Seeds."[11]

Still the Acadians did not thrive, and they seemed much on the conscience of the Governor. Near the end of the year (1757) he had observed their plight and reported to the Council that a great many were in a "distressed starving Condition . . . and so afflicted by Sickness that there were not more than five Persons able to Work for the Maintenance and Support of One hundred." He thought that the Council should provide for their immediate relief, which it did by supplying them with five barrels of rice.[12]

It seems that little of what the Georgia authorities provided for the Acadians was carried out, largely because the Acadians failed to act. Probably few planters ever asked for Acadian laborers, and just as likely the Acadians never applied for land. It seems that few ever moved beyond the vicinity of Savannah, as long as they remained in the colony. But it is also evident that if land was allotted to the Acadians, they were not given the ownership of it, for in 1761 it appeared that the land on which the Acadians resided near Savannah, had become private property and the owners had demanded that the Acadians vacate it. They were required to move and they were now set down on land to the westward up the Savannah River where they were to be allowed to build huts and reside, but no nearer the bluff than a hundred feet.[13]

Indeed, the lot of the Acadians was a hard one. They were a strange people in a strange land, speaking no English, and professing a religion outlawed in Georgia. Yet they were not interfered with in their worship, which without priests consisted of meeting in some convenient house where they recited their prayers in common.[14]

The Acadians could never consider Georgia their permanent home. Expelled from Nova Scotia, they had not elected to come to Georgia or to any other region to which they had been sent. From the very beginning they were biding the time when they might get away. Very soon some began to cross the Savannah River into South Carolina, where 1,500 of their compatriots had been sent, or to make their way up the coast in small boats. In 1761 two families set out for Rhode Island,[15] and two years later twenty-one individuals left for Mobile to continue on to New Orleans, as opportunity afforded.[16] Others had preceded them to Louisiana and more would follow.[17]

The Duke of Nivernois, who was the French ambassador in London, had taken a special interest in the Acadians who had been sent to England when the Virginians had refused to let them land, and was finally able to have them removed to France. The Duke was equally interested in gathering up the Acadians all up and down the English colonies in America and sending them to France. In 1763 there were left in Georgia thirty-seven families, consisting of 187 people. When they heard of the Duke's plans they were overcome with joy. In August of that year they wrote to him an account of their hardships in Georgia, how they had lived eight years there without priests.[18]

It is not known how many, if any, went to France under the Duke's patronage, but the days of the Acadians in Georgia were now numbered, for they soon began leaving for the island of Santo Domingo, in the West Indies. In the very month they had complained to the Duke of their hard lot, it was reported that "a number of Acadians who have been here for a few years" boarded a sloop "for Monte-Christi."[19] This place was on the north side of the island in the Spanish part. A few months later they were followed by a group going to another part of the island, according to this report which came out of Savannah: "All the Acadians here are about leaving the place; yesterday upwards of 90 of them went on board a vessel in the river to Cape Francois."[20] And on January 12, 1764, finis was written to the sojourn of the Acadians in Georgia: "The Acadians have entirely left this place; 44 of them went for Cape-Francois on Friday in the brigt. Polly and Deborah, Capt. George Anderson."[21]

Cape Francois was the largest town in the French end of the island, where later the Negro slaves and mulattoes rebelled, slaughtered all the whites they could find, and set up the independent country of Haiti. It was on the northern coast on the edges of an extensive fertile plain, well watered and under high cultivation.[22] These Acadians were to have "settlement there, with plantation tools, and two years provisions," furnished by the French authorities.[23] The horrors of the war were especially marked in the Cape Francois region, and a considerable number of the whites who escaped came to Georgia, and among them may well have been some of the Acadians who had once lived there.

Notes

Numbers in brackets at the top of the following pages indicate the pages in the text to which these notes refer.

CHAPTER I

¹A. L. Hull, *A Historical Sketch of the University of Georgia* (Athens, 1894), 19.

²E. Merton Coulter, *College Life in the Old South* (New York, 1928), 99-100.

³Ulrich B. Phillips, *The Life of Robert Toombs* (New York, 1913), 13-14.

⁴Pleasant A. Stovall, *Robert Toombs, Statesman, Speaker, Soldier, Sage* . . . (New York, 1892), 12.

⁵Hull, *Historical Sketch of the University of Georgia*, 45. The linking of Toombs' death with lightning striking the old oak persisted. See *Athens Daily Banner* (Georgia), June 16 (p. 9), 1901; A. B. Bernd, "Robert Toombs and the University," in *The Georgian* (Athens, Ga.), June, 1911 (Vol. XV, No. VIII), 307. Even Mrs. Toombs' death was linked with the withering of a tree in the Toombs yard, in Washington, Ga. It "turned yellow in the gasp of death also." *Athens Daily Banner*, November 5, (1, 7), 1891. Henry Tuck, who was a student at the University from 1877 to 1881 and who remained a citizen of Athens for many years thereafter until his death, stated as a definite fact that the tree was struck by lightning on July 4, 1884. In less than two years Toombs died—December 15, 1885. The tree lingered on until 1908. Tuck declares that the Toombs speech under the tree was "another fiction." Henry C. Tuck, *Four Years at the University of Georgia, 1877-1881* (Athens, 1938), 141.

⁶Joel Chandler Harris, *Life of Henry W. Grady, Including his Speeches and Writings* (New York, 1890), 91.

⁷The Henry W. Grady scrapbooks are in the Emory University Library. They contain a great many newspaper clippings of Grady's writings, including the two articles on Toombs. In a rather close search, no other article on Toombs was found by this writer.

⁸*The Pandora '86*, p. 4. This was the first number of the University of Georgia student yearbook.

⁹*Athens Daily Banner*, May 26 (2, 1), 1891.

¹⁰*Athens Weekly Banner*, November 6 (2, 1), 1891.

¹¹*Athens Daily Banner*, November 5 (1, 7), 1891.

¹²*Georgian*, November, 1899 (Vol. IV, No. I), 15.

¹³*Pandora, 1898* (XI), 176.

¹⁴*Georgian*, December, 1903 (Vol. VIII, No. III), 17.

¹⁵*Pandora, 1902*, p. 240.

¹⁶*Athens Banner*, July 10 (?, 5), 1908. The author of this article has a small block of the old oak, presented by an alumnus, Professor George Heidler, who inherited it.

CHAPTER II

[1]Ruth Blair, comp., *Georgia's Official Register, 1925* (Publication of the Department of Archives and History), 305; *ibid., 1927*, p. 449; Thomas W. Reed MS (in University of Georgia Library), 94-96.

[2]A. L. Hull, *A Historical Sketch of the University of Georgia* (Atlanta, 1894), "Catalogue, Trustees [no page numbers]."

[3]*Biographical Directory of the American Congress, 1774-1927* (Washington, 1928), 1143; Lucian Lamar Knight, *Georgia's Landmarks, Memorials and Legends* (2 vols., Atlanta, 1913, 1914), II, 1016-17.

[4]Clarke County Deed Record P (in Office of Clerk of the Court), 9.

[5]*Ibid.*, 507-508. The plantation was about seven miles east of Athens, near the present town of Winterville.

[6]*Ibid.*, S, 300-301. See also Clarke County Record of Bills of Sale, Mortgages, etc. (in Office of Clerk of the Court), Book L, 18-21, 81.

[7]Lucian Lamar Knight, *A Standard History of Georgia and Georgians* (6 vols., Chicago, 1917), VI, 3002.

[8]The present writer made a thorough search.

[9]These sketches were entitled, " 'Tis Sixty-Five Years Since," and appeared in the following issues: April 20; May 4, 11, 25; June 1, 8, 15, 22, 29; July 6, 13, 20; August 3, 10; September 7; October 19; and November 9.

[10]*Georgia Weekly Telegraph* (Macon), August 17 (4, 2), 1875. The figures within the parentheses represent page and column respectively.

[11]*North-East Georgian* (Athens), August 11 (2, 7), 1875.

[12]*Southern Watchman* (Athens, weekly), March 16 (3, 8), 1882; *Banner-Watchman* (Athens, weekly), January 3 (4, 1), 1883; Katharine Stanley Nicholson, *Historic American Trees* (New York, 1922), 46; D. Pricilla Edgerton, *Famous Trees* (U. S. Department of Agriculture Forest Service, Washington, D. C. October 1, 1935), 8. The Washington elm fell October 27, 1923.

[13]Augustus Longstreet Hull, *Annals of Athens, Georgia, 1801-1901. With an Introductory Sketch by Dr. Henry Hull* (Athens, 1907), 281.

[14]*Atlanta Constitution*, August 11 (2, 4-5), 1906.

[15]Nicholson, *Historic American Trees*, 19.

[16]Edgerton, *Famous Trees*, 31.

[17]Ulrich B. Phillips made an inventory of the Athens Archives in 1904 and noted that he found no records prior to 1858. The present writer found records as far back as 1847. See Ulrich B. Phillips. "Georgia Local Archives," in *Annual Report of the American Historical Association for the Year 1904* (Washington, 1905), 592.

[18]An unsigned typed sheet in the folder entitled "Tree that Owns Itself," in Rare Book Collection of the University of Georgia Library.

[19]*Atlanta Constitution*, August 11 (2, 4-5), 1906.

[20]Lena E. Bliss, "A Legal Conundrum," in *The Law Student, a Magazine for Law Students* (Brooklyn, N. Y.), Vol. 18, no. 3 (March, 1941), 6-7.

[21]If the neighborhood of the tree had been settled long before 1890, in addition to Malthus Ward's residence across on Dearing Street, which ran into Finley at right angles and stopped there, then the tree could have developed as a playground for the children of the vicinity, and it might have been for that reason that the tree was left unmolested. The following statement which was made in 1901 suggests that answer: "It is tall and symmetrical, its great limbs are shaped as if by the hand of an artist, and under its shade several generations have sheltered themselves from the heat or disported playfully in frolic and amusement." *Athens Daily Banner*, June 16 (8-3), 1901. But there is this additional puzzling question: Why was it that Malthus Ward was not selected to write that mythical deed? Ward lived opposite the tree for nearly forty years; he loved trees and nature, for he was long the director of the University Botanical Garden, which was located along the small branch meandering through the valley at the foot

of the hill. Why should William H. Jackson have been chosen, a man who lived at most a dozen years and possibly only three years in the vicinity of the tree, who then moved away seven miles from Athens, to a plantation, where he lived for ten years, and who thereafter lived in various parts of Georgia but never again in Athens. The fact that Jackson should have been practically unknown in Athens in 1890, except among hs kinsmen the Cobbs and their proliferation, makes it difficult to understand why he should have been selected to make the deed, unless one of his kinsmen invented the story. Jackson's name appears in the Deed Records in the Courthouse of Clarke County, but never as the owner of the land on which the tree stood or of any other land in Athens, but rather as a resident on a plantation seven miles away always, borrowing money, giving mortgages on his property, and finally being sold out.

22*Athens Banner-Herald*, December 5 (1, 2-3; 5, 4-6), 1946; *Atlanta Constitution*, December 19 (p. 16), 1946. The mayor was Robert L. McWhorter and the minister who said the prayer was the Reverend E. L. Hill of the First Presbyterian Church.

23A tree in Oxford, Georgia was deeded to itself in official exercises held September 30, 1929. Katherine Pope Merritt, "Two Trees Own Themselves," in *Atlanta Journal* (Magazine Section, page 12), December 7, 1930. A citizen of New York has set aside in California an area of forty acres to protect a huge oak, measuring thirty-one feet in circumference, and reckoned to be from 600 to 700 years old. Nicholson, *Historical American Trees*, 19.

CHAPTER III

1Robert and George Watkins, eds., *A Digest of the Laws of the State of Georgia. From its First Establishment as a British Province down to the Year 1798, Inclusive, and the Principal Acts of 1799* . . . (Philadelphia, 1800), 765-97.

2*Ibid.*, 290.   3*Ibid.*, 299-302.   4*Ibid.*, 258-65.

5*Ibid.*, 238; William Bacon Stevens, *A History of Georgia, from the First Discovery by Europeans to the Adoption of the Present Constitution in MDCCXCVIII* (2 vols., New York, 1847; Philadelphia, 1859), II, 358-59.

6Watkins, eds., *Digest*, 295. For an excellent discussion of land boundaries, see Milton Sydney Heath, *Constructive Liberalism. The Role of the State in Economic Development in Georgia to 1860* (Cambridge, Mass., 1954), 93-97.

7Watkins, eds., 293.

8*Ibid.*, 294.   9*Ibid.*, 291, 294.

10Allen D. Candler, ed., *The Revolutionary Records of the State of Georgia* (3 vols., Atlanta, 1908), III, 208, 219, 225, 281, 332.

11Watkins, eds., *Digest*, 292,

12Candler, ed., *Revolutionary Records*, II, 791, 792, 793, 794-95.

13For an extensive account of these Virginians by one of them, see [George R. Gilmer], *Sketches of Some of the First Settlers of Upper Georgia, of the Cherokees, and the Author* (New York, 1855), 587 pp.

14Stevens, *History of Georgia*, II, 355-58; Watkins, eds., *Digest*, 294.

15Watkins, eds., *Digest*, 291, 308-309.

16*Georgia State Gazette or Independent Register* (Augusta), September 29 (3, 1-2), 1787. The first number inside the parentheses refers to the page, and the following numbers to the columns. Elijah's son John omitted the final letter from the family name, making it Clark.

17*Ibid.*, March 15 (3, 1), 1788.

18*Ibid.*, September 22 (3, 1-2), 1787. For an account of the stolen child, see *Georgia Gazette* (Savannah), July 28, 1796.

19*Augusta Chronicle*, April 27 (2, 2), 1793. The full title of this paper is *Georgia. The Augusta Chronicle and Gazette of the State*. It is a continuation, beginning with April 11, 1789, of *Georgia State Gazette or Independent Register*, previously cited.

20*Augusta Chronicle*, May 4 (2, 3), 1793.

21*Ibid.*, April 27 (2, 2), 1793.   22*Ibid.*, May 4 (3, 1).

23*Ibid.*, February 23 (1, 1-2).

24*Ibid.*, March 16 (1, 1).   25*Ibid.*, May 11 (2, 1).

26*Ibid.*, February 23 (1, 1).

27Watkins, eds., *Digest*, 575-76. The act was approved February 11, 1796.

28*Augusta Chronicle*, April 25 (4, 1), 1801.

29*Ibid.*, July 18 (3, 1).   30*Ibid.*, August 1 (3, 1).

31*Ibid.*, September 5 (3, 2), See also *ibid.*, July 25 (3, 2).

32Watkins, eds., *Digest*, 575-76.

33*Ibid.*, 678-79; Augustin Smith Clayton, ed., *A Compilation of the Laws of the State of Georgia, Passed by the Legislature Since the Political Year 1800, to the Year 1810, Inclusive* . . . (Augusta, 1812), 35-36.

34Jackson County Deed Record A-B, 73-74, 296. It seems worth while to note here that the site of the University and of the town of Athens was originally owned by a man of unusual interest in Georgia history. He was William Few. Born in Maryland in 1748, Few moved his family first to North Carolina and then to Georgia in 1776, where he took part in the Revolution. He served as a delegate to the Continental Congress from 1780 to 1782 and from 1785 to 1788. He was a member of the Constitutional Convention which made the United States Constitution and was one of the two signers for Georgia. He was one of the first two Georgia senators in the new government. Also he was one of the members of the Board of Trustees named in the charter of the University. In 1799 he moved to New York, where he had a political and financial career of note. He died in 1828.

35*Augusta Chronicle*, August 1 (3, 1) 1801. Easley had been appointed by the University Trustees to be their land agent for Jackson County.

36*Ibid.*, July 25 (3, 2). Easley knew a great deal about the lands in this section of Georgia, for he and Ezequiel Offutt had been appointed by the Trustees to lay off and chequer into 100-acres lots the two 5,000-acre tracts of University land in Jackson County. Minutes of the Trustees, University of Georgia, Vol. I (1794-1817), p. 31. (In the University of Georgia Library). And it might well be inferred that the Trustees advised the Committee to use Easley as a scout and guide in their search for the best location for the University; and it might have been John Milledge's faith in the good judgment of Easley as well as a sense of obligation to him that led Milledge to buy the tract from Easley.

37*Ibid.*, October 17 (3, 1). A. L. Hull in his *A Historical Sketch of the University of Georgia* (Atlanta, 1894) erroneously states on page 15 that the contract for building Old College was let to John Billups.

38*Augusta Chronicle*, July 25 (3, 2), 1801.

39Clayton, ed., *Compilation*, 35.

40See E. Merton Coulter, "Nancy Hart, Georgia Heroine of the Revolution: The Story of the Growth of a Tradition," in *Georgia Historical Quarterly*, XXXIX, 2 (June, 1955), 124.

41Clarke County Minutes of Superior Court, 1801-1808, p. 13. In Office of Clerk of Court, Athens, Ga.

42*Ibid.*, 28; Clarke County Deed Record, B, 58.

43Clarke County Deed Record, B, 59.

44Clarke County Minutes of Inferior Court, 1802-1810, p. 7. In Office of Clerk of Court, Athens, Ga.

45Jackson County Deed Record A-B, 224-25, 306; F, 72; Clarke County Minutes of Inferior Court, 1802-1810, p. 19.

46Clarke County Minutes of Superior Court, 1801-1808, p. 66.

47*Ibid.*, 67.

48Clarke County Minutes of Inferior Court, 1802-1810, p. 196.

49*Ibid.*, 180.　　　50*Ibid.*, 195, 234.　　　51*Ibid.*, 234.

52Clarke County Minutes of Superior Court, 1801-1808, p. 32.

53*Ibid.*, 44; Clarke County Minutes of Inferior Court, 1802-1810, p. 46.

54Clarke County Minutes of Superior Court, 1801-1808, p. 67.

55Clarke County Deed Record, B, 285.　　　56*Ibid.*, 281.

57Clarke County Minutes of Inferior Court, 1802-1810, p. 196.

58*Ibid.*, 200-203.　　　59Jackson County Deed Record, A-B, 126, 218.

60*Ibid.*, 218-19, 255, 350, 353.

61Jackson County Minutes of Inferior Court, 1796-1802, no page numbers.

62Clarke County Minutes of Superior Court, 1801-1808, p. 19.

63*Ibid.*, 93.

64Clarke County Minutes of Inferior Court, 1802-1810, p. 21.

65*The Georgia Justice of Peace, Containing the Duties, Powers and Authorities of that Office, as Regulated by the Laws now in Force in this State* . . . (Augusta, 1804), 41, 48, 62, 100.

66Clarke County Minutes of Superior Court, 1801-1808, pp. 21-22.

67Clarke County Minutes of Inferior Court, 1802-1810, pp. 7, 20, 28, 39, 54.

68Clarke County Minutes of Superior Court, 1801-1808, p. 42.

69Clarke County Minutes of Inferior Court, 1802-1810, p. 144.

70*Ibid.*, 7.　　　71*Georgia Justice of Peace*, 171.

72Clarke County Minutes of Inferior Court, 1802-1810, p. 44. For rates fixed in 1803, see *ibid.*, 19.

73Page 3, column 2.

74Jackson County Inferior Court Minutes, 1796-1802, no page numbers. In Office of the Ordinary, Jefferson, Ga.

75See footnote 42.　　　76Clarke County Deed Record, P, 150-51; Q, 19.

77Athens *Southern Banner*, July 13 (3, 1), 1843.

78Clarke County Marriage Licenses, C, 82. In Office of the Ordinary, Athens, Ga.

79Hull, *Annals of Athens*, 22.　　　80Page 11.

81*Oglethorpe Echo* (Lexington, Ga.), December 11 (3, 2), 1925.

82Jackson County Deed Record, A-B, 327. See also *ibid.*, 162, 190, 196, 243, 332; Clarke County Deed Record, A, 240, 251-52.

83Clarke County Deed Record, A, 238, 289; Oglethorpe County Deed Record, C, 509; Oglethorpe County Will Book, B, 160. Billups was one of the leading citizens of this region and doubtless aided the Committee in their work, which would indicate that they made his tavern their headquarters. During the first five years following the selection of the site, when the "collegiate building" was under construction, Billups received two separate contracts to make a total of 600,000 bricks at $7.50 a thousand to go into the structure. Trustee Minutes, I, 1794-1817, pp. 54, 60, 61, 64, 111.

84Milledgeville *Georgia Journal*, June 7 (1, 2), 1815.

85Minutes of the Senatus Academicus, 29. In the University of Georgia Library.

86XII (June, 1899), 14.　　　87Page 18.

88Page 11-A, columns 1-2.

89Horatio Marbury & William H. Crawford, eds., *Digest of the Laws of the State of Georgia from* . . . *1755, to* . . . *1800, Inclusive* (Savannah, 1802), 563.

90Trustee Minutes I (1794-1817).

91Watkins, eds., *Digest*, 322-23.　　　92*Ibid.*, 323.

93Trustee Minutes, I (1794-1817), 4.　　　94Watkins, eds., *Digest*, 320.

95Trustee Minutes, I (1794-1817), 9-10.

96The Trustees either did not understand the meaning of the Act with regard to the method of their appointment or they chose to disregard it, for they themselves continued to fill vacancies, despite a reasonable interpretation of the Act which would leave the appointment to the legislature. See Trustee Minutes, I (1794-1817), 43 ff. The Act repealed the Charter "so far as respects the appointment of trustees."

[97]Minutes of the Senatus Academicus, 5.

CHAPTER IV

[1]*A Catalogue of the Officers and Students of Franklin College (University of Georgia) Athens. 1851-'52* (Athens, 1851) and catalogues for subsequent years.

[2]The life of a student at the University of Georgia is set forth in E. Merton Coulter, *College Life in the Old South* (New York, 1928; second edition, Athens, Ga., 1951).

[3]Demosthenian Literary Society Minutes, 1847-1854 (typescript of the original MS volume, both in the University of Georgia Library), 90, 91, 95, 103, 104, 117, 139, 142; *ibid.*, 1854-1859, pp. 13, 14, 19, 20, 24, 27, 36, 37.

[4]Minutes of Faculty, 1850-1873 (MS in University of Georgia Library), 37. See also United States Census, 1860, Population Schedule, Clarke County, Georgia, 142. Microfilm in University of Georgia Library.

[5]Faculty Minutes, 1850-1873, p. 45.

[6]*Ibid.*, 73.

[7]*Athens Daily Banner*, January 11 (2, 3), 189. Numbers within parentheses represent page and column, respectively.

[8]Minutes of the Board of Trustees, 1835-1858 (typescript of the original MS volume, both in the University of Georgia Library), 347. See also A. L. Hull, *A Historical Sketch of the University of Georgia* (Atlanta, 1894), 64.

[9]Trustee Minutes, 1835-1858, p. 469.

[10]Minutes of the Board of Trustees, 1858-1871 (typescript of the original MS volume, both in the University of Georgia Library), 30, 38-39.

[11]Coulter, *College Life in the Old South* (second edition), 194-96.

[12]Faculty Minutes, 1850-1873, p. 83 (MS copy).

[13]William D. Sullivan, Gray Court, S. C., April, 1926 to E. M. Coulter, Athens, Ga. (Letter in possession of recipient). Sullivan was a student at the University at that time.

[14]Faculty Minutes, 1850-1873, pp. 122-23 (MS copy).

[15]*Ibid.*, 87. April 10, 1857.   [16]*Ibid.*, 114-15. April 20, 1858.

[17]*Ibid.*, 138-39. June 20, 1859.   [18]*Ibid.*, 112. March 8, 1858.

[19]*Ibid.*, 113. March 17, 1858. [20]*Ibid.*, 134. April 21, 1859.

[21]*Ibid.*, 84. February 24, 1857. For another classroom incident, see A. L. Hull, *Annals of Athens, Georgia, 1801-1901* (Athens, 1906), 340-41.

[22]Athens *Southern Banner*, September 18 (2, 5), 1861. On January 22, 1862 Wash was admitted to the practice of law, taking the oath to support the Constitution of the Confederate States of America and the Constitution of the State of Georgia, Minutes of the Superior Court of Clarke County, Records No. 21 (August, 1860-September, 1862).

[23]*Ibid.*, June 10 (3, 2), 1863.   [24]*Ibid.*, February 27 (3, 2), 1861.

[25]*Southern Banner*, September 18 (2, 3), 1861.

[26]Athens *Southern Watchman*, November 13 (2, 1), 1861.

[27]*Athens Daily Banner*, January 11 (2, 3), 1890. In describing this fight, Mrs. Howell Cobb wrote her husband, November 17, 1861, that "fists, pen knives & walking canes flourished in dangerous proximity to the faces & limbs of the pious contestants—'no body hurt.'" This letter is in the Howell Cobb Collection, on deposit in the University of Georgia Library.

[28]*Southern Banner*, December 18 (3, 4), 1861.

[29]*War of the Rebellion. Official Records of the Union and Confederate Armies* (128 vols. Washington, 1880-1901), Ser. I, Vol. XXIII, Pt. I, 65-70; Hull, *Historical Sketch of the University of Georgia*, 72, 75 (for quotation); Hull, *Annals of Athens, Georgia, 1801-1901*, 248; *Southern Banner*, June 10 (3, 2), 1863; *Southern Watchman*, June 24 (3, 3), 1863.

[30]Faculty Minutes, 1850-1873, pp. 170-72 (MS copy), June 8, 1863 (a copy being in *Southern Banner*, June 10 [3, 2], 1863); Hull, *Historical Sketch of the University of Georgia*, 75.

[31]*Southern Watchman*, June 24 (3, 3), 1863.

CHAPTER V

1R. H. Clark, T. R. R. Cobb, and D. Irwin, *The Code of the State of Georgia* (Atlanta, 1861), 319, 877, 878, 879, 880, 881.

2*Acts of the State of Georgia, 1849-50* (Milledgeville, 1850), 377; Athens (Ga.) *Southern Watchman*, July 6 (3, 3); December 6 (3, 4), 1864. The first number in the parentheses indicates the page, subsequent numbers indicate the columns.

3*Georgia Acts, 1849-50*, p. 377; Clark, et al., *Code of Georgia*, 878.

4*Acts of the General Assembly of the State of Georgia . . . November and December, 1835* (Milledgeville, 1836), 101-103; Clark, et al., *Code of Georgia*, 319.

5Clark, et al., *Code of Georgia*, 321, 322.

6*Population of the United States in 1860; . . . Eighth Census* (Washington, 1864), 58-59, 62-63, 66-67, 74.

7*Southern Watchman*, April 28 (2, 5), 1859.

8Athens (Ga.) *Southern Banner*, November 15 (3, 3), 1860.

9*Southern Watchman*, June 26 (2, 3), 1861.

10Minutes of the Superior Court August 1860, pp. 132-33. Manuscript ledger in Office of the Clerk of the Court, Athens, Clarke County.

11*Southern Watchman*, February 19 (3, 5), 1862.

12Augustin Smith Clayton, *A Compilation of the Laws of the State of Georgia, . . . 1800, to the Year 1810, Inclusive, . . .* (Augusta, 1812), 329-30.

13Lucius Q. C. Lamar, *A Compilation of the Laws of the State of Georgia, . . . Since the year 1810 to . . . 1819. Inclusive, . . .* (Augusta, 1821), 1006-07.

14William C. Dawson, *A Compilation of the Laws of the State of Georgia, . . . Since the Year 1819 to the Year 1829, Inclusive, . . .* (Milledgeville, 1831), 442.

15*Acts of the State of Georgia, 1847* (Milledgeville, 1848), 26-28.

16*Acts of the General Assembly of the State of Georgia, . . . November and December, 1831* (Milledgeville, 1832), 243.

17*Acts of the General Assembly of the State of Georgia, . . . November, December, January, February & March, 1855-'56* (Milledgeville, 1856), 400-401.

18*Acts of the General Assembly of the State of Georgia, . . . November and December, 1842* (Milledgeville, 1843), 96-97.

19Augustus Longstreet Hull, *Annals of Athens, Georgia, 1801-1901 . . .* (Athens, 1906), 127.

20*Southern Watchman*, January 23 (3, 5), 1861; January 22 (3, 3), 1862.

21*Ibid.*, January 22 (3, 3), 1862.

22*Ibid.*, January 11 (3, 3), 1865. See also *ibid.*, January 14 (3, 3), 1863; January 5 (3, 3), 1864.

23*Ibid.*, January 22 (3, 3), 1862.

24*Ibid.*, December 4 (3, 4), 1861; January 13 (3, 3), 1864.

25Hull, *Annals of Athens*, 283-84.

26*Southern Watchman*, February 27 (3, 3), 1861; March 19 (3, 5), 1862; *Southern Banner*, September 18 (3, 4), 1861; Proceedings of City Council, II, 57. These minutes of the City Council are in the City Hall in Athens. Since these minutes were published in the two Athens newspapers, the newspaper source has been used in most cases as being much more accessible. Also there is a microfilm of the minutes in the University of Georgia Library.

27*Southern Watchman*, March 13 (3, 5); April 17 (3, 5); July 17 (3, 6), 1861.

28*Ibid.*, January 22 (3, 4), 1862. See also *ibid.*, February 5 (3, 3); April 2 (3, 4), 1862.

29*Ibid.*, January 13 (3, 3), 1864. See also *Southern Banner*, February 18 (3, 5), 1863.

30*Southern Watchman*, January 13 (3, 4); January 15 (3, 5); March 15 (3, 3), 1864.

31*Ibid.*, January 25 (3, 4); February 8 (3, 4); April 12 (3, 4), 1865.

32*Ibid.*, January 13 (2, 1), 1864.

33*Ibid.*, June 15 (3, 1), 1864. Christy said that Negroes could "be seen perambulating your streets all hours of the day. There are crowds of them idle, or doing such work as might be easily despensed with." He said there were 500 to 1,000 who could be spared for a year or so. *Ibid.*, November 4 (2, 2), 1863.

34*Ibid.*, March 8 (2, 3), 1865.   35*Ibid.*, January 18 (2, 1-2), 1865.

36*Ibid.*, December 11 (2, 5), 1861.   37*Ibid.*, January 22 (3, 3), 1862.

38*Ibid.*, November 6 (3, 4), 1861.   39*Ibid.*, April 8 (3, 3), 1863.

40*Ibid.*, April 2 (3, 4), 1862.   41*Ibid.*, October 7 (3, 4), 1863.

42*Ibid.*, September 16 (3, 3), 1863.   43*Ibid.*, March 15 (3, 3), 1864.

44*Ibid.*, January 25 (3, 4), 1865.   45*Ibid.*, June 5 (2, 1), 1861.

46*Ibid.*, June 16 (3, 1), 1864.

47*Ibid.*, February 11 (3, 4), 1863; April 6 (3, 4), 1864.

48*Ibid.*, December 31 (2, 5), 1862.   49*Ibid.*, June 15 (3, 5), 1864.

50*Ibid.*, September 16 (3, 3), 1863.   51*Ibid.*, June 1 (2, 3), 1864.

52*Ibid.*, January 14 (3, 3), 1863; Hull, *Annals of Athens*, 286.

53*Southern Watchman*, March 18 (3, 4), 1863.

54*Ibid.*, April 13 (2, 1), 1864; *Southern Banner*, April 20 (3, 5), 1864.

55*Southern Watchman*, February 5 (3, 3), 1862.

56Minutes of Superior Court August 1860, p. 51.

57*Southern Watchman*, January 22 (3, 3), 1862. See also *ibid.*, January 8 (2, 4), 1862.

58*Ibid.*, July 23 (2, 5), 1862; *Southern Banner*, July 23 (3, 1), 1862; Hull *Annals of Athens*, 255-56.

59*Southern Watchman*, April 1 (3, 4), 1863.

60*Ibid.*, July 8 (3, 4), 1863.

61*Ibid.*, July-August, *passim*, September 14 (2, 1), 1864; Mary Ann Cobb, Athens, Ga., August 4, 1864, to Col. Wm. M. Browne (MS Letter in possession of present writer). The "Thunderbolts" were a home guard of old and infirm men, who facetiously gave themselves this name.

62*Ibid.*, May 18 (2, 1), 1864.

63*Ibid.*, July 6 (2, 3); October 26 (2, 2), 1864; Hull *Annals of Athens*, 295.

64*Southern Watchman*, August 24 (3, 5), 1864.

65*Ibid.*, January 27 (2, 1), 1864.

66*Ibid.*, April 26 (2, 1), 1865; Hull, *Annals of Athens*, 297-98.

67*Southern Watchman*, May 3 (2, 2), 1865.   68Hull, *Annals of Athens*, 298; Athens *Weekly Banner-Watchman*, August 3 (1, 3), 1886.

69*The War of the Rebellion: A Compilation of the Official Records of the Union and Confederate Armies* (127 books and index. Washington, 1880-1901), Series I, Vol. XLIX, Part II, 615, 630; Hull, *Annals of Athens*, 299.

70P. M. Mell, Jr., *Life of Patrick Hues Mell by his Son* (Louisville, Ky., 1895), 145-46.

71*Southern Watchman*, May 17 (1, 1-2), 1865.

72*Official Records of Union and Confederate Armies*, Ser. I, Vol. XLIX, Pt. II, 998, 999-1000, 1032-33; Dallas D. Irvine, "The Fate of Confederate Archives," in *The American Historical Review* (New York, N. Y.), XLIV (1938-1939), 838-39; Hull, *Annals of Athens*, 307.

73*Southern Watchman*, May 17 (1, 2), 1865.   74*Ibid.*, June 28 (1, 4), 1865.

75*Ibid.*, May 31 (1, 1); (2, 4), 1865.

76*Ibid.*, September 13 (1, 3-4); November 8 (3, 1), 1865.

77Minutes of Superior Court, 1864-1868, pp. 22-26.

78*Southern Watchman*, June 7 (1, 3), 1865.

79*Ibid.*, May 31 (2, 4), 1865. See also *ibid.* (1, 1), 1865.

80*Ibid.*, June 21 (1, 1); 28 (1, 3), 1865.   81Hull, *Annals of Athens*, 305-306.

82*Southern Watchman*, October 25 (2, 1), 1865.

83Proceedings of City Council, II, 232.

84*Southern Watchman*, December 13 (3, 2), 1865.

85Hull, *Annals of Athens*, 306.   86*Southern Watchman*, July 5 (1, 2), 1865.
87Hull, *Annals of Athens*, 302.   88*Southern Watchman*, February (2, 5; 3; 1), 1865.
89*Southern Watchman*, May 3 (2, 2), 1865.
90*Ibid.*, May 24 (1, 2), 1865; Proceedings of City Council, II, 222.
91*Southern Watchman*, May 31 (1, 3), 1865.   92*Ibid.*, June 14 (1, 2), 1865.
93*Ibid.*, June 21 (1, 1), 1865.   94*Ibid.*, May 31 (1, 3), 1865.
95*Ibid.*, May 31 (1, 2), 1865.   96Hull, *Annals of Athens*, 292.
97*Southern Watchman*, May 17 (1, 1), 1865.   98*Ibid.*, June 7 (1, 3), 1865.
99*Ibid.*, June 21 (1, 1), 1865.   100*Ibid.*, June 5 (1, 1), 1865.
101*Ibid.*, October 4 (2, 2), 1865.
102*Ibid.*, June 14 (1, 1), 1865; Hull, *Annals of Athens*, 303.
103*Southern Watchman*, August 30 (1, 1), 1865.   104*Ibid.*, October 4 (2, 2), 1865.
105*Ibid.*, July 12 (1, 1-2), 1865.   106*Ibid.*, December 20 (2, 4), 1865.
107*Ibid.*, December 20 (3, 1), 1865.
108*Ibid.*, August 9 (1, 1); September 20 (1, 3), 1865.
109*Ibid.*, July 26 (1, 1), 1865.   110*Ibid.*, October 18 (2, 2-3), 1865.
111*Ibid.*, December 13 (3, 2), 1865.

CHAPTER VI

1Charles H. Brainard, *John Howard Payne, A Biographical Sketch of the Author of "Home, Sweet Home"*. . . (Boston, 1885), 13, 17; Willis T. Hanson, *The Early Life of John Howard Payne* . . . (Boston, 1913), 207 ff.; Gabriel Harrison, *The Life and Writings of John Howard Payne* . . . (Albany, N. Y., 1875), 12, 28, 32, 174, 221; Stanley T. Williams, *The Life of Washington Irving*, (2 vols. New York, 1935), I, 286. See also Grant Foreman, ed., *Indian Justice. A Cherokee Murder Trial at Tahlequah in 1840, as Reported by John Howard Payne* (Oklahoma City, 1934), ii-iv; *New York Times*, June 16 (22, 5-6), 1958. No satisfactory life of Payne has yet been published.
2Brainard, *Payne*, 137. This quotation is from the oration delivered at the Payne funeral at the Oak Hill Cemetery, Washington, D. C.
3Milledgeville *Georgia Journal*, September 22 (1, 2), 1835. The prospectus of *Jam Jehan Nima* is published here in full.
4*Ibid.*   5*Ibid.* (1, 2-3).   6*Ibid.* (1, 2; 1, 3).
7Harrison, *Payne*, 170, 171. The Green Corn Dance is described in Payne's letter to his sister, the complete text of which is included in Harrison's book, pages, 157-72. Payne described the course he took to Georgia in his "John Howard Payne to his Countrymen," which was published in various newspapers, but all references to it in this article are taken from its republication in a pamphlet edited by Clemens de Baillou, under the same title (Athens, Ga., 1961). The reference here is to page 14. Payne's address was also published in George Magruder Battey, Jr., *A History of Rome and Floyd County* (Atlanta, 1922), I (no more published), 55-74.
8Harrison, *Payne*, 157.   9Milledgeville *Federal Union*, December 11 (2, 4), 1835.
10Lucian Lamar Knight, *Georgia's Landmarks, Memorials and Legends* (2 vols. Atlanta, 1913, 1914), II, 67.
11Quoted in Augustus Longstreet Hull, *Annals of Athens, Georgia, 1801-1901. With an Introductory Sketch by Dr. Henry Hull* (Athens, Ga., 1906), 115.
12de Baillou, ed., *Payne to his Countrymen*, 14
13Quoted in the Augusta *Weekly Constitutionalist*, April 22 (6, 3), 1857, from the *Charleston News*.
14de Baillou, ed., *Payne to his Countrymen*, 14   15*Ibid.*
16Battey, Jr., *Rome and Floyd County*, I, 54.
17de Baillou, ed., *Payne to his Countrymen*, 17. It has been often repeated,

without any evidence being cited, that Edward Harden gave Payne a letter of introduction to Ross. For instance, see Laura Speer, "John Howard Payne's Southern Sweetheart," in *The New England Magazine* (New Series), V (November, 1891), 359.

18"Report from the Secretary of War, in Compliance with a Resolution of the Senate of the 13th October, 1837, in Relation to the Cherokee Treaty of 1835," being Number 120 in United States *Senate Documents*, 25th Cong., 2d Sess., Serial Number 315, p. 574.

19For the text of the March 14th treaty, see Athens (Georgia) *Southern Banner*, April 16 (1, 2-6), 1835.

20*Ibid.*, June 18 (2, 1-2).

21For a general account of this period of Cherokee history, see Charles C. Royce, "The Cherokee Nation of Indians: A Narrative of their Official Relations with the Colonial and Federal Governments," in J. W. Powell, Director, *Fifth Annual Report of the Bureau of Ethnology* . . . *1883-'84* (Washington, 1887), 279-83. See also "Report from the Secretary of War," 396-448.

22"Report from the Secretary of War," 574.

The location of Red Clay was in a beautiful long shallow valley a stone's throw north of what was considered the Georgia-Tennessee boundary, a line much in dispute then and for years thereafter. The twentieth century village of Red Clay lay in Georgia, with its northern extremities in Tennessee. It has been variously stated that the Ross cabin was at Blue Springs and at Flint Springs, both in Tennessee. Flint Spring is bold, fast-flowing, and beautifully located, only three or four miles from Red Clay; whereas Blue Spring is much farther away. Payne describes the Indians as they passed by Ross's Cabin the day before the Council meeting. Since they intended to reach the place that day, the distance must have been short. After the meeting of the Council, Payne and Ross were arrested at the Ross cabin about eleven o'clock at night, and were taken on to Spring Place, arriving there the next morning. This fact indicates that the cabin must have been at Flint Springs, for the distance from Blue Springs to Spring Place could not have been covered in part of one night. As further and indisputable proof of Flint Springs being the location of Ross's cabin, letters to the present writer from Burton Jones, June 1, 2, and 13, 1962, of Cleveland, Tennessee, now 85 years old, state that he often saw the old Ross cabin at the Flint Spring, and that he made a picture of it before it was moved and later torn down, a copy of which he presented to the present writer. Jones was born in the village of Red Clay, north of which (in Tennessee) his father owned 250 acreas (part of the Red Clay Council area). Jones grew up on another farm of his father's at Flint Spring. Preparatory to migrating to the West, no fewer than 5,000 Cherokee gathered at Red Clay in 1837 to meet with Ross. *Georgia Journal*, August 22 (3, 2), 1837.

23"Report from the Secretary of War," 578.   24*Ibid.*, 483.

25*Ibid.*, 566. Payne was telling the Indians and others that "the day of retribution will come for these wrongs." *Ibid.*, 569. See also de Baillou, ed., *Payne to his Countrymen*, 18.

26Royce, "Cherokee Nation of Indians," 279-83; Ralph Henry Gabriel, *Ellias Boudinot, Cherokee & his America* (Norman, Okla., 1941), 146-55; George White, *Historical Collections of Georgia:* . . . (New York, 1854), 148-50.

27de Baillou, ed., *Payne to his Countrymen*, 18.

28*Acts of the General Assembly of the State of Georgia* . . . *November and December, 1830* (Milledgeville, 1931), 116-17.

29[William Gilmore Simms,] *Guy Rivers: A Tale of Georgia* (2 vols. New York, 1834), I, 200-201.

30de Baillou, ed., *Payne to his Countrymen*, 19-20.

31*Huntsville* (Ala.) *Weekly Democrat*, June 21 (1, 4), 1882.

32Williams Forrest, *Trail of Tears* (New York, 1959), 82-83.

33From *Cassville* (Ga.) *Pioneer*, November 13, quoted in *Federal Union*, November 27 (2, 6), 1835.

34Battey, Jr., *Rome and Floyd County*, I, 54.

35"Report from the Secretary of War," 568.

36Battey, Jr., *Rome and Floyd County*, I, 84.

37"Report from the Secretary of War," 490.

38Knight, *Landmarks*, II, 67. In an earlier account Knight said that the Ridge faction made the arrest. *Ibid.*, I, 172, 173.

39Athens (Georgia) *Southern Watchman*, March 29 (2, 3), 1871.

04de Baillou, ed., *Payne to his Countrymen*, 20-21.

41*Ibid.*, 30, 32; Marion L. Starkey, *The Cherokee Nation* (New York, 1946), 260-63; Milledgeville *Southern Record*, December 15 (3, 1), 1835.

42de Baillou, ed., *Payne to his Countrymen*, 24; Speer, "John Howard Payne's Southern Sweetheart," 359; Mildred Lewis Rutherford, "John Howard Payne," in *Flags and Flowers*, 12 (col. 2).

43"Report from the Secretary of War," 490.

44*Niles' Weekly Register* . . . (Baltimore), XLIX (September, 1835-March, 1836), 239.

45de Baillou, ed., *Payne to his Countrymen*, 30.

46"Report from the Secretary of War," 538-39.

47*Federal Union*, December 11 (2, 4), 1835.

48For first quotation, see "Report from the Secretary of War," 570; for second, *ibid.*, 552. See also *ibid.*, 490; Starkey, *Cherokee Nation*, 262.

49"Report from the Secretary of War," 552, 553.   50*Ibid.*, 489-90.

51*Journal of the House of Representatives of the State of Georgia . . . November and December, 1835* (Milledgeville, 1836), 326-27.

52*Federal Union*, December 11 (2, 4), 1835.

53"Report from the Secretary of War," 552, 564.

54*Southern Watchman*, March 29 (2, 2), 1871.

55de Baillou, ed., *Payne to his Countrymen*, 43.

56December 11 (2, 4), 1835. The letter was published also in the *Southern Banner*, December 17 (2, 4-5), 1835.

57"Report from the Secretary of War," 503.   58*Ibid.*, 549-91.

59*Ibid.*, 550.   60*Ibid.*, 552.

61*Southern Record*, December 22 (3, 4), 1835.

62*Ibid.*, November 24 (3, 2).

63*Georgia Journal*, November 24 (3, 1), 1835.

64*Ibid.*, December 8 (2, 5-6).

65*Ibid.*, January 5 (3, 2). The editor of the *Federal Union*, November 20 (2, 4), 1835 said, "We fear that this gentleman has suffered injury from the excited temper of the times."

66*Niles' Weekly Register*, XLIX, 307.

67"Report from the Secretary of War," 492.

68*Ibid.*, 587.   69December 3 (3, 1), 1835.

70December 31 (3, 1-2), 1835.

71Wilson Lumpkin, *The Removal of the Cherokee Indians from Georgia* (2 vols. Wormsloe, Ga., 1907), II, 265.

72*Federal Union*, December 18 (3, 2), 1835.

73*Journal of the Georgia House, 1835*, pp. 205, 248.

74*Southern Record*, December 22 (3, 4), 1835. The report and resolutions may be found also in *Georgia Journal*, December 29 (3, 1-3), 1835; *Journal of the Georgia House, 1835*, pp. 427-33; *Acts of the General Assembly of the State of Georgia . . . November and December, 1835* (Milledgeville, 1836), 336-43.

75Louis Leary, "John Howard Payne's Southern Adventure: 1835," in *Library Notes. A Bulletin issued for the Friends of Duke University Library* (Durham, N. C.), No. 19 (February, 1948), 9.

76January 1 (3, 1), 1836.

77For the correspondence, see *Federal Union*, January 1 (3, 1-2), 1836; *Niles' Weekly Register*, XLIX, 343.

78For a copy of this article, see "Report from the Secretary of War," 573-79. Commenting on it, Payne said that he had considered it a public service to write a series of articles on the Cherokee problem, and "For this purpose I commenced such a series as I have spoken of, but having written one number, I thought I would lay it by for reconsideration, and forbear to make up my mind finally until I saw how matters were carried on at the Council then approaching." de Baillou, ed., *Payne to his Countrymen*, 16.

79de Baillou, ed., *Payne to his Countrymen*, 16.

80"Report from the Secretary of War," 577. See also *idid.*, 575.

81*Ibid.*, 575-76.   82de Baillou, ed., *Payne to his Countrymen*, 38.

83"Report from the Secretary of War," 576.   84*Ibid.*, 578.

85For a copy, see *Southern Banner*, December 10 (3, 2), 1835; *Federal Union*, December 11 (3, 3), 1835; *Richmond* (Virginia) *Enquirer*, December 10 (2, 5), 1835.

86de Baillou, ed., *Payne to his Countrymen*, 11.

87Battey, Jr., *Rome and Floyd County*, 78.

88A copy of this letter may be found in Leary, "John Howard Payne's Southern Adventure," 7.

89"Report from the Secretary of War," 488-89.

90December 12 (3, 4), 1835. It was reprinted in, at least, two Georgia newspapers, the *Augusta Constitutionalist*, December 24 (from which the de Baillou copy was taken) and the *Georgia Journal*, January 5 (1, 5-6; 2, 1-6; 3, 1), 1836.

91Quoted by Leary, "John Howard Payne's Southern Adventure," 6.

92de Baillou, ed., *Payne to his Countrymen*, 46-48.

93*Ibid.*, 16. For the text, see *ibid.*, 49-61.   94*Ibid.*, 49.

95*Ibid.*, 51.   96Leary, "John Howard Payne's Southern Adventure," 9.

97*Ibid.*

98*Georgia Journal*, December 22 (3, 1), 1835; "Report from the Secretary of War," 556.

99de Baillou, ed., *Payne to his Countrymen*, 38, 39.

100Leary, "John Howard Payne's Southern Adventure," 7.

101de Baillou, ed., *Payne to his Countrymen*, 18.

102Leary, "John Howard Payne's Southern Adventure," 9.

103*Ibid.*, 10.   104Hull, *Annals of Athens*, 116.

105Rutherford, *Flags and Flowers*, 12 (cols. 2-3).

106Hull, *Annals of Athens*, 117.

107A picture may be found in Evelyn Harden Jackson, *Souvenir of the Harden Home* (Athens, 1918), 6.

108Brainard, *Payne*, 59-60. The sketch of Payne in the *Dictionary of American Biography*, XIV, 327-29 does not mention the Mary Harden affair; and more remarkable, neither the *National Cyclopaedia of American Biography* nor *Appleton's Cyclopaedia of American Biography* mentions Payne's trip through the South.

109Harrison, *Payne*, 225.

110For some examples of how fiction is presented as fact, see Speer, "John Howard Payne's Southern Sweetheart," 359, *passim;* Rutherford, *Flags and Flowers*, 12; Knight, *Landmarks*, II, 62; Elinor Hillyer, "When Payne Courted Athens Girl," in *Atlanta Journal Magazine*, March 17 (4), 1929; Annie Hornady Howard and Florine Harden Smith, "The Romances of 'Home, Sweet Home'," in *Holland's The Magazine of the South*, Vol. 48 (October, 1929), 18, *passim*; Annie Hornady Howard, "A Red Rose for Love," in *Georgia Magazine* (Decatur), I (April-May, 1958), 24-27.

111Hull, *Annals of Athens*, 115.

112Howard and Smith, "Romance of 'Home, Sweet Home'," 18 (col. 3);

Speer, "John Howard Payne's Southern Sweetheart," 358-59; "John Howard Payne," in *Oglethorpe Echo* (Lexington, Ga.), October 12 (5, 2-3), 1906.

113Knight, *Landmarks*, II, 66; Rutherford, *Flags and Flowers*, 12 (col. 2); Howard and Smith, "Romance of 'Home, Sweet Home'," 18 (col. 3) Frances Letcher Mitchell, *Georgia Land and People* (Atlanta, 1893), 211 says that Payne came South to write articles for a newspaper with which he "was connected." In fact his own *Jam Jehan Nima* magazine never saw the light of day, and he was at no time connected with a newspaper.

114Knight, *Landmarks*, II, 67; Rutherford, *Flags and Flowers*, 12 (col. 2); Speer, "John Howard Payne's Southern Sweetheart," 359; undated clipping by "Cheshire" in folder in Evelyn Harden Jackson Collection, in University of Georgia Library.

115"Cheshire" clipping. See footnote above.

116Howard and Smith, "Romance of 'Home, Sweet Home'," 18. The place was misread as Gainesville for Carnesville. See Leary, "John Howard Payne's Southern Adventure," 7 (footnote 16).

117The album is in the Evelyn Harden Jackson Collection, in the University of Georgia Library. Mary Harden's signature may be found in this album.

118Athens *Daily Banner*, November 4 (2, 2), 1891. See also Athens *Daily and Weekly Banner* (Special Issue), November 24 (18, 6-7), 1899; Hull, *Annals of Athens*, 116; Knight, *Landmarks*, II, 68.

119*Dade County* (Trenton, Ga.) *Weekly Times*, June 24 (3, 4), 1887; Athens *Weekly Banner*, December 29 (5, 1-2), 1891; "Callaway" clipping in Mary Harden Album; "Carithers" Clipping in Mary Harden Album; "Cheshire" clipping, in Evelyn Harden Jackson Collection; Rutherford, *Flags and Flowers*, 12 (col. 4); Howard and Smith, "Romance of 'Home, Sweet Home'," 18 (col. 1). Hillyer, "When Payne Courted Athens Girl," says that Mary Harden's copy of "Home, Sweet Home" is mentioned in her will. Her will is recorded in Record of Wills, E, 107-108, in Office of Ordinary Clarke County, Georgia; but the MS is not mentioned.

120Evelyn Harden Diary, May 14, 1887. This diary is part of the Evelyn Harden Jackson Collection, in the University of Georgia Library.

121May 17 (2, 3), 1887. Evelyn Harden Jackson wrote in her Diary, May 25, 1887, "I trust she now has a home Sweeter than any earthly Home Sweet Home." Mary Harden willed to Evelyn Harden Jackson, after all her debts and expenses were paid, "the balance of my estate of every kind and description." Record of Wills, E, 107-108. When Miss Jackson opened the box in which Mary Harden kept her special mementoes and valuables, she found not only jewelry, silverware, and so on, "and the sweetest thing of all One little gold heart presented by her lover John Howard Payne & his love letters." Diary, May 19, 1887.

122Jackson, *Souvenir of the Harden Home*, 19; Letter from Helmer L. Webb, Librarian, Schaffer Library, Union College, Schnectady, N. Y., May 7, 1962, to E. M. Coulter. In Brainard, *Payne*, opposite page 53 is a facsimile of a copy of the song, which Payne made for Brainard, and autographed on August 10, 1850.

123An undated clipping from the *Murray County* (Georgia) *Messenger*, in Evelyn Harden Jackson Collection. See also Knight, *Landmarks*, II, 68.

124Quoted in *Federal Union*, December 4 (2, 6), 1835.

125"Memoirs of the Early Life and Times of Judge Junius Hillyer" (a typescript), 230-34. In University of Georgia Library.

126Quoted from undated *Charleston News* by *Weekly Constitutionalist*, April 22 (6, 3), 1857.

127Quoted by *Southern Watchman*, March 29 (2, 2), 1871.

128*Ibid.*

129*Huntsville* (Alabama) *Weekly Democrat*, June 21 (1, 4), 1882.

130See Foreman, ed., *Indian Justice*. See also Grant Foreman, "John Howard Payne and the Cherokee Indians," in *American Historical Review*,

XXXVII (July, 1932), 724. A large collection of Payne's Indian manuscripts are in the Ayer Collection, Newberry Library, Chicago.

131Harrison, *Payne*, 174, 310; Jackson, *Souvenir of the Harden Home*, 16; Sandersville *General Georgian*, April 2 (2, 3), 1857. See also Horace Montgomery, "Howell Cobb, Daniel Webster, and Jenny Lind," in *Georgia Historical Quarterly*, XLV (March, 1961), 37-41.

132Brainard, *Payne*, 99-100.

133Howard, "A Red Rose for Love," 27.

134It was a few days after the incident in New York, that Mary Harden spent the day with Evelyn Harden Jackson, as she mentions in her diary. Mary Harden was now very old and feeble and never visited outside of Athens.

135*Southern Watchman*, March 29 (2, 3), 1871.

Chapter VII

1M. M. Ponton, *Life and Times of Henry M. Turner* (Atlanta, 1917), 173; John W. Cromwell, "The First Negro Churches in the District of Columbia," in *Journal of Negro History*, VII (1922), 69.

2Dumas Malone, ed., *Dictionary of American Biography*, XIX, 65.

3*National Cyclopaedia of American Biography*, II (1899), 206.

4*Testimony Taken by the Joint Select Committee to Inquire into the Condition of Affairs in the Late Insurrectionary States* (13 vols. Washington, 1872), VII, Pt. 2, pp. 1084, 1085. Cited hereafter under the binder's title, *Ku Klux Conspiracy*.

5Athens *Southern Watchman*, July 21 (2, 2), 1868. In newspaper citations, the first number in the parentheses represents the page; subsequent number, the column.

6*Ku Klux Conspiracy*, VII, Pt. 2, p. 1085.

7Macon *American Union*, July 30 (2, 4), 1869.   8*Ibid*., July 16 (2, 1), 1869.

9For information on Turner's early life, see Ponton, *Turner*, 33-35; Albert Nelson Marquis, ed., *Who's Who in America* (Chicago), VIII (1914-1915), 2382; "Rev. H. M. Turner," in *Harper's Weekly* (New York), VII (December 12, 1863), 796; *Ku Klux Conspiracy*, VII, Pt. 2, p. 1034; Malone, ed., *Dictionary of American Biography*, XIX, 65; *National Cyclopaedia of American Biography*, II, 206; Ethel Maude Christler, "Participation of Negroes in the Government of Georgia, 1867-1870" (MS Thesis, Atlanta University, June 1932), 23.

10*Ku Klux Conspiracy*, VII, Pt. 2, p. 1034. See also Malone, ed., *Dictionary of American Biography*, XIX, 65-66; *Appletons' Cyclopaedia of American Biography* (Revised edition), VI (1900), 186.

11Ponton, *Turner*, 69.

12"Condition of Affairs in Georgia," being *House of Representatives Miscellaneous Document*, No. 52, 40th Cong., 3d sess (1869), 12; *Appletons' Cyclopaedia of American Biography*, VI, 186.

13*Ku Klux Conspiracy*, VII, Pt. 2, p. 1034.   14*Ibid*., 1041.

15*Ibid*., 1188-89.   16*Ibid*., 1187.   17*Ibid*., 1184.

18Milledgeville *Southern Recorder*, January 30 (1, 4), 1866.

19*National Cyclopaedia of American Biography*, II, 206. See also **Griffin** *American Union*, January 24 (3, 2), March 20 (2, 4), 1868. J. Clarke Swayze started the *American Union* in Griffin, Georgia, on August 16, 1867. He transferred it to Macon in 1868, the last issue in Griffin being May 1, 1868. He said that he founded the paper to "tend to diminish the lustre of Rebel honor." *Ibid*., August 16 (2, 1), 1867. The last issue of the paper was January 2, 1873.

20*Ku Klux Conspiracy*, VII, Pt. 2, p. 1188.

21Griffin *American Union*, November 8 (3, 1), 1867.

22*Ibid*. (Macon), July 6 (2, 1), 1871.

[23]Christler, "Negroes in Government of Georgia," 93.

[24]*Journal of the Proceedings of the Constitutional Convention of the People of Georgia, Held in the City of Atlanta in the Months of December, 1867, and January, February and March*, 1868 (Augusta, 1868), 68, 75.

[25]Macon *American Union*, June 5 (2, 5), 1868.

[26]*Constitutional Convention, 1867-1868*, p. 279; *Ku Klux Conspiracy*, VII, Pt. 2, p. 1041.

[27]Macon *American Union*, August 28 (2, 1), 1868.

[28]Macon *Georgia Weekly Telegraph*, March 13 (4, 1), 1868. See also Christler, "Negroes in Government of Georgia," 85.

[29]Atlanta *Georgia Weekly Opinion*, October 8 (1, 2), 1867.

[30]"Condition of Affairs in Georgia," 12.

[31]Christler, "Negroes in Government of Georgia," 93.

[32]"Condition of Affairs in Georgia," 11.

[33]Macon *Georgia Weekly Telegraph*, May 29 (2, 2), 1868.

[34]*Ibid.*, May 15 (8, 5), 1868.   [35]*Ibid.*, May 29 (2, 2), 1868.

[36]*Ibid.*, May 22 (5, 3), 1868.   [37]*Ibid.*, June 5 (3, 3), 1868.

[38]*Ibid.*, May 22 (5, 3), 1868. While in Washington, Turner had a conference with Salmon P. Chase, Chief Justice of the United States Supreme Court, relative to education.

[39]*Ibid.*, June 5 (3, 3), 1868.   [40]*Ku Klux Conspiracy*, VII, Pt. 2, p. 1034.

[41]*Constitutional Convention, 1867-1868, passim;* Griffin *American Union*, January 24 (2, 6), 1868; C. Mildred Thompson, *Reconstruction in Georgia, Economic, Social, Political, 1865-1872* (Studies in History, Economics and Public Law, Vol. LXIV, Columbia University, New York, 1915), 189, 190. "The Atlanta Intelligencer published, a few days ago, a speech delivered by a negro delegate in the Bradley Convention, calling himself Mr. Turner. The negro is, perhaps, the most intellectual man of his race in that body— the most intelligent, polished and experienced public speaker among them— for he has been a preacher for several years. Well, we read the speech calmly and cooly, just to see what a negro could do, and frankly admit that it was a little better than we expected; but notwithstanding all this, we will venture the opinion that every man who reads it, will come to the conclusion that negroes are entirely unfitted for intellectual employment. It is the most abominable attempt at speaking we have ever met with, and would, if circulated among the Northern people, cure them at once of every thing like negro worship.

"The career of [Aaron Alpeoria] Bradley, Turner, and their sable brethern, as legislators, will, we think, satisfy all sensible darkies that legislation is not 'Sambo's' *forte!*" Athens *Southern Watchman*, February 19 (2, 3), 1868.

[42]*Ku Klux Conspiracy*, VII, Pt. 2, p. 1035.

[43]*Journal of the House of Representatives of the State of Georgia . . . Commenced . . . July 4th, 1868* (Macon, 1868), 169, 219; Augusta *Weekly Chronicle & Sentinel*, September 2 (2, 6), 1868. On one occasion, Turner's wife insisted on riding in the railway car with the white people, and on refusing to move to the Negro car when asked to do so, she was taken by the arm and ejected. Augusta *Weekly Constitutionalist*, August 25 (4, 6), 1869. As further evidence of Turner's conservative attitude toward the white people, he voted for a resolution calling for the removal of disabilities imposed in the Third Section of of the XIV Amendment. The editor of the *Southern Watchman*, July 29 (2, 3), 1868, praised Turner for his vote and also for his "sensible speech—claiming that it was unjust to give the negroes unrestricted privileges and discriminate against the whites!"

[44]Augusta *Weekly Chronicle & Sentinel*, September 9 (2, 8), 1868.

[45]*Weekly Atlanta Intelligencer*, September 9 (4, 1), 1868.

[46]Turner's speech was printed in pamphlet form. It is copied in Christler, "Negroes in Government of Georgia," 82-96 (for quotations, 82, 83, 94). See also *Georgia House Journal, 1868*, p. 241; *Weekly Atlanta Intelligencer*, September 9 (4, 1), 1868; Augusta *Weekly Chronicle & Sentinel*, July, August,

passim, 1868; W. E. Burghardt Du Bois, *Black Reconstruction* . . . (New York, 1935), 502.

47*Georgia House Journal, 1868*, p. 243.

48*The Nation* (New York), VII (September 10, 1868), 201. See also Athens *Southern Watchman*, September 9 (2, 3), 1868.

49*Ibid.*

50Macon *American Union*, March 16 (2, 1), 1871. See also Christler, "Negroes in Government of Georgia," 92.

51Macon *American Union*, September 25 (3, 2), 1868.

52*Ibid.*, September 18 (3, 2), October 9 (3, 2), 1868.

53*Ibid.*, December 4 (3, 3), 1868.

54*Journal of the House of Representatives of the State of Georgia . . . Session . . . Commenced . . . January 10, 1870* (Atlanta, 1870), Pt. 1, p. 126.

55*Ibid.*, 428; Augusta *Weekly Chronicle & Sentinel*, August 31 (4, 3), 1870.

56Macon *American Union*, May 27 (2, 5), 1870.   57*Ibid.*, July 30 (2, 4), 1869.

58*Ku Klux Conspiracy*, VII, Pt. 2, pp 1091-92.

59Macon *American Union*, December 15 (2, 5), 1870.

60*Ibid.*, August 3 (2, 1), 1871.   61*Ibid.*, January 19 (2, 1-2), 1871.

62*Ibid.*, August 31 (2, 1), 1871.   63*Ibid.*, October 29 (2, 1), 1869.

64*Ibid.*, November 6 (3, 2), 1868.

65*Ibid.*, June 22 (1, 1), 1871. On another occasion there had to be a "kallecshun fur to furnish brudder Turner . . wid bacca and beer money." *Ibid.*

66Ponton, *Turner*, 70.

67Augusta *Weekly Chronicle & Sentinel*, July 28 (1, 7), 1869; Augusta *Weekly Constitutionalist*, July 28 (3, 2), 1868; Macon *American Union*, September 12 (2, 3), 1872.

68*Ku Klux Conspiracy*, VII, pt. 2, p. 1085.

69Augusta *Weekly Constitutionalist*, June 9 (5, 5), 1869, quoting the *Macon Telegraph*, without date.

70Athens *Southern Watchman*, June 30 (2, 1), 1869.

71Augusta *Weekly Chronicle & Sentinel*, July 21 (3, 1), 1869.

72*Ibid.*, July 14 (1, 8), 1869.

73*Ibid.*, July 21 (2, 7), July 28 (1, 7; 4, 2-3), 1869.

74Augusta *Weekly Constitutionalist*, July 21 (3, 5), July 28 (3, 5), 1869; Augusta *Weekly Chronicle & Sentinel*, July 21 (3, 1), July 28 (4, 3), 1869; Macon *American Union*, August 13 (2, 5), August 27 (1, 5), August 27 (1, 2), September 24 (2, 5), 1869.

75Augusta *Weekly Chronicle & Sentinel*, July 14 (1, 4), July 21 (2, 7), July 28 (2, 2; 4, 3), August 4 (2, 5), November 17 (3, 1), 1869; Augusta *Weekly Constitutionalist*, July 28 (3, 4; 3, 5), 1869; *Greensboro Herald*, August 12 (2, 2), 1869.

76Macon *American Union*, July 23 (2, 5-6), 1869. See also Augusta *Weekly Chronicle & Sentinel*, July 21 (2, 7), August 4 (1, 8), 1869.

77*Ku Klux Conspiracy*, VII, Pt. 2, pp. 1084, 1090; Augusta *Weekly Constitutionalist*, July 21 (3, 6), July 28 (3, 3; 3, 6), 1869; Augusta *Weekly Chronicle & Sentinel*, July 21 (2, 7; 4, 5), July 28 (1, 7-8), August 4 (2, 5), 1869; Macon *American Union*, August 6 (2, 2), 1869; Athens *Southern Watchman*, July 21 (2, 2), 1869; *Weekly Atlanta Intelligencer*, July 21 (3, 5), 1869.

78Augusta *Chronicle & Sentinel*, August 4 (2, 5), 1869.

79*Ibid.*, July 28 (4, 4), 1869. See also *ibid.*, July 28 (1, 8), 1869.

80Macon *American Union*, July 30 (3, 3), 1869.

81*Greensboro Herald*, July 22 (2, 1), 1869.   82*Ibid*, August 12 (2, 2), 1869.

83Macon *American Union*, August 13 (2, 5), 1869, quoting *Macon Telegraph* without date.

84Augusta *Weekly Chronicle & Sentinel*, August 4 (2, 1), 1869.

85*Ibid.*, July 28 (2, 2), 1869. "The Government should not be permitted to shield him for fear of the political effect that his punishment might have on the Radical party." Editorial in *Greensboro Herald*, August 12 (2, 2), 1869.

[86]Macon *American Union*, August 27 (2, 1), 1869.

[87]*Ibid.*, March 7 (2, 3), 1872. [88]*Ibid.*, August 27 (2, 6), 1869.

[89]Augusta *Weekly Chronicle & Sentinel*, August 4 (2, 5), 1869.

[90]*Ibid.*, September 22 (2, 4), 1869; Macon *American Union*, September 24 (2, 5), October 1 (2, 4), 1869.

[91]*Ku Klux Conspiracy*, VII, Pt. 2, p. 1085. See also Augusta *Weekly Chronicle & Sentinel*, August 4 (2, 5), 1869.

[92]*Ku Klux Conspiracy*, VII, Pt. 2, p. 1091. [93]*Ibid.*, 1094.

[94]*Ibid.*, 1196. [95]Macon *American Union*, March 7 (2, 3), 1872.

[96]*Ibid.*, June 15 (2, 3), 1871.

[97]*Ku Klux Conspiracy*, VII, Pt. 2, pp. 1085, 1193, 1196, 1197; Augusta *Weekly Constitutionalist*, June 9 (5, 5), August 25 (2, 6), 1869; *Greensboro Herald*, August 26 (3, 4), 1869; Macon *American Union*, June 11 (3, 2), 1869.

[98]Athens *Southern Watchman*, July 28 (3, 3), 1868.

[99]Macon *American Union*, January 29 (2, 3), 1869.

[100]*Ku Klux Conspiracy*, VII, Pt. 2, p. 1036. See also "Condition of Affairs in Georgia," 11; Macon *American Union*, October 22 (3, 4-5), 1869; June 15 (2, 2), 1871.

[101]Macon *American Union*, February 26 (3, 4), 1869.

[102]"Condition of Affairs in Georgia," 10-12.

[103]Macon *American Union*, March 26 (2, 4), 1869.

[104]*Ku Klux Conspiracy*, VII, Pt. 2, p. 1036.

[105]Macon *American Union*, September 25 (3, 2), 1868.

[106]*Ibid.*, November 20 (1, 3), 1868. [107]*Ibid.*, October 23 (2, 3), 1868.

[108]"Condition of Affairs in Georgia," 12.

[109]*Ku Klux Conspiracy*, VII, Pt. 2, p. 1037. [110]*Ibid.*, 1042.

[111]*Ibid.*, 1189. [112]*Ibid.*, 1086.

[113]*Greensboro Herald*, October 7 (2, 3), 1869.

[114]*Ku Klux Conspiracy*, VII, Pt. 2, p. 1039.

[115]*Ibid.*, 1035. [116]*Ibid.*, 1042. [117]*Ibid.*, 1187.

[118]*Ibid.*, 1091. See also *ibid.*, 1084, 1085, 1090.

[119]*Ibid.*, I, 353. For text of the law, see *Acts and Resolutions of the General Assembly of the State of Georgia . . . 1870* (Atlanta, 1870), 62-66.

[120]*Ku Klux Conspiracy*, VII, Pt. 2, 1184. See also *ibid.*, 1188, 1189.

[121]*Ibid.*, 1039-38. [122]*Greensboro Herald*, November 17 (2, 1), 1870.

[123]Augusta *Weekly Chronicle & Sentinel*, January 4, (1, 4), 1871.

[124]*Ibid.*, January 4 (1, 6), 1871.

[125]*Journal of the House of Representatives of the State of Georgia . . . 1871* (Atlanta, 1872), 8, 11, 23-24.

[126]Macon *American Union*, December 29 (2, 4), 1870.

[127]*Ibid.*, June 15, 1871.

[128]Malone, ed., *Dictionary of American Biography*, XIX, 66; *Appletons' Cyclopaedia of American Biography*, VI, 186.

[129]Macon *American Union*, March 7 (2, 3), 1872.

[130]Malone, ed., *Dictionary of American Biography*, XIX, 66; *Journal of Negro History*, XLIV (1959), 237; *Atlanta Constitution*, May 9 (8a, 4), 1915.

[131]*Atlanta Constitution*, November 15 (1, 5), 1887.

[132]Macon *American Union*, January 11 (2, 2), 1872.

[133]H. M. Turner, *The Barbarous Decision of the United States Supreme Court Declaring the Civil Rights Act Unconstitutional and Disrobing the Colored Race of Civil Protection. The most Cruel and Inhumane Verdict against a Loyal People in the History of the World* (Atlanta, 1893), 3; *Atlanta Constitution*, July 14 (5, 1), 1890.

[134]Turner, *Barbarous Decision*, 64. [135]*Ibid.*, 64. [136]*Ibid.*, 4.

[137]*Ibid.*, 62. [138]*Ibid.*, 3.

[139]Marquis, ed., *Who's Who in America*, VIII (1914-1915), 2382.

[140]*Atlanta Constitution*, July 14 (5, 1), 1890.

141*Ibid.*, September 22 (1, 2), 1891.

142*Ibid.*, July 14 (5, 1), 1890.   143*Ibid.*, September 26 (4, 1), 1891.

144Marquis, ed., *Who's Who in America*, VIII (1914-1915), 2382. In 1872 Turner was awarded the LL. D. degree by the University of Pennsylvania; and the next year Wilberforce University conferred on him the degree of Doctor of Divinty. *Ibid.*, 2382; Ponton, *Turner*, 36.

145Ponton, *Turner*, 60, 142; *Elberton Star* (Georgia), February 22 (4, 3), 1906.

146Malone, ed., *Dictionary of American Biography*, XIX, 66; *Atlanta Journal*, May 9 (7, 3), 1915; *Atlanta Constitution*, December 4 (1, 5), 1907. The obituary in the *Atlanta Journal* contained much misinformation. Turner had a flair for literary activities. He started several periodicals, wrote a book on Methodism, a catechism, and a hymn book.

CHAPTER VIII

1John C. Butler, *Historical Record of Macon and Central Georgia* . . . (Macon, 1879), 74; *Acts of the General Assembly of the State of Georgia* . . . *November and December, 1829* (Milledgeville, 1830), 181-82; Greensboro *Herald and Journal*, August 12 (1, 1), 1887. The numbers in parentheses in newspaper citations refer to the page and the column, respectively.

2*Atlanta Constitution*, August 17 (4, 6), 1887.

3Athens *Weekly Banner-Watchman*, August 9 (3, 3), 1887.

4*Atlanta Constitution*, August 10 (3, 3), 1889.

5*Ibid.*, August 7 (5, 3), 1887.

6*Calhoun Times* (Georgia), August 11 (1, 1), 1887. This writer visited the site of the house on April 16, 1964. Nothing was left except two large piles of brick and stones, marking the chimney places; a depression, appearing to have been the cellar; a well nearly filled up near a cedar tree; some shrubbery; and a large holly tree, marking the site where Susan M. Woolfolk, Richard's first wife, was buried. On the bottom terrace were two wells; remnants of chimneys; and a pile of stone between two trees, which appeared to be a grave.

7*Atlanta Constitution*, August 11 (3, 3), 1887.

8Athens *Weekly Banner-Watchman*, August 16 (1, 3), 1887; *Calhoun Times*, August 11 (1, 10), 1887; *Macon Telegraph*, December 13 (1, 3), 1887. All references to the *Macon Telegraph* are to the weekly edition.

9Bibb County Deed Record (in courthouse in Macon), Vol. U, 271; *Atlanta Constitution*, August 14 (6, 1), 1887; Greensboro *Herald and Journal*, August 12 (1, 1), 1887.

10Bibb County Deed Record, Vol. X, 243.

11*Ibid.*, Vol. QQ, 401; *Atlanta Constitution*, August 11 (3, 3), 1887.

12*Macon Telegraph*, December 13 (1, 5), 1887; *Atlanta Constitution*, August 7 (5, 4), 1887.

13*Atlanta Constitution*, August 12 (3, 4), 1887; *ibid.*, February 16 (2, 2), 1888; *Calhoun Times*, August 11 (1, 2), 1887; Greensboro *Herald and Journal*, August 12 (2, 2), 1887.

14*Atlanta Constitution*, August 8 (2, 2), 1887.

15*Ibid.*, August 13 (3, 1), 1887.   16*Ibid.*, March 9 (3, 2), 1888.

17*Ibid.*, August 11 (3, 3), 1887.   18*Ibid.*, August 13 (3, 1), 1887.

19*Ibid.*, August 8 (2, 1-2), 1887.

20Athens *Weekly Banner-Watchman*, August 9 (3, 3), August 16 (1, 3), 1887.

21*Calhoun Times*, August 11 (1, 2), 1887.

22*Atlanta Constitution*, August 12 (3, 4), August 18 (4, 6), 1887.

23*Macon Telegraph*, December 13 (6, 6), 1887.

24*Atlanta Constitution*, August 20 (4, 6), 1887.

25Athens *Weekly Banner-Watchman*, August 9 (3, 4), 1887; *Atlanta Constitution*, August 7 (5), 1887.

26Athens *Weekly Banner-Watchman*, August 16 (1, 4), 1887; *Atlanta Constitution*, August 10 (3, 3), 1887.

27*Atlanta Constitution*, August 16 (3, 3), 1887.

28*Ibid.*, August 8 (2, 1-2), 1887; Greensboro *Herald and Journal*, August 12 (2, 2), 1887.

29*Atlanta Constitution*, August 7 (5, 2; 5, 3; 5, 5), 1887; Athens *Weekly Banner-Watchman*, August 9 (3, 3), December 13 (3, 2), 1887; Athens *Weekly Banner*, August 5 (4, 2), 1890; *Calhoun Times*, August 11 (1, 1), 1887; Greensboro *Herald and Journal*, August 12 (1, 1; 2, 2; 2, 2-3), 1887. Tom said, "I had to jump out of the window when they came or they would have gotten me too." *Calhoun Times* (quoting the *Atlanta Constitution*), August 11 (1, 1), 1887. The quotation in the narrative is from the *Atlanta Constitution*, August 7 (5, 4), 1887.

30*Atlanta Constitution*, August 7 (5, 1), August 8 (1, 1-3; 1, 6; 2, 6), 1887.

31*Ibid.*, August 7 (5, 1), 1887; *Calhoun Times*, August 11 (1, 1), 1887.

32Greensboro *Herald and Journal*, August 12 (1, 1; 4, 4), December 9 (1, 1), 1887.

33*Calhoun Times*, August 11 (2, 1), 1887.

34*Atlanta Constitution*, August 25 (8, 2), 1887.

35*Ibid.*, August 16 (3, 3), 1887.

36*Macon Telegraph*, August 9 (1, 2), 1887.

37*Atlanta Constitution*, August 11 (8, 3), 1887.

38Athens *Weekly Banner-Watchman*, August 16 (4, 2), 1887.

39*Ibid.*, August 9 (3, 3), 1887.

40Quoted in *Atlanta Constitution*, August 10 (4, 4), 1887.

41*Ibid.*, August 8 (1, 3), 1887. See also *ibid.*, August 7 (5, 5), 1887.

42Athens *Weekly Banner-Watchman*, August 16 (1, 1), 1887. The undertaker's charges were $583.50. *Atlanta Constitution*, August 20 (4, 6), 1887. This writer visited the graves on April 16, 1964. They were entirely bricked-over level with the ground, without markers of any kind. But on the top step, of marble, leading down to the plot, was engraved the name WOOLFOLK.

43*Atlanta Constitution*, August 8 (1, 1), 1887.

44*Ibid.*, August 8 (1, 4), 1887.   45*Ibid.*, October 30 (2, 1), 1890.

46*Ibid.*, August 13 (7, 1), 1887.

47*Ibid.*, August 10 (7, 1), August 11 (8, 3), 1887.

48*Ibid.*, August 9 (7, 1), 1887.   49*Ibid.*, August 13 (7. 1), 1887.

50*Macon Telegraph*, August 30 (1, 2), 1887.

51*Atlanta Constitution*, August 10 (7, 1), 1887. See also Athens *Weekly Banner-Watchman*, August 16 (1, 1), 1887.

52Athens *Weekly Banner-Watchman*, August 23 (2, 7), 1887; *Atlanta Constitution*, November 9 (3, 3), 1887. Rutherford died in March, 1891. *Ibid.*, March 11 (2, 1), March 13 (2, 2), 1891.

53Bibb County Deed Record, Vol. QQ, 481.   54*Ibid.*, 482.

55*Ibid.*, Vol. TT, 496, 497.

56*Calhoun Times*, September 8 (2, 3), 1887; Athens *Weekly Banner-Watchman*, August 23 (2, 7), 1887.

57*Atlanta Constitution*, October 27 (2, 4), 1887.

58*Ibid.*, November 22 (2, 2), 1887; *Macon Telegraph*, August 23 (7, 6), 1887.

59Athens *Weekly Banner-Watchman*, December 13 (3, 1; 3, 3-4), 1887; *Macon Telegraph*, December 13 (5, 4), 1887; *Atlanta Constitution*, December 7 (2, 3), 1887.

60Athens *Weekly Banner-Watchman*, December 13 (3, 1), 1887.

61*Atlanta Constitution*, December 15 (2, 1), 1887.

62Greensboro *Herald and Journal*, December 9 (1, 1), 1887; *Macon Telegraph*, December 13 (1, 4), December 20 (4, 6), 1887; Athens *Weekly Banner-Watchman*, December 13 (3, 2-3), 1887.

63Woolfolk *vs* The State of Georgia, in *Reports of Cases in Law and Equity, Argued and Determined in the Supreme Court of Georgia. Parts of March and October Terms, 1888* (Atlanta, 1889), Vol. 81, p. 553.

64*Atlanta Constitution*, December 9 (2, 1), 1887.

65*Georgia Reports*, Vol. 81, p. 558.

66*Macon Telegraph*, December 13 (12, 1), 1887; *Atlanta Constitution*, December 11 (10, 3), 1887.

67*Macon Telegraph*, December 13 (6, 6), 1887.

68*Atlanta Constitution*, December 10 (2, 3), 1887.

69*Georgia Reports*, Vol. 81, p. 565; Athens *Weekly Banner-Watchman*, December 20 (1, 2), 1887; *Atlanta Constitution*, March 1 (3, 3), 1889; *Macon Telegraph*, August 14 (8, 4), 1889.

70*Reports of Cases Argued and Decided in the Supreme Court of Georgia at the March Term, 1890* (Atlanta, 1891), Vol. 85, p. 108; *Macon Telegraph*, December 13 (7, 2), 1887.

71*Atlanta Constitution*, December 11 (12, 2), 1887.

72*Ibid.*, December 13 (1, 6), 1887; Athens *Weekly Banner-Watchman*, December 20 (1, 6-7), 1887; *Macon Telegraph*, December 20 (4, 2-3), 1887.

73*Atlanta Constitution*, December 18 (15, 1), 1887.

74*Macon Telegraph*, December 20 (6, 2-3), 1887; Athens *Weekly Banner-Watchman*, December 20 (1, 6), 1887.

75*Macon Telegraph*, December 20 (4, 5-6), 1887; Athens *Weekly Banner-Watchman*, December 20 (1, 6), 1887.

76*Macon Telegraph*, December 20 (6, 6), 1887; Athens *Weekly Banner-Watchman*, December 20 (3, 8), 1887.

77Athens *Weekly Banner-Watchman*, December 20 (3, 1), 1887; *Atlanta Constitution*, December 17 (7, 1), 1887.

78*Oglethorpe Echo* (Lexington, Ga.) December 23 (2, 2), 1887.

79Athens *Weekly Banner-Watchman*, December 20 (2, 2), 1887.

80*Atlanta Constitution*, December 17 (7, 1), 1887.

81*Ibid.*, December 17 (7, 1), 1887; Athens *Weekly Banner-Watchman*, December 20 (3, 7), 1887.

82*Atlanta Constitution*, December 30 (2, 1), 1887; *Macon Telegraph*, January 3 (3, 4), 1887.

83*Macon Telegraph*, December 20 (1, 1), 1887.

84*Atlanta Constitution*, December 20 (4, 5), 1887. See also *Calhoun Times*, January 26 (2, 2), 1888; *Macon Telegraph*, December 27 (8, 1), 1887; *ibid.*, February 14 (10, 3-4), 1888.

85*Atlanta Constitution*, July 23 (5, 3), 1888.

86*Ibid.*, January 31 (4, 4), February 12 (8, 2), 1889.

87*Georgia Reports*, Vol. 81, pp. 559-60. See also *ibid.*, 551-53, 558; *Atlanta Constitution*, February 1 (8, 1), 1889.

88*Atlanta Constitution*, February 12 (8, 2), 1889.

89*Ibid.*, March 6 (8, 3), 1889.   90*Ibid.*, March 8 (3, 1), March 12 (3, 2), 1889.

91*Ibid.*, March 7 (3, 3), 1889.   92*Ibid.*, March 8 (3, 1), 1889.

93*Ibid.*, March 9 (3, 1), 1889.   94*Ibid.*, March 12 (3, 1), 1889.

95*Ibid.*, March 13 (3, 3), March 14 (3, 2), 1889.

96*Ibid.*, March 15 (3, 3), 1889.

97Athens *Banner-Watchman* (daily), May 19 (1, 4), 1889.

98*Ibid.*, May 8 (1, 1), 1889; *Atlanta Constitution*, March 14 (7, 1), May 29 (3, 3), May 30 (3, 3), June 8 (3, 3), June 15 (4, 6), 1889.

99*Atlanta Constitution*, June 4 (3, 4), June 5 (3, 5), June 7 (3, 5), 1889. See also *Georgia Reports*, Vol. 85, pp. 83-97.

100*Atlanta Constitution*, June 6 (3, 5), June 8 (3, 3), June 9 (3, 5), June 11 (1, 1), 1889.

101*Athens Weekly Chronicle*, June 22 (2, 7), 1889; *Atlanta Constitution*, June 18 (3, 3), 1889.

102*Athens Weekly Chronicle*, April 27 (2, 2), 1889; *Atlanta Constitution*, April 23 (3, 4), June 16 (12, 5-6), 1889.

103*Atlanta Constitution*, September 20 (3, 1), September 22 (5, 4), 1887; Athens *Weekly Banner-Watchman*, September 27 (1, 3; 1, 5), 1887; *Macon Telegraph*, December 13 (1, 6), 1887.

104*Macon Telegraph*, December 13 (5, 1-2), 1887; *Atlanta Constitution*, September 21 (7, 1), 1887.

105*Macon Telegraph*, October 25 (11, 2), 1887; *Atlanta Constitution*, May 10 (3, 3), June 11 (3, 5), July 3 (5, 5), July 7 (2, 3), 1889.

106*Atlanta Constitution*, June 16 (12, 5), 1889.

107*Ibid.*, June 17 (3, 6), 1889.

108*Ibid.*, June 13 (2, 2), 1889. Property was much on Tom's mind both before the murder and afterwards. Assuming that Tom did the murder, some people believed that he had used an axe or might have used some other method to wreak his vengenance, but not to burn the house, for that was property which he wanted. And he killed everyone, even the infant, for he wanted no one to come betwen him and his inheritance. The homestead and fifty acres of land belonged to his stepmother and would have descended to her children if any had been spared. If she had died first, and none of her children were left, then her husband would have received the property and after his death it would have gone to Tom and his two sisters. In a mass killing, it was held to be the presumption in law that the strongest die last (as in a shipwreck), but in the Woolfolk murder case it might be presumed that the assassin killed the strongest first, who would be trying to defend the weak. For contemporary discussions, see *Macon Telegraph*, January 10 (1, 3), 1888; *Atlanta Constitution*, August 7 (5, 4), August 9 (7, 1), August 10 (7, 1), October 9 (10, 1), November 6 (10, 1), November 13 (11, 5), December 20 (4, 5-6), 1887; *ibid.*, November 5 (5, 2), 1890.

109*Atlanta Constitution*, June 19 (3, 3), June 20 (3, 4), June 21 (3, 5), June 22 (3, 3), June 23 (10, 1), June 25 (1, 1), 1889.

110*Athens Weekly Chronicle*, June 29 (2, 5), 1889; *Atlanta Constitution*, June 26 (2, 3), July 22 (3, 3), 1889.

111*Athens Weekly Chronicle*, August 23 (1, 8), 1889; *Atlanta Constitution*, July 7 (2, 2), 1889.

112*Macon Telegraph*, November 15 (10, 2), 1887; *Atlanta Constitution*, July 22 (3, 3), 1889; *ibid.*, May 13 (3, 1), 1890.

113*Atlanta Constitution*, July 7 (2, 3), 1889. See also *ibid.*, August 29 (3, 1), 1889.

114*Ibid.*, July 20 (3, 5), 1889.

115*Athens Weekly Chronicle*, August 17 (3, 3), August 23 (1, 4), 1889; *Atlanta Constitution*, August 11 (12, 4), August 15 (3, 3), August 31 (3, 3), 1889.

116*Atlanta Constitution*, May 13 (3, 1), 1890. See also *ibid.*, March 3 (2, 3), May 11 (14, 2), July 8 (4, 4), 1890.

117*Georgia Reports*, Vol. 85, pp. 75, 76, 83-97. See also *Atlanta Constitution*, June 4 (5, 3), 1890.

118*Georgia Reports*, Vol. 85, pp. 108-109. See also *ibid.*, 105-106.

119*Ibid.*, 99.   120*Ibid.*, 104.   121*Ibid.*, 79

122*Athens Weekly Banner*, August 5 (4, 2), 1890; *Atlanta Constitution*, July 29 (6, 1-3), 1890; *Macon Telegraph*, August 6 (3, 1), 1890. The Woolfolk trials were a great expense to Bibb County. Up to June, 1890, four months before the further expenses of keeping Tom in jail and hanging him, the county had spent $25,000. *Atlanta Constitution*, June 5 (6, 1), 1890. See also *Athens Weekly Chronicle*, June 15 (1, 2), 1890; *Atlanta Constitution*, June 12 (3, 4), August 11 (12, 4), 1889.

123*Atlanta Constitution*, January 15 (5, 3), 1890.

124Athens *Weekly Banner-Watchman*, November 15 (4, 1), 1887; *Macon Telegraph*, November 22 (8, 3), 1887; January 10 (8, 5), March 27 (1, 6),

1888; November 5 (5, 6), 1890; *Atlanta Constitution*, November 16 (3, 1), 1887; January 4 (2, 4), March 24 (9, 1), 1888.

125*Macon Telegraph*, April 24 (2, 7), 1888.

126*Ibid.*, December 13 (6, 3), 1887; *Atlanta Constitution*, February 18 (2, 2), 1888; March 13 (3, 3-4), June 12 (3, 1), 1889.

127*Macon Telegraph*, April 24 (2, 7), 1888.

128*Atlanta Constitution*, April 6 (4, 1-4), 1890. For an article on death by hanging or by electricity, see *Macon Telegraph*, January 31 (4, 4), 1888.

129Athens *Banner-Watchman* (daily), May 8 (1, 1), 1889.

130For quotation, see *Macon Telegraph*, October 4 (11, 3), 1887. See also *Athens Weekly Chronicle*, August 10 (1, 7), 1889; *Atlanta Constitution*, July 26 (3, 4), August 2 (3, 2), 1889.

131For quotation, see *Macon Telegraph*, November 15 (10, 2), 1887. See also *ibid.*, August 14 (8, 3), 1889; *Athens Weekly Chronicle*, August 23 (1, 8), 1889.

132For quotation, see *Athens Weekly Banner*, February 25 (3, 5), 1890. See also *Macon Telegraph*, December 27 (8, 1), 1887; *Calhoun Times*, December 5 (2, 2), 1889; *Atlanta Constitution*, December 2 (2, 2), 1889.

133*Atlanta Constitution*, July 29 (6, 3), 1890.

134*Macon Telegraph*, August 6 (3, 1-2), 1890.

135*Ibid.*, August 6 (3, 2), 1890.

136*Ibid.*, August 6 (6, 8), 1890.   137*Ibid.*, August 6 (3, 2), 1890.

138*Atlanta Constitution*, January 2 (2, 2), January 5 (page 4), January 16 (2, 3), October 3 (2, 2), 1890.

139*Ibid.*, September 17 (3, 2), October 8 (2, 1), October 10 (1, 6), 1890; *Macon Telegraph*, October 15 (2, 6), 1890.

140*Atlanta Constitution*, October 29 (1, 3), 1890.

141*Macon Telegraph*, October 29 (7, 6), 1890. See also *ibid.*, November 5 (5, 1; 5, 2), 1890.

142*Atlanta Constitution*, October 29 (1, 1-3), 1890.

143*Ibid.*, October 30 (1, 1), 1890; *Macon Telegraph*, November 5 (5, 2), 1890.

144*Macon Telegraph*, November 5 (5, 3), 1890.

145*Athens Weekly Banner*, November 4 (5, 1), 1890.

146*Atlanta Constitution*, October 25 (3, 2), 1890; *Macon Telegraph*, October 29 (7, 6-7), 1890. The branch was sometimes erroneously called Fanny Graham.

147*Macon Telegraph*, November 5 (5, 3), 1890. See also *Athens Weekly Banner*, November 4 (5, 1), 1890.

148*Macon Telegraph*, November 5 (5, 1-6), 1890. See also *Atlanta Constitution*, October 31 (2, 1), 1890. The inscription on the tombstone gives the date of Tom's death as October 28, 1890. He was sentenced to hang on the 29th, and that was the date of his hanging.

149Greensboro *Herald-Journal*, October 31 (1, 6), 1890.

150*Athens Weekly Banner*, November 4 (5, 2), 1890.

151*Atlanta Constitution*, October 30 (4, 2), 1890.

152For example, see *ibid.*, January 25 (15, 5), 1891.

CHAPTER IX

1For a full and scholarly discussion of the dispersal of the Acadians, see Oscar William Winzerling, *Acadian Odyssey* (Baton Rouge, 1955). Note here page 155.

2*Ibid.*, 11.

3The two Georgia historians Stevens and Jones treat the subject of the Acadians in Georgia in a very cursory fashion, devoting most of their attention to the Acadians in general without reference to Georgia. See William Bacon Stevens, *A History of Georgia from the First Discovery by Europeans* to the *Adoption of the Present Constitution* MDCCXCVIII (2 vols., New York, 1847; Philadelphia, 1859), I, 413-17; Charles C. Jones, Jr., *The History of Georgia* (2 vols. Boston, 1883), I, 502-505.

4Allen D. Candler, ed., *The Colonial Records of the State of Georgia* (26 vols. Atlanta, 1904-1916), VII, 301-302.

5*Ibid.*, 304.

6Colonial Records of Georgia (MS copies in Department of Archives and History, Atlanta, Ga., of originals in the Public Record Office, London, England), XXVIII, Pt. 1, p. 192.

7*Ibid.*, XXXIV (MS), 170.   8*Ibid.*, 182-84; XXXIX (MS), 207-10.

9*Ibid.*, XVIII, 188-91. See also *ibid.*, XIII, 87, 157; XVI, 76, 115.

10*Ibid.*, XXVIII (MS), Pt. 1, p. 8.   11*Ibid.*, VII, 506-507.

12*Ibid.*, 625.

13*Ibid.*, XIII, 492-93.   14Winzerling, *Acadian Odyssey*, 22.

15Candler, ed., *Colonial Records of Georgia*, VIII, 512.

16*Georgia Gazette* (Savannah), December 22 (2, 2), 1763. (The first number in parentheses denotes page, the second, column.)

17Shelby T. McCloy, "French Charities to the Acadians, 1755-1799," in *Louisiana Historical Quarterly*, XXI (July, 1938), 8.

18Winzerling, *Acadian Odyssey*, 22. See also *ibid.*, 45.

19*Georgia Gazette*, August 18 (3, 1), 1763.   20*Ibid.*, December 15 (2, 2).

21*Ibid.*, January 12 (1, 2), 1764.

22Sidney E. Morse, *A New System of Modern Geography, or a View of the Present State of the World* (Boston, 1822), 241.

23*Georgia Gazette*, February 9 (2, 1), 1764.

Bibilography

I. BOOKS

Bass, Althea, *Cherokee Messenger*. Norman: University of Oklahoma Press, 1936.

Battey, George Magruder, Jr., *A History of Rome and Floyd County*. Vol. I (no more published). Atlanta: The Webb and Vary Company, 1922.

Biographical Directory of the American Congress, 1774-1927. Washington: Government Printing Office, 1928.

Blair, Ruth, comp., *Georgia's Official Register, 1925*. Publication of the Department of Archives and History.

Bliss, Lena E., "A Legal Conundrum," in *The Law Student, A Magazine for Law Students* (Brooklyn, N. Y.), Vol. 18, no. 3 (March, 1941).

Brainard, Charles H., *John Howard Payne, A Biographical Sketch of the Author of "Home, Sweet Home," with a Narrative of the Removal of his Remains from Tunis to Washington*. Boston: Cupples, Upham & Company, 1885.

Butler, John C., *Historical Record of Macon and Central Georgia.* . . . Macon: J. W. Burke & Co., 1879.

Candler, Allen D., comp., *The Colonial Records of the State of Georgia*. Vols. VII, VIII, XIII, XVI, XVIII. Atlanta: Publishers vary, 1906, 1907, 1910. (A continuation of these records which were never published, Vols. XXVIII, pt. 1, XXXIV, XXXIX. Typed copies of the originals are in the Department of Archives and History, Atlanta.)

Candler, Allen D., comp., *The Revolutionary Records of the State of Georgia*. Vol. II. Atlanta: The Franklin-Turner Company, 1908.

Coulter, E. Merton, *College Life in the Old South*. New York: The Macmillan Company, 1928.

de Baillou, Clemens, ed., *John Howard Payne to his Countrymen*. University of Georgia Libraries Miscellanea Publications, No. 2. Athens: University of Georgia Press, 1961.

Du Bois, W. E. Burghardt, *Black Reconstruction.* . . . New York: Harcourt, Brace and Company, 1935.

Foreman, Grant, ed., *Indian Justice. A Cherokee Murder Trial at Tahlequah in 1840. As Reported by John Howard Payne*. Oklahoma City: Harlow Publishing Company, 1934.

Forrest, Williams, *Trail of Tears*. New York: Crown Publishers, Inc., 1959.

Gabriel, Ralph Henry, *Elias Boudinot, Cherokee & his America.* Norman: University of Oklahoma Press, 1941.

Georgia Justice of Peace, Containing the Duties, Powers and Authorities of that Office, as Regulated by the Laws now in Force in this State. Augusta: Printed by George F. Randolph, 1804.

(Gilmer, George R.), *Sketches of Some of the First Settlers of Upper Georgia, of the Cherokees, and the Author.* New York: D. Appleton and Company, 1855.

Hanson, Willis T., *The Early Life of John Howard Payne.* . . . Boston: The Bibliophile Society, MCMXIII.

Harris, Joel Chandler, *Joel Chandler Harris' Life of Henry W. Grady, Including his Writings and Speeches.* New York: Cassell Publishing Company, 1890.

Harrison, Gabriel, *John Howard Payne, Dramatist, Poet, Actor, and Author of Home, Sweet Home. His Life and Writings.* Philadelphia: J. B. Lippincott & Co., 1885. (An earlier edition: Albany, N. Y.: Joel Munsell, 1875.)

Heath, Milton Sydney, *Constructive Liberalism. The Role of the State in Economic Development in Georgia to 1860.* Cambridge: Harvard University Press, 1954.

Hull, A. L., *Annals of Athens, Georgia, 1801-1901. With an Introductory Sketch by Dr. Henry Hull.* Athens: Banner Job Office, 1906.

Hull, A. L., *A Historical Sketch of the University of Georgia.* Atlanta: The Foote & Davies Co., 1894.

Jones, Charles C., Jr., *The History of Georgia.* Vol. 1 of 2 vols. Boston: Houghton, Mifflin and Company, 1883.

Knight, Lucian Lamar, *Standard History of Georgia and Georgians.* 6 vols. Chicago: The Lewis Publishing Company, 1917.

Knight, Lucian Lamar, *Georgia's Landmarks, Memorials and Legends.* 2 vols. Atlanta: The Byrd Printing Co., 1913, 1914.

Lumpkin, Wilson, *The Removal of the Cherokee Indians from Georgia.* 2 vols. Wormsloe (Savannah): Privately printed, 1907.

Malone, Dumas, ed., *Dictionary of American Biography.* Vol. XIX. New York: Charles Scribner's Sons, 1936. (Twenty volumes were edited in the first printing. Since the first publication, supplementary volumes have periodically appeared. The first three volumes of the original edition were edited by Allen Johnson; volumes IV to VII, inclusive, by Johnson and Malone; and volumes eight through twenty, by Malone.)

Marquis, Albert Nelson, ed., *Who's Who in America.* Vol. VIII (1914-1915). Chicago: A. N. Marquis & Company, 1914. Volumes appear every two years.

Mell, P. H., *Life of Patrick Hues Mell by his Son.* Louisville, Ky.: Baptist Book Concern, 1895.

Mitchell, Frances Letcher, *Georgia Land and People.* Atlanta: Franklin Printing and Publishing Company, 1893.

Morse, Sidney E., *A New System of Modern Geography, or a View of the Present State of the World. . . .* Boston: George Clark, 1822.

National Cyclopaedia of American Biography. 13 vols. New York: James T. White & Company, 1898-1906. (Supplementary volumes were later added.)

Pandora '86; ibid., 1898. (University of Georgia Yearbooks.)

Phillips, Ulrich B., "Georgia Local Archives," in *Annual Report of the American Historical Association for the Year 1904.* Washington: Government Printing Office, 1905.

Phillips, Ulrich B., *The Life of Robert Toombs.* New York: The Macmillan Company, 1913.

Ponton, M. M., *Life and Times of Henry M. Turner.* Atlanta: A. B. Caldwell Publishing Company, 1917.

(Simms, William Gilmore) By the Author of "Martin Faber," *Guy Rivers: A Tale of Georgia.* 2 vols. New York: Harper & Brothers, 1834.

Starkey, Marion L., *The Cherokee Nation.* New York: Alfred A. Knopf, 1946.

Stevens, William Bacon, *A History of Georgia from its First Discovery by Europeans to the Adoption of the Present Constitution in MDCCXCVIII.* 2 vols. I. New York: D. Appleton and Co., 1847; II. Philadelphia: E. H. Butler & Co., 1859.

Stovall, Pleasant A., *Robert Toombs, Statesman, Speaker, Soldier, Sage. . . .* New York: Cassell Publishing Company, 1892.

Thompson, C. Mildred, *Reconstruction in Georgia, Economic, Social, Political, 1865-1872.* Studies in History, Economics and Public Law, Vol. LXIV, no. 1, Whole Number 154. New York: The Columbia University Press, 1915.

Tuck, Henry C., *Four Years at the University of Georgia, 1877-1881.* Athens: Published by the Author, 1938.

Williams, Stanley T., *The Life of Washington Irving.* 2 vols. New York: Oxford University Press, 1935.

Winzerling, Oscar William, *Acadian Odyssey.* Baton Rouge: Louisiana State University Press, 1955.

White, George, *Historical Collections of Georgia. . . .* New York: Pudney & Russell, 1854.

Wilson, Grant and John Fiske, eds. *Appletons' Cyclopaedia of American Biography.* Revised edition. Vol. VI (6 vols. and supplement in all). New York: D. Appleton and Company, 1900.

II. GOVERNMENT DOCUMENTS (Printed)

A. Georgia

Acts of the General Assembly of the State of Georgia. . . . 1829; ibid., 1830; ibid., 1831; ibid., 1835; ibid., 1842; ibid., 1847; ibid., 1849-50; ibid., 1855-'56; ibid., 1870. Titles, places and dates of publication, and printers vary.

Clark, R. H., T. R. R. Cobb, and D. Irwin, comps., Code of the State of Georgia. Atlanta: John S. Seals, 1861.

Clayton, Augustin Smith, comp., A Compilation of the Laws of Georgia, . . . 1800, to the Year 1810, Inclusive. . . . Augusta: Adams & Duyckinck, 1812.

Dawson, William C., comp., A Compilation of the Laws of the State of Georgia, . . . Since the Year 1819 to the Year 1829, Inclusive. . . . Milledgeville: Grantland and Orme, 1831.

Journal of the House of Representatives of the State of Georgia . . . November and December, 1835; ibid., commenced July 4, 1868; ibid., commenced January 10, 1870; ibid., 1871. Titles, places and dates of publication, and printers vary.

Journal of the Proceedings of the Constitutional Convention of the People of Georgia, Held in the City of Atlanta in the Months of December, 1867, and January, February and March, 1868. And Ordinances and Resolutions Adopted. Augusta: E. H. Pughe, 1868.

Lamar, Lucius L. Q., comp., A Compilation of the Laws of Georgia, . . . Since the Year 1810 to the Year 1819. . . . Augusta: T. S. Hannon, 1821.

Marbury, Horatio and William Harris Crawford, comps., Digest of the Laws of the State of Georgia, from its Settlement as a British Province, in 1755 to the Session of the General Assembly in 1800. . . . Savannah: Seymour, Woolhopter & Stebbins, 1802.

Report of Cases Argued and Decided in the Supreme Court of Georgia at the March Term, 1890. Vol. 85. Peeples and Stevens, Reporters. Atlanta: Franklin Publishing House, 1891.

Report of Cases in Law and Equity, Argued and Determined in the Supreme Court of Georgia. Parts of March and October Terms, 1888. Vol. 81. Peeples and Stevens, Reporters. Atlanta: Franklin Publishing House, 1889.

Watkins, Robert and George Watkins, comps., A Digest of the Laws of the State of Georgia . . . to the Year 1798, Inclusive, and the Principal Acts of 1799. . . . Philadelphia: R. Aitken, 1800.

B. United States

"Condition of Affairs in Georgia," being *House of Representatives Miscellaneous Documents*, No. 52 of 40th Cong., 3d sess.

Edgerton, Priscilla, *Famous Trees*. United States Department of Agriculture Forest Service. Washington, D. C., October 1, 1935.

Population of the United States in 1860; . . . *Eighth Census*. . . . Washington: Government Printing Office, 1864.

"Report from the Secretary of War, in Compliance with a Resolution of the Senate of the 13th of October, 1837, in Relation to the Cherokee Treaty of 1835," being *Senate Document*, No. 120 of 25th Cong., 2d sess. Serial No. 315.

Royce, Charles C., "The Cherokee Nation of Indians: A Narrative of their Official Relations with the Colonial and Federal Government," in J. W. Powell, Director, *Fifth Annual Report of the Bureau of Ethnology . . . 1883-'84*. Washington: Government Printing Office, 1887.

Testimony Taken by the Joint Select Committee to Inquire into the Condition of Affairs in the Late Insurrectionary States. Georgia. Vol. II. 13 vols. in all. Washington: Government Printing Office, 1872. Generally cited by the binder's title, *Ku Klux Conspiracy*.

War of the Rebellion: A Compilation of the Official Records of the Union and Confederate Armies. 127 books and index. Washington: Government Printing Office, 1880-1901.

III. MANUSCRIPTS (official and unofficial)

Christler, Ethel Maude, "Participation of Negroes in the Government of Georgia, 1867-1870." Master of Arts Thesis, Atlanta University, June, 1932.

Georgia County Archives:

Bibb County Deed Record, Q, T, U, X. Courthouse in Macon.

Clarke County Deed Record, A, B, P, Q; Marriage Licenses, C; Minutes of Inferior Court, 1802-1810; Minutes of Superior Court, 1801-1808, 1860, 1864-1868, Vol. 21; Record of Bills of Sale, Mortgages, etc., Book L; Record of Wills, E. Courthouse in Athens.

Jackson County Deed Record, A-B; Minutes of Inferior Court, 1796-1802. Courthouse in Jefferson.

Oglethorpe County Deed Record, C; Will Book, B. Courthouse in Lexington.

Hillyer, Junius, "Memoirs of the Early Life and Times of Judge Junius Hillyer." A typescript in the General Library of the University of Georgia.

Jackson, Evelyn Harden, "Evelyn Harden Jackson Collection." Box I.
In the General Library of the University of Georgia.
Jackson, Evelyn Harden, "Diary of Evelyn Jackson, 1864-1928." In
the General Library of the University of Georgia.
Read, Keith, "Keith Read Manuscript Collection." In the General
Library of the University of Georgia.
University of Georgia: Minutes of the Demosthenian Literary Society,
1847-1854; Minutes of the Faculty, 1850-1873; Minutes of the
Senatus Academicus, 1799-1842; Minutes of the Trustees, 1794-
1817, 1835-1858, 1858-1877.

IV. NEWSPAPERS

Athens Daily *Banner*, 1890, 1891, 1901, 1908.
Athens Daily and Weekly *Banner*. A combination special edition,
November 24, 1899.
Athens Weekly *Banner*, 1890, 1891.
Athens *Southern Banner*, 1835-1836, 1843, 1861-1865.
Athens *Banner-Herald*, 1946.
Athens Daily *Banner-Watchman*, 1889.
Athens Weekly *Banner-Watchman*, 1883, 1887.
Athens Weekly *Chronicle*, 1889.
Athens *North-East Georgian*, 1875.
Athens *Southern Watchman*, 1859-1866, 1868-1871, 1882.
Atlanta *Constitution*, 1887-1891, 1906, 1915, 1946.
Atlanta *Georgia Weekly Opinion*, 1867.
Atlanta Weekly *Intelligencer*, 1868.
Atlanta *Journal*, 1929, 1930, 1915.
Augusta *Chronicle*, 1793, 1801, 1835, 1836. Title varies.
Augusta Weekly *Chronicle & Sentinel*, 1868, 1869.
Augusta Weekly *Constitutionalist*, 1869.
Augusta *Georgia Constitutionalist*, 1835-1836.
Augusta *Georgia State Gazette or Independent Register*, 1787.
Calhoun *Times*, 1887-1889.
Elberton *Star*, 1906.
Greensboro *Herald*, 1869, 1870.
Greensboro *Herald and Journal*, 1887.
Greensboro *Herald-Journal*, 1890.
Griffin *American Union*, 1867-1868. Moved to Macon.
Huntsville (Alabama) Weekly *Democrat*, 1882.
Lexington *Oglethorpe Echo*, 1887, 1906, 1925.
Macon *American Union*, 1868-1873. Moved from Griffin.
Macon *Georgia Weekly Telegraph*, 1868, 1875.

Macon Weekly *Telegraph*, 1887, 1890.
Milledgeville *Federal Union*, 1835-1836.
Milledgeville *Georgia Journal*, 1815, 1835-1836.
Milledgeville *Southern Recorder*, 1835-1836, 1866.
New York *Times*, 1958.
Richmond (Virginia) *Enquirer*, 1835.
Sandersville *Central Georgian*, 1857.
Savannah *Georgia Gazette*, 1763, 1764, 1796.
Savannah Daily *Georgian*, 1835-1836.
Trenton *Dade County Weekly Times*, 1887.

All of the above papers were published in Georgia except as indicated. In some the name of the town appeared in the title, but in the interest of uniformity, the town has not been italicized.

V. PAMPHLETS AND LEAFLETS

A Catalogue of the Officers and Students of Franklin College (University of Georgia) *Athens, 1851-'52*. Athens, 1851.
Jackson, Miss Evelyn Harden, *Souvenir of the Harden Home*. Athens: W. J. Gardner, 1918.
Rutherford, Mildred Lewis, *Flags and Flowers*. Athens, though no place or date is given.
Turner, H. M., *The Barbarous Decision of the United States Supreme Court Declaring the Civil Rights Act Unconstitutional and Disrobing the Colored Race of all Civil Protection. The Most Cruel and Inhumane Verdict against a Loyal People in the History of the World*. Atlanta: Compiled and published by Turner, 1893.

VI. PERIODICALS

Coulter, E. Merton, "Nancy Hart, Georgia Heroine of the Revolution: The Story of the Growth of a Tradition," in *Georgia Historical Quarterly*, XXXIX, 2 (June, 1955).
Cromwell, John W., "The First Negro Churches in the District of Columbia," in *Journal of Negro History*, VII (1922).
Foreman, Grant, "John Howard Payne and the Cherokee Indians," in *American Historical Review*, XXXVII (July, 1932).
Howard, Annie Hornady, "A Red Rose for Love," in *Georgia Magazine* (Decatur), I, 6 (April-May, 1958).
Howard, Annie Hornady and Florine Harden Smith, "The Romance of Home, Sweet Home," in *Holland's, The Magazine of the South*, Vol. 48, no. 10 (October, 1929).
Georgian, IV, 1 (November, 1899); VIII, 3 (December, 1903); XV, 8 (June, 1911). A student publication at the University of Georgia.

Harper's Weekly. A Journal of Civilization. VII (December 12, 1863).

Irvine, Dallas D., "The Fate of Confederate Archives," in *American Historical Review*, XLIV (1938-1939).

Leary, Lewis, "John Howard Payne's Southern Adventure: 1835," in *Library Notes. A Bulletin Issued for the Friends of Duke University.* No. 19 (February, 1948). Durham: Duke University Library, 1948.

McCloy, Shelby T., "French Charities to the Acadians, 1755-1799," in *Louisiana Historical Quarterly*, XXI, 3 (July, 1938).

Montgomery, Horace, "Howell Cobb, Daniel Webster, and Jenny Lind," in *Georgia Historical Quarterly*, XLV (March, 1961).

Nation (New York). VII (1868).

Niles, Hezekiah, ed., *Niles' Weekly Register. . . .* XLIX (September, 1835-March, 1836).

Speer, Laura, "John Howard Payne's Southern Sweetheart," in *New England Magazine*, New Series, Vol. V (November, 1891).

United States Magazine and Democratic Review, I (February, 1838).

Index